"Nicholas Johnson and Brendan Markey-Towler have written a must-read guide to understanding the fourth industrial revolution, its socioeconomic impact, and ways to seize opportunities and overcome possible challenges. I'm definitely recommending this to anyone who wants to stay ahead as we continue to integrate technology in different industries and business processes."

Tasmin Trezise, President of Workforce.com

"*Economics of the Fourth Industrial Revolution* is an essential explainer on the future of socio-economic development. Without oversimplifying, it comprehensively dissects the vast terrains of General Purpose Technologies and Mega Technologies through the lens of Brisbane Club Model and its network effect. Nicholas and Brendan highlight the critical structural transformation that is presently underway, and provide the theoretical framework required to understand this change and its future implications. As we navigate the complex cascading effects of globalisation, *Economics of the Fourth Industrial Revolution* explores crucial insights on how individuals, groups, and communities can effectively leverage these technological advancements. The book uniquely captures the cultural, behavioural, and society metamorphosis propelled by the Fourth Industrial Revolution. Backed with insightful case studies and a coherent conceptual understanding, Nicholas and Brendan's writing flows between meta-themes of evolutionary economic and social organisation to practical advice to leverage the potential of emerging technologies. For developing countries like India, and entrepreneurial individuals and communities, *Economics of the Fourth Industrial Revolution* is a must read. It will help you realise your untapped economic capabilities and orient them to leverage the Fourth Industrial Revolution. In times of disconcerting uncertainty and upheaval, Nicholas and Brendan write with astounding clarity."

Utkarsh Amitabh, Founder of Network Capital

ECONOMICS OF THE FOURTH INDUSTRIAL REVOLUTION

This book applies cutting-edge economic analysis and social science to unpack the rich complexities and paradoxes of the Fourth Industrial Revolution. The book takes the reader on a bold, refreshing, and informative tour through its technological drivers, its profound impact on human ecosystems, and its potential for sustainable human development. The overarching message to the reader is that the Fourth Industrial Revolution is not merely something to be feared or survived; rather, this dramatic collision of technologies, disciplines, and ideas presents a magnificent opportunity for a generation of new pioneers to rewrite "accepted rules" and find new avenues to empower billions of people to thrive. This book will help readers to discern the difference between disruption and transformation.

The reader will come away from this book with a deeply intuitive and highly contextual understanding of the core technological advances transforming the world as we know it. Beyond this, the reader will clearly appreciate the future impacts on our economies and social structures. Most importantly, the reader will receive an insightful and actionable set of guidelines to assist them in harnessing the Fourth Industrial Revolution so that both they and their communities may flourish.

The authors do not primarily seek to make prescriptions for government policy, but rather to speak directly to people about what they can do for themselves, their families, and their communities to be future-proofed and ready to adapt to life in a rapidly evolving world ecosystem.

Nicholas Johnson is an economist and mathematician. He is the Principal Economist at Economists Without Borders. He also holds research and teaching positions at the University of Queensland and Queensland University of Technology. He holds a Master of Public Policy from the Australian National University, and undergraduate degrees in mathematics and economics (with First Class Honours) from Queensland University of Technology. Nicholas is a World Economic Forum Global Shaper.

Brendan Markey-Towler is a behavioural, institutional, evolutionary economist and an Associate with Economists Without Borders. He was previously a Senior Advisor at Evidn, a global behavioural science company headquartered in Brisbane, Australia. He has researched and taught at the University of Queensland, RMIT University, and University College London and holds a PhD in behavioural, institutional, and evolutionary economics and Bachelor of Economics with First Class Honours and a University Medal from the University of Queensland.

Innovation and Technology Horizons

Series Editor: Vanessa Ratten

La Trobe University, Australia

As business landscape constantly shifts in today's digital age, this timely series looks at how business and society can harness technological innovation to succeed and drive progress. The books in this series identify new innovation capabilities and emerging technologies and investigate the managerial implications of such technologies. As business processes become increasingly complex, the series also explores how businesses can transform themselves with new digital technologies while aligning themselves with today's societal goals. This series provides direction through research on innovation and technology management and will be of benefit to anyone who is keen to thrive in an evolving business environment.

Tourism, Hospitality and Digital Transformation
Strategic Management Aspects
Edited by Kayhan Tajeddini, Vanessa Ratten and Thorsten Merkle

Managing Sustainable Innovation
Edited by Vanessa Ratten, Marcela Ramirez-Pasillas and Hans Lundberg

The Business of Data
Commercial Opportunities and Social Challenges in a World Fuelled by Data
Martin De Saulles

Economics of the Fourth Industrial Revolution
Internet, Artificial Intelligence and Blockchain
Nicholas Johnson and Brendan Markey-Towler

For more information about this series, please visit www.routledge.com/Innovation-and-Technology-Horizons/book-series/ITH

ECONOMICS OF THE FOURTH INDUSTRIAL REVOLUTION

Internet, Artificial Intelligence and Blockchain

*Nicholas Johnson and
Brendan Markey-Towler*

Routledge
Taylor & Francis Group

LONDON AND NEW YORK

First published 2021
by Routledge
2 Park Square, Milton Park, Abingdon, Oxon OX14 4RN

and by Routledge
52 Vanderbilt Avenue, New York, NY 10017

Routledge is an imprint of the Taylor & Francis Group, an informa business

© 2021 Nicholas Johnson and Brendan Markey-Towler

British Library Cataloguing-in-Publication Data
A catalogue record for this book is available from the British Library

Library of Congress Cataloging-in-Publication Data
Names: Johnson, Nicholas (Economist and mathematician) author. |
    Markey-Towler, Brendan, author.
Title: Economics of the fourth industrial revolution : internet, artificial
    intelligence and blockchain / Nicholas Johnson and Brendan
    Markey-Towler.
Description: 1 Edition. | New York : Routledge, 2020. |
    Series: Innovation and technology horizons | Includes bibliographical
    references and index.
Identifiers: LCCN 2020027312 (print) | LCCN 2020027313 (ebook) |
    ISBN 9781138366923 (hardback) | ISBN 9781138366947 (paperback) |
    ISBN 9780429430015 (ebook)
Subjects: LCSH: Technological innovations—Economic aspects. |
    Technological innovations—Social aspects. | Technology and
    civilization.
Classification: LCC HC79.T4 J64 2020 (print) | LCC HC79.T4 (ebook) |
    DDC 303.48/34—dc23
LC record available at https://lccn.loc.gov/2020027312
LC ebook record available at https://lccn.loc.gov/2020027313

ISBN: 978-1-138-36692-3 (hbk)
ISBN: 978-1-138-36694-7 (pbk)
ISBN: 978-0-429-43001-5 (ebk)

Typeset in Bembo
by Apex CoVantage, LLC

MIX
Paper from
responsible sources
FSC™ C013985

Printed in the United Kingdom
by Henry Ling Limited

CONTENTS

FIGURES

ACKNOWLEDGMENTS

Naturally there are many people to whom we are grateful for contributing intellectual and personal support in writing this book. As they say, a man should do three things in life: plant a tree, write a book, and have a child. It takes a village to raise a child, and it takes not much less to write a book. Without the support of our global village this book would not have been feasible, let alone intellectually stimulating.

In the first instance, thanks must go to our editor at Routledge, Kristina Abbott, for having given us the opportunity to publish this work and encouraging us to take it. Brendan first met Kristina at the DRUID 2017 conference in New York, where she approached him to explore the potential for publishing a book on technology diffusion. We (Nicholas and Brendan) had been kicking around the idea for this book for some time, and Kristina was wonderful in continuing for the next year to encourage us to bring it into reality. We are immensely grateful to her for giving us this opportunity and providing us with encouragement to seize upon it to put our ideas into the world.

Nicholas wishes to thank several people for their professional and academic advice in recent years, perhaps unrelated to this book itself but instrumental during the period in which the book was written, and therefore affecting it indirectly. From the Queensland University of Technology, special thanks go to his former supervisor Professor Stan Hurn. He also wishes to thank Dr. Annastiina Silvennoinen and Professor Timo Teräsvirta. From the University of Queensland, thanks go to Dr. Thomas Taimre. Although there are too many other people to list, Nicholas also wishes to thank a few of his many colleagues in Economists Without Borders, the World Economic Forum Global Shapers Community, the Horasis Global Visions Community, the UNLEASH Innovation Lab, the Economic Society of Australia (Queensland), and Pro Bono Econos, who happened to provide various inputs into this book.

For intellectual support and development, Brendan thanks his constant mentors Professor John Foster and Associate Professor Peter Earl of the University of Queensland. These two men were at the core of the Brisbane Club and made seminal contributions to the model which emerged from it. They also took unreasonable amounts of time and effort to help a young man in his early twenties understand it. He is also particularly grateful to his colleagues at the RMIT Blockchain Innovation Hub for their unique insights into blockchain technology. Jason Potts, Sinclair Davidson, Chris Berg, Mikayla Novak, Darcy Allen, and Al Berg are pioneers of the emerging field of institutional cryptoeconomics and we commend their work to anyone interested in the institutional technology that is blockchain. To his mentors at the University of Queensland and colleagues at RMIT Blockchain Innovation Hub, Brendan is especially grateful for the personal support they have offered in a difficult period. Often a single sentence in conversation or piece of work with them has made the difference between quitting and keeping at his work.

Thanks from both of us must also go to John "Muppet" Humphreys, whose sharp intellect and willingness to participate in lengthy philosophical discussions is always well-appreciated. Within our circle, the phrase "to be Muppeted" denotes an experience similar to that which Bertrand Russell recounted with John Maynard Keynes: "When I argued with him, I felt that I took my life in my hands, and I seldom emerged without feeling something of a fool." Where our ideas have held up to Muppet's scrutiny, we have known them to pass muster.

As ambitious young men with much of our respective careers still ahead of us, both of us are acutely aware of the support our families have provided us in various ways. Nicholas would like to thank his parents, Craig and Susan, for their loving support, ongoing advice, and personal sacrifices over the course of many years, all of which have helped him to seek and seize opportunities he never would have had otherwise. Further, Nicholas would like to thank his three brothers, Mitchell, Andrew, and Joshua, for their support and close friendship. Brendan can't ever repay the debt he owes to his parents, Paul and Di, for their support during what has been a difficult period, both material and moral, and he would not have been able to keep working at this project without the devotion of his wife Lucy. To these great people, both of us extend our deepest gratitude and affection. We hope the sacrifice they have made is justified by the value this book brings to the lives of others.

1

INTRODUCTION

How and why to understand the Fourth Industrial Revolution

We might be tempted to think that we're living out a Dickens novel. We could well say of our times that "it was the best of times, it was the worst of times." We might be tempted to say that our lives increasingly resemble the unfeeling, harsh world of the industrial revolution painted by the great author in *Hard Times*. Our rustic, comfortable past is increasingly being swept away in a torrent of industry and innovation. The world around is constantly, radically changing as new technologies replace old ways of doing things with which we were comfortable.

It's no accident that we might feel this way. We are currently experiencing the beginnings of the Fourth Industrial Revolution. In this, the first fifth of the twenty-first century, we are observing the convergence of innovations which are changing the technological basis for our industrial systems at their most fundamental level. Globalisation seems to have become less of an idea and more of an everyday reality as we increasingly live in a global marketplace through the medium of platforms like Amazon, Google, and Facebook. Where the Luddites felt the cotton weaver might be threatened by the advent of the loom, the machines we're now inventing are creating fear that humanity itself might be superseded. We're just beginning to observe the advent of technologies which challenge the very notion of nation-states to which we have become so accustomed. And every which way it seems we have prophets of doom and of glory telling us about our dystopian or utopian future.

One thing is for sure as we observe radical changes to the technological basis for our industrial systems – the economy of the future is going to look substantially different to the economy of the present. As with the third, second, and first industrial revolutions before it, the Fourth Industrial Revolution will radically alter the structure and function of our socioeconomic systems, and what was a successful or even viable way of life and doing business in the past will by no means necessarily be so in the future. The Fourth Industrial Revolution will present profound opportunities for harnessing technology to extend the range of human capability in the production and distribution of resources. But it will also present profound challenges for individuals, organisations, and communities whose systems for securing the necessary goods and services for life and its enjoyment will be disrupted by the emergence of these technologies. In order to be able to seize the opportunities the Fourth Industrial Revolution offers, and substantially mitigate the challenges it presents in terms of disruption for everyday people, we need to understand the dynamics of how the technologies which characterise it will affect the structure and function of our socioeconomic systems. Hence our purpose in this book.

Our purpose in this book is to bring economic analysis to bear on the convergent innovations which are fundamentally changing the structure of our socioeconomic systems as the Fourth Industrial Revolution emerges. We seek to form a view of the dynamics by which they are affecting that structure, project a likely future from those dynamics, and identify opportunities to be seized and challenges to be mitigated against. We also seek to develop a high-level perspective on what can be done by individuals, groups of individuals within organisations, and communities to so seize those opportunities and mitigate those challenges. In doing this we don't pretend in any way to have established the final word on the economics of the Fourth Industrial Revolution – far from it. We hope, with this book, to contribute to an ongoing conversation about how we can harness the technologies converging to create the Fourth Industrial Revolution to seize the profound opportunities they offer, while mitigating against the profound disruptive challenges they will present to existing socioeconomic systems.

We were motivated to write this book as an extension of Klaus Schwab's *The Fourth Industrial Revolution (2016)*. Schwab was among the first to recognise the convergence of innovations we are observing as an industrial revolution, coining the term "Fourth Industrial Revolution," and the first to give a comprehensive overview of the technologies driving it. Schwab's work has contributed to a substantial literature discussing and debating various aspects of the technologies which comprise the Fourth Industrial Revolution, and is a superb introduction to it. Where we hope to extend that contribution is by bringing a coherent and unique theoretical perspective from economics to bear on what we call the "megatechnologies" which underlie the convergent innovations which are driving the Fourth Industrial Revolution.

We believe that this contribution is important because it is necessary at some point, when faced with a phenomenon so massive and complicated as an industrial revolution, to simplify it as much as possible and apply a coherent theory to discover what dynamics give rise to it. A good deal of the literature on the Fourth Industrial Revolution to date has been motivated by a close analysis of various case studies of the technology using a diverse toolbox of theories. This has been valuable but can have the effect of losing sight of the proverbial forest for the trees, and can leave people arguing about what they do not realise to be different trees. That is to say, we feel that it is now important to delve deeper beyond case studies of particular technologies to see what we can say about the core dynamics of the way the convergence of technologies is causing socioeconomic systems to evolve.

By bringing a coherent and unique theoretical perspective from economics to bear on what we believe to be the "mega-technologies" of the Fourth Industrial Revolution from which the various innovations which comprise it emerge, we reduce the complexity of the problem greatly and reveal the core dynamics of the phenomenon. By this contribution to the literature we hope to obtain a coherent perspective on the dynamics underlying the evolving structure of socioeconomic systems in response to the emerging "mega-technologies" of the Fourth Industrial Revolution. By bringing that theoretical perspective to bear on these "mega-technologies" we hope also to respond to and extend Schwab's contribution in particular by identifying, in a systematic manner, the opportunities and challenges presented by these technologies, as well as high-level strategies to seize the former and mitigate the latter. By this contribution to the literature, in short, we hope to offer readers an understanding of the dynamics of the Fourth Industrial Revolution which allows them to adapt their approaches to life and business in response to its disruptions and to realise its profound advancements.

1 Our approach to the economics of the Fourth Industrial Revolution

To develop an economic analysis of the convergent technologies of the Fourth Industrial Revolution, we will apply two theoretical perspectives. The first allows us to identify and justify a focus on the "mega-technologies" of the Fourth Industrial Revolution, while the second, unique perspective allows us to think about how those technologies will affect the structural evolution of the socioeconomic system. The first allows us to significantly reduce the complexity of the problem of analysing the convergent technological innovations which comprise the Fourth Industrial Revolution surveyed by Schwab (2016) in particular, among others, and the second allows us to then understand the function of those technologies within a theoretical economy.

The first theoretical perspective we adopt is that of "General Purpose Technologies," particularly as outlined by Richard Lipsey in *Economic Transformations* (Lipsey, Carlaw and Bekar, 2005). A General Purpose Technology is one which has wide scope for application across an economy, and becomes a core part of the technological basis for its structure and function. It is one from which a range of more specific technologies emerge as a sort of "spillover." We might think of it as the core "theme" to a cluster of different technologies – the common technological structure underlying a group of specific technologies. As those various specific technologies cause the socioeconomic system to evolve as they emerge, we can observe commonalities in the evolution they cause due to the commonality of their technological structure. We can thus analyse the evolution of socioeconomic structures by analysing the way the common technological structure brings about sufficiently similar evolutionary dynamics within the structure of socioeconomic systems. That is to say, we can analyse a General Purpose Technology to come to an understanding of the common, core dynamics technologies which emerge from it bring about.

We applied this perspective to the range of different technologies which Schwab (2016), among others, have identified as comprising the Fourth Industrial Revolution, and believe it to be constituted by the convergence and interaction of three General Purpose Technologies, which we call the "mega-technologies" of the Fourth Industrial Revolution. These three technologies, we believe, and we argue throughout, underlie the more specific technologies from which the Fourth Industrial Revolution emerges, and are generating large scale evolutionary change across our socioeconomic systems. Hence the subtitle of this book. We believe that the Fourth Industrial Revolution is characterised by the emergence, convergence, *and interaction* of three General Purpose Technologies, "mega-technologies": internet, artificial intelligence, and blockchain.

When we say that the internet is a General Purpose Technology underlying the Fourth Industrial Revolution we are aware of the fact that it can rightly be said to have been one underlying the Third Industrial Revolution as well. What we think makes the internet a part of the troika of technologies converging to create the Fourth Industrial Revolution is the switch of its application from being, properly speaking, a communication technology, to a technology which provides the basic infrastructure for socioeconomic interaction. The first iteration of the internet as a technology involved its capabilities as an information communication technology. In this application, the internet made the communications processes upon which *any* economic system relies significantly faster. It could have been said to have made our socioeconomic systems vastly more efficient, rather than changing their core structural dynamics. The internet as a mega-technology of the Fourth Industrial Revolution is a technology which is used as an infrastructure for *economic* exchange, as a technology for supporting new forms of economic interaction rather than making existing ones more efficient.

What transformed the technology radically enough for this to be the case, and for the internet to become a mega-technology of the Fourth Industrial Revolution as well as the third, was the rise of the smartphone. The smartphone's effect was to embed internet access points in mobile devices which could be accessed readily and conveniently at any point and in any space, and therefore to make the internet ubiquitous and pervasive in everyday life and not just a network to connect to when necessary. As a mega-technology of the Fourth Industrial Revolution, the internet in this form makes social media possible and ubiquitous; similarly with e-commerce platforms, it facilitates the spread of "apps" to manage everything from your finances to your fridge, and serves as the backbone of the Internet of Things. It is what helps to make Big Data sets possible, as well as augmented reality. It is, essentially, the basic infrastructure for the Fourth Industrial Revolution, providing the base technology with which our future socioeconomic interactions will be enabled.

Where the internet provides the basic infrastructure with which our future socioeconomic interactions will be enabled, artificial intelligence is the General Purpose Technology underlying the Fourth Industrial Revolution which provides its *production* technology. Artificial intelligence, especially that endowed with machine learning capabilities, is a mega-technology of the Fourth Industrial Revolution which radically reduces the labour required for a given production system to function and thus radically expands production capabilities. Obviously enough, it makes radical automation possible, not only of physical tasks but also of tasks which traditionally involved human information processing. But artificial intelligence also makes the "drone" economy possible by endowing machines with artificial intelligence which allows them to complete tasks from delivery to development of draft documents. It further enhances our computing power to stupendous degrees, allowing for advances in scientific discovery, especially when coupled with the Big Data generated by the internet, as well as with biomedical sciences, where it can be used to improve diagnostic and genetic sequencing procedures. It is, essentially, the basic production technology for the Fourth Industrial Revolution, allowing any activity which can be reduced to the operation of an algorithm to be automated.

The Fourth Industrial Revolution is not only a revolution of platforms for socioeconomic interaction and production techniques, however; it is also a revolution of governance technology, and this is why we include blockchain as a General Purpose Technology underlying it. Blockchain is an *institutional* technology which allows for privatised governance to emerge on internet-based platforms for socioeconomic interaction. As a mega-technology of the Fourth Industrial Revolution, it allows communities to design and develop governance structures organised around the keeping of a decentralised, immutable book of true records of socioeconomic facts which are bespoke to their needs. It has applications from cryptocurrency, to smart contracts, to the keeping of voting records and identity. Where the internet provides the basic infrastructure for socioeconomic interaction in the Fourth Industrial Revolution, and artificial intelligence provides its production technology, blockchain will provide the technology for institutional, privatised governance of the socioeconomic systems which emerge from it.

With this simplification of the convergent technologies underlying the Fourth Industrial Revolution in hand, we adopt a unique theoretical perspective on socioeconomic systems and their evolution: the "Brisbane Club" model. The reason for this is that the technologies of the Fourth Industrial Revolution lend themselves not so much to an analysis which focusses on the increased outputs for similar inputs which are made possible by new technologies, but rather to an analysis which focusses on the evolutionary pressures they introduce to the *structure* of socioeconomic systems. The Fourth Industrial Revolution will be characterised by the disruption of existing structures within socioeconomic systems and the building of new ones even more so than the increase of output for given inputs. The Brisbane Club model is suited to analysing these dynamics because it was *developed* in order to understand how new technologies introduce evolutionary dynamics to the structure of socioeconomic systems.

The Brisbane Club model is so named because it was developed in the early twenty-first century by a group of evolutionary and behavioural economists interested in complex systems theory at the University of Queensland. It crystallised around *The New Evolutionary Microeconomics (2000)* by Jason Potts, and was further developed in contributions from John Foster (2005), Kurt Dopfer (Dopfer, Foster and Potts, 2004; Dopfer and Potts, 2008), and Peter Earl and Tim Wakeley (2010). It was substantially formalised by one of the present authors (Markey-Towler) in his doctoral thesis, and it is this model that we apply in the present work. The Brisbane Club model presents the economy as a complex, evolving network system of value-creating exchange formed by individuals acting on the basis of their psychology and socioeconomic environment enabled by technology. It allows us to take a technology, examine the manner in which it expands human capabilities, then place it within a model of the economy as a complex evolving network of value-creating exchange and observe the effects it has. We adopt this model here to analyse and project the likely dynamics created by the mega-technologies of the Fourth Industrial Revolution on our socioeconomic systems. In each case we will identify what the technology *is* and how it expands human capability for action, and then apply the Brisbane Club model to this in order to analyse the likely dynamics the technologies will create as the Fourth Industrial Revolution progresses.

As a result of the approach we took to the economic analysis of the Fourth Industrial Revolution, we arrived at a different, but complementary, analysis to that offered by Brynjolfsson and McAfee in their 2017 book *Machine, Platform, Crowd*. Brynjolfsson and McAfee (2017) take a rich set of case studies and academic work in technology, psychology, and economics, and continue to develop the view of the trends being brought about by the advent of artificial intelligence and other digital technologies put forth in their earlier work (Brynjolfsson and McAfee 2011, 2014). They argue that myriad digital technologies, particularly artificial intelligence, machine learning, and internet-enabled communications technologies are converging to promote the rise of the *machine* over the mind, the *platform* over the product, and the knowledge of the *crowd* over the knowledge of what they call the "core" – the knowledge of an organisation or group. For Brynjolfsson and McAfee (2017), harnessing the technologies which give rise to these trends is a question of designing organisations to get the balance of utilisation in organisational function "right" between mind-machine, product-platform, and crowd-core, knowing that the balance is increasingly toward machine, platform, and crowd.

While also drawing on a variety of case studies, we instead, as we have outlined, took those offered by Schwab (2016), among others, and drove our analysis by applying a coherent theoretical framework designed for understanding the evolutionary dynamics brought about by new technologies. Our contribution is therefore highly systematic, seeking to identify a particular mega-technology, understand its function, relate this function to the extension of human capabilities, and understand the change to the structure of socioeconomic systems it is likely to bring about. So, while our work seeks to reduce and systematise the problem of the Fourth Industrial Revolution somewhat further than Brynjolfsson and

McAfee (2017), and therefore offers a different perspective on it, our work ought to be read as a companion to their contributions.

2 A preview of our arguments

We approach this work in four parts. In the next chapter we introduce the Brisbane Club model of socioeconomic systems as complex, evolving networks formed by individuals acting on the basis of their psychology and socioeconomic environment enabled by technology, which we will use as a model for analysing the mega-technologies of the Fourth Industrial Revolution. Then, in the first three parts of this book we first present a theoretical analysis of each mega-technology of the Fourth Industrial Revolution, making use of the Brisbane Club model of socioeconomic systems, and then use a series of case studies to demonstrate how the dynamics we identify are emerging. In each of the chapters which provides a theoretical analysis we provide a technical appendix which outlines a sketch of how our argument proceeds in the formal context of the Brisbane Club model for those readers who are interested. In the final part of this book we draw together our analyses of the various mega-technologies of the Fourth Industrial Revolution to present a view of the socioeconomic system which will emerge from it. In this we draw together an assessment of the various opportunities and challenges presented by this new socioeconomic system, and also make use of the Brisbane Club model to develop a perspective on how individuals, groups, and communities may take certain actions to develop a high-level capability to seize opportunities and mitigate challenges presented by the Fourth Industrial Revolution.

In the first part of our book, after introducing the Brisbane Club model of socioeconomic systems, we apply it to the mega-technology of the internet, revealing it to be a technology which is causing the emergence of genuinely global markets in which everyday life will take place through internet-enabled search. We will establish that this creates opportunities for hyper-growth into global markets if an individual or organisation has a unique capability to produce a globally best good or service, or one for which no substitutes exist. But we also establish that for those who do not, the effect of the internet is to introduce hyper-competition from global marketplaces. We further show how the internet interacts with the cognitive constraints of human beings to make the struggle for the *attention* of prospective buyers central to the socioeconomic systems of the Fourth Industrial Revolution. Finally, we discuss how the interconnectedness of the world of the Fourth Industrial Revolution, where the internet provides the basic infrastructure for socioeconomic interaction, is a more chaotic one where evolutionary processes take place over a period of months or years rather than decades. In the second chapter of this part, we introduce a variety of case studies to elaborate how the effects we identify are beginning to emerge within the economy already as the Fourth Industrial Revolution gathers pace.

In the second part of our book, we apply the Brisbane Club model to the mega-technology of artificial intelligence, revealing it to be a technology which has both whisperings of utopia *and* dystopia. We find that it does present very real challenges in terms of the spectre of mass unemployment it raises as a substitute for much human labour. But we also find that it offers profound opportunities for expanding human production capability as a complement for human labour in production plans which require the exercising of judgment, the cultivation of creativity, and the application of tacit knowledge in social and physical activity. In the second chapter of this part we will introduce a variety of case studies to elaborate how these dynamics are beginning to emerge, with both the challenges of automation and opportunities for expanding production capabilities presenting themselves as the Fourth Industrial Revolution progresses.

In the third part of our book, we draw on the institutional cryptoeconomics literature to study the nature of the mega-technology that is blockchain before applying the Brisbane Club model to it to discover the potential for greater entrepreneurial action in the development of institutional governance. We will argue that this creates significant opportunities for community-based solutions to specific problems facing those communities which require institutional governance, but that there are challenges to implementing those solutions concerning the adoption of blockchain technologies. We show how the developers of blockchain-based systems of institutional governance face challenges in terms of forming and coordinating expectations of institutional governance meeting certain requirements, and offering sufficient scope for complementarities to be realised across the population of potential adopters. In the second chapter of this part we again introduce a variety of case studies to elaborate how these dynamics – an entrepreneurship of rules if you will – are already beginning to develop, with a new era of community-based solutions to problems requiring institutional governance emerging at the beginning of the Fourth Industrial Revolution.

In the final, fourth part of our book, we bring together these various analyses in order to formulate a perspective on the economy of the future, the one which emerges from the Fourth Industrial Revolution, and systematise a categorisation of the various challenges and opportunities it presents. We see an economic system which is truly global, with networks of value creating exchange enabled by the internet being largely unbounded by location and rapidly evolving due to hyper-growth and hyper-competitive dynamics. We see an economy with vast production potential due to substantial automation of production systems within those global networks implemented on the internet, where human beings need only input judgment, creativity, and tacit knowledge. We see an economic system largely subject to bespoke governance implemented using blockchain designed and developed by communities relative to their needs. These trends present quite profound challenges to individuals, groups, and communities in terms of the hyper-competition and the struggle for attention global markets enabled by the internet bring, the mass unemployment radical automation threatens, and the difficulty of coordinating adoption of privatised systems of governance. But they also present profound opportunities to individuals, groups, and communities in terms of the potential for hyper-growth in the building of networks of value-creating exchange in global markets, the radical expansion of human production capabilities, and the design of bespoke systems for institutional governance.

In this part of the book we also present a high-level analysis of what can be done by individuals, groups, and communities to mitigate the disruptive challenges posed by the Fourth Industrial Revolution and seize the opportunities it presents. The challenge at every level is one of systems-building – developing the capability to build networks of value-creating exchange. The key to mitigating disruptive challenges and seizing opportunities in the Fourth Industrial Revolution at the level of the individual and organisation, we argue, is development and cultivation of knowledge and an antifragile mindset. The key to both of these, the Brisbane Club model suggests, is the pursuit of what might be called a "classical" education – a highly generalist program for building knowledge across a range of different areas which creates a basis for further growth of knowledge. At the level of the organisation also, the ability to organise individual contributions to a production plan so that capability prerequisites are met given the new technologies available to them is essential for building systems of value creating exchange now as ever before. At the level of the community, the ability to harness blockchain to promote bespoke solutions requiring institutional governance such as (in particular) income insurance and wealth management will be crucial to seizing the opportunities and mitigating the challenges presented by the Fourth Industrial Revolution.

In the final chapter of this part, and of our book, we provide an epilogue which reflects on what we have found in our analysis of the mega-technologies of the Fourth Industrial Revolution, and casts an optimistic perspective for the future. We encourage individuals, groups, and communities to take action to engage with the mega-technologies of the Fourth Industrial Revolution to make their promise of a better everyday life a reality, and give a final warning to pay heed to their contingency on certain basic infrastructure by developing redundancies and contingency. We believe that the Fourth Industrial Revolution, like the first, second, and third before it, will radically change human life for the better, and we hope that our work contributes to the project of harnessing its technologies to that end.

References

Brynjolfsson, Erik and McAfee, Andrew, (2011) *Race Against the Machine*, Digital Frontier Press, Lexington

Brynjolfsson, Erik and McAfee, Andrew, (2014) *The Second Machine Age*, W.W. Norton & Co., New York

Brynjolfsson, Erik and McAfee, Andrew, (2017) *Machine, Platform, Crowd*, W.W. Norton & Co., New York

Dopfer, Kurt, Foster, John and Potts, Jason, (2004) "Micro-meso-macro", *Journal of Evolutionary Economics,* 14(3), pp. 263–279

Dopfer, Kurt and Potts, Jason, (2008) *The General Theory of Economic Evolution*, Routledge, London.

Earl, Peter and Wakeley, Tim, (2010) "Alternative perspectives on connections in economic systems", *Journal of Evolutionary Economics*, 20(2), pp. 163–183

Foster, John, (2005) "From simplistic to complex systems in economics", *Cambridge Journal of Economics*, 29(6), pp. 873–892

Lipsey, Richard G., Carlaw, Kenneth I. and Bekar, Clifford T., (2005) *Economic Transformations: General Purpose Technologies and Long-term Economic Growth*, Oxford University Press, Oxford

Potts, Jason, (2000) *The New Evolutionary Microeconomics*, Edward Elgar, Cheltenham

Schwab, Klaus, (2016) *The Fourth Industrial Revolution*, World Economic Forum

PART I

Industrial revolutions

What they are, why they matter,
how to analyse them

2

INDUSTRIAL REVOLUTIONS PAST, PRESENT, AND FUTURE

A brief overview of how we got here and where we're going

Before launching into a book which purports to discuss technological mega-trends and how they relate to the economics of the Fourth Industrial Revolution, it is wise to pause momentarily and ensure we are all familiar with how the term "industrial revolution" is used and defined. Further, if we are to speak of a fourth industrial revolution, surely it is useful to briefly discuss the first, second, and third in both an historical and an economic context.

From an economic point of view, we define "industrial revolutions" as historical periods featuring major systematic and industry-independent breakthrough applications of innovative technology which permit new manifestations of essential economic institutions or marketplaces, and which tend to shift the aggregate production possibilities frontier outward while permanently raising the standard of living.

Let us break that definition down into its components. The term "systematic" highlights the organised and pervasive nature of the changes within an industry, permeating most aspects of how goods and services are sourced, produced, and sold. The term "industry-independent" highlights the observation that industrial revolutions are not limited to the confines of just one industry, such as agriculture, aviation, or banking. Rather, the nature of the breakthrough applications is such that they affect the core operational processes common to most industries. In other words, the breakthrough applications solve widespread fundamental problems or "pain" points which are not the exclusive domain of any industry. Innovative technologies are the enabler for industrial revolutions. Economic progress is impossible without new knowledge and new ideas which can be implemented and commercialised.

There are three important qualifiers in our definition. The first entails that the applied technology must enable essential economic institutions to exist in another form or operate in substantially different ways. Alternatively, the applied technology must create brand new marketplaces for economic buyers and sellers, in which they can exchange goods and services which either previously did not exist or were exchanged in other, older marketplace formats. The second qualifier entails that the aggregate production possibilities frontier for the society must expand outward. This implies that the applied technologies must enable the society to increase the economic output it can create from the same amount of resources used. In other words, economic productivity must increase in relation to the factors of production. The third qualifier entails that the standard of living must increase for the representative member of the population. Traditionally, this would be measured using GDP per capita as a proxy, however modern approaches may consider a wider array of metrics to gain a fuller picture of living standards. Historically, this is relevant in identifying industrial revolutions because GDP per capita was approximately constant for millennia despite many new technological innovations.

1 From economic stagnation to economic growth

Before the mid-eighteenth century, economic growth rates in per capita terms across most of the world were minute and barely discernible. Income per capita witnessed no substantial change for many centuries. Figure 2.1 illustrates this for

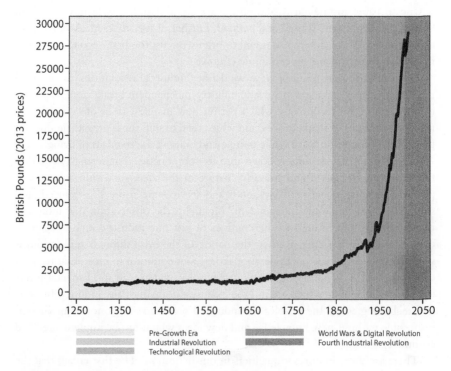

FIGURE 2.1   Economic prosperity over time.

Real GDP per capita for England (1270–2017).

Source: Historical data compiled by Broadberry et al. (2015), obtained from Thomas and Dimsdale (2017) via the Bank of England.

England, which was chosen due to the economy possessing relatively accurate and tractable long-run historical datasets. England was also a first-mover in leading the world into the Industrial Revolution. The next two hundred years witnessed economic per capita growth rates sustained at levels never seen before in human history.

The transition from economic stagnation to economic prosperity remains enigmatic, since it cannot adequately be described within the framework of the neoclassical models of economic growth (with endogenous or exogenous technological change) designed exclusively to account for the last 150 years of data. The characteristics of pre-industrial economies have not typically been emphasised in the creation of modern growth theory. There has subsequently emerged a substantial body of scholarship devoted to answering the following questions:

- Why has most of economic history been characterized by little if any sustained growth in GDP per capita?
- What technological developments and behavioural or institutional structures created the right conditions for the economy to break out of this growth stagnation?
- Why did the demographic transition take place?
- Why was there a large divergence in world economic development? Why did some economies around the world develop faster and earlier than others?

Several attempts have been made to create a unified growth theory which exposes the underlying micro-foundations of economic development in its various stages throughout history. The seminal paper by Galor and Weil (2000) introduced "a unified model that encompasses the transition between three distinct regimes that have characterized the process of economic development: the 'Malthusian Regime,' the 'Post-Malthusian Regime,' and the 'Modern Growth Regime'" Galor (2011) further expanded upon these ideas in the book *Unified Growth Theory*.

The model assumes that the economy began in a stable steady state equilibrium of the Malthusian variety in the pre-growth era. It then suggests that gradual technological progress helped to create an expansion of resources sufficient to outpace the dynamics of the delayed population adjustment, meaning that GDP per capita began to rise. The authors posit that the technological progress led to a greater demand for human capital, with the result that more resources within household budget constraints could be allocated towards child-rearing, while simultaneously incentivising a greater allocation of the same resources to child quality.

According to unified growth theory, the Post-Malthusian Regime witnessed an increase of both family size and child quality due to the increased income per capita (Dalgaard and Strulik 2016). Before long, greater human capital investments disentangled population size and per-capita income. The new dynamic was represented by the Modern Growth Regime, where technological progress increased the demand for human capital, which further incentivised a household budget reallocation towards child quality over family size (Strulik and Weisdorf 2008).

Galindev (2011) suggest that this democratic transition is accentuated by a fall in the relative price of leisure goods compared to child-rearing.

The resulting demographic transition is thus accounted for (Doepke 2004; Chatterjee and Vogl 2018), and the vast divergence in world economic development is explained by the heterogeneity of initial conditions faced by each economy, encompassing matters of geography, institutions, demographics, natural accidents, and prior history. Madsen and Murtin (2017) examine the role of education and find that it is the most important determinant of income growth in Britain from 1270 to 2010 out of a range of macroeconomic factors. The importance of human capital to any long-term growth model is further supported by Baten and Van Zanden (2008).

The unified growth theorists have received criticism for the apparent ad hoc nature by which the three regimes mentioned above were selected. For example, authors such as Nielsen (2016) suggest that the unified growth theory of Galor et al. is not the best representation of the data, instead arguing that the Malthusian trap did not truly exist in the first place and that growth rates can be better modelled using hyperbolic distributions. Other authors have extended the unified growth theory framework with research and development-based innovations to describe the emergence of productivity growth (Strulik, Prettner, and Prskawetz 2013), or have integrated elements of unified growth theory with neoclassical models (Dalgaard and Strulik 2013).

An alternative modelling approach was put forward by Hansen and Prescott (2002), who treat economic growth as exogenous in both a land-based "Malthus" sector and an industrial "Solow" sector. The model contains a threshold of profitability for the Solow sector which must be surpassed for the Solow sector to be used in production processes. As Berg and Staley (2015) point out, however, the Hansen-Prescott model has received various criticisms. For instance, the higher modern productivity growth is assumed, not explained; human capital is excluded from the analysis; and the demographic transition is explained without reference to appropriate micro-foundations.

The following sections provide a brief overview of the journey from economic stagnation to economic growth, highlighting the interesting economic features of the first, second, and third industrial revolutions, as well as the pre-growth epoch. We refer our readers to a list of other texts which cover these economic periods in more empirical and theoretical detail. We use these sections to stimulate a discussion on how people derive utility, how this creates economic value, and how this drives industrial revolutions. We also examine unique features of the Fourth Industrial Revolution which distinguish it from those periods of economic development which preceded it.

2 Malthusian dynamics and the pre-growth era

Most of economic history around the world prior to the early eighteenth century epitomised the Malthusian Trap – a state of the economy where an expansion of

resources derived from technological advances led to a counter-balancing population expansion, with the result that long-run per-capita living standards generally
remained unchanged (Boserup 1965). This phenomenon was reflected in the "iron
law of wages" from the works of Thomas R. Malthus (Malthus 1798), whose pes-
simistic view of the prospects for growth based on the historical data at that time is
one reason economics was once dubbed the "dismal science."

The essence of the Malthusian economy is displayed in Figure 2.2 and in Figure 2.3. Figure 2.2 portrays the data showing that earnings began to rise soon after
the Black Death plague led to the deaths of many tens of millions of people across
Europe around 1350. Eventually as the population levels recovered, earnings began
to fall. Figure 2.3 illustrates this in a more abstract form; any technological advances
made during these centuries tended to increase the population size without any
substantial impact on the wage levels (Voigtländer and Voth 2013). A more comprehensive and dynamic Malthusian model involving overlapping generations was
introduced by Ashraf and Galor (2011), who showed that land productivity was
linked to population density in the pre-growth era, rather than per capita income.
These observations motivated Adam Smith's statement in his Wealth of Nations
that "[t]he most decisive mark of the prosperity of any country is the increase of
the number of its inhabitants" (Smith 1776).

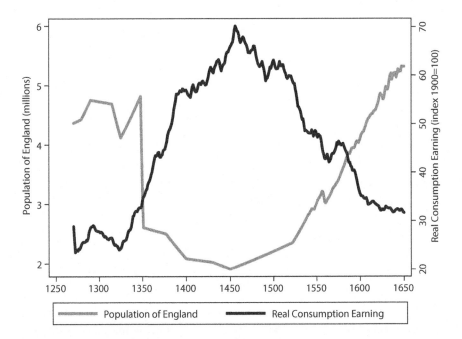

FIGURE 2.2   An empirical illustration of the Malthusian trap.

The population of England versus the real consumption earning index with a moving average filter applied
(1270–1650).

Source: Historical data obtained from Thomas and Dimsdale (2017) via the Bank of England.

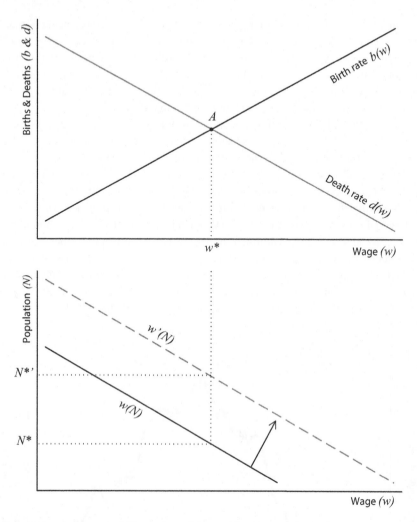

FIGURE 2.3   A theoretical illustration of the Malthusian trap.

The basic Malthusian model has a positive relationship between birth rates and wages, and negative relationships between death rates and wages, and between the population size and wages. The latter is caused by decreasing returns to labour when the available land resources are fixed. Point A maintains a stable population N★. Mortality events such as the Black Death lead to wages w > w★, which leads to population growth, returning the economy to equilibrium at Point A. Technological improvement moves the economy from w(N) to w′(N), but ceteris paribus this eventually leads to a larger population (N★) with equilibrium wages w★ left unchanged (Voigtländer and Voth 2013).

Still, the economic reality was a little more nuanced. Chaney and Hornbeck (2016) analysed data from the 1609 expulsion of Moriscos from Spain to show that particular social institutions and cultural factors influenced the speed of convergence in the Malthusian dynamics, enabling significantly higher per capita incomes to be sustained in subsets of the economy. As Fouquet and Broadberry (2015) point out, there is also plenty of data to suggest that European economies experienced episodes of economic growth following events of the Italian Renaissance and the Golden Age of Holland; however, these growth periods were short-lived. Other European economies witnessed economic deterioration.

Malthusian stagnation should not be interpreted to suggest that macroeconomic variables were stable and nothing of interest was taking place. Although GDP per capita fluctuated quite dramatically in relative terms due to various wars and other economic events or natural disasters, the point is that there was little evidence of any sustained growth in per capita income. Aiyar, Dalgaard, and Moav (2008) argue that the periods of technological and economic deterioration could partly be explained by realising that, historically, technology and human capital were not always as conceptually distinct as they are often assumed to be today. Interestingly, Madsen, Ang, and Banerjee (2010) conclude that the data on technological innovation in Britain supports a Schumpeterian model of economic growth more strongly than it supports a semi-endogenous growth model.

There are ample studies in the economic history literature showing that economies tended to have stable populations if they did not see substantial advances in technology or an acquisition of new land. They also tended to maintain a relatively constant level of per capita income (Woodward 1981). The countries which possessed greater technological capability were eventually able to support larger populations, but the average standard of living remained little different from that of less advanced economies.

3 The industrial revolution: the first

The First Industrial Revolution, or simply, the Industrial Revolution, is widely understood to have occurred from about 1760 to about 1840 in Great Britain, which is often cited as the example economy due to its first-runner status in the list of world economies moving out of the Malthusian stagnation (Berg and Hudson 1992). Its defining features were the invention of the steam engine and the widespread construction of railroads (Taylor 1951), which made mechanical production possible and opened new possibilities for communication and trade networks (Inikori 2002). Put simply, technology was developed which enabled the construction of infrastructure to support the production of more valuable goods and services within a given timeframe, with the same resources (Rosenberg 1983). Infrastructure was also developed, which allowed for the development of larger global marketplaces for communication, trade, and investment. A greater proportion of GDP began to be sourced from non-agrarian sectors (Overton 1996).

This general period of economic history has also been referred to as the "Post-Malthusian Regime" by Galor (2005) and other scholars. Møller and Sharp (2014), however, argues that England had "already escaped the Malthusian Epoch" about two hundred years before the onset of the Industrial Revolution. Their empirical conclusions are based on estimating a cointegrated vector autoregression (CVAR) Malthusian model between birth (and death) rates and income. Klemp and Møller

(2016) raise the salient point that a transitory post-Malthusian era is probably not a necessary step for economies as they pass out of economic stagnation to sustained growth. Instead, it may be a unique characteristic of the English economy.

Vast amounts have been written on the subject of the Industrial Revolution. Economic historians over the last 150 years have engaged in many lively and scholarly debates about the detail and nature of its origins (Hudson 1992). Advances in statistical methods in the latter half of the twentieth century opened up new tools, such as Granger causality testing (Granger 1969), with which to carry out these debates of predictive causality and significance. In his renowned chapter "The Industrial Revolution and the New Economic History" (Mokyr 1985), Joel Mokyr identifies the following four primary schools of thought which help to make sense of the various scholarly and professional contributions to the subject:

1 **The social change school**

These contributions tended to view the Industrial Revolution as primarily an institutional change in the nature of economic marketplaces where people and legal entities could come together to exchange goods and services. An emphasis was also placed upon the birth of new markets for both final goods and factors of production higher up in the supply chain. As an early example of authors from this school, Mokyr points out that Arnold Toynbee's (1884) well-known *Lectures on the Industrial Revolution* contains the quote that "the essence of the Industrial Revolution is the substitution of competition for the medieval regulations which had previously controlled the production and distribution of wealth."

2 **The industrial organization school**

These contributions tend to narrow in on the noticeable changes to the economic and managerial structure of the firm and the changing role of capital in production processes. Technological advances led to the development of new capital goods such as steam engines and cotton-spinning machinery. Being mostly machines and structures, many of these capital items were markedly fixed in nature, in contrast to circulating capital items such as agricultural seed and raw materials. An early author who falls squarely within this school is Mantoux (1928).

3 **The macroeconomic school**

This body of literature focuses on the evolution of economic growth models and the theoretical and empirical relationships between various aggregated macroeconomic variables. Kuznets (1959) and Rostow (1960) are typical early examples of this approach to looking at the Industrial Revolution.

4 **The technological school**

These contributions tend to examine the developments in new technology over time and track how certain inventions and innovation impact the labour market, marketing processes, production processes, and productivity growth. An excellent early example of this school of thought, according to Mokyr, is Landes (1969).

In practical terms, the Industrial Revolution saw the first widespread replacement of muscle power with machine power in a wide variety of production processes (Musson and Robinson 1989). The era marked the first period in history when the population and the per capita income increased simultaneously. The sources of increased productivity are numerous, but oft-quoted examples include cotton spinning (Lakwete 2005), iron making (Gordon 1996), steam power, and machine tools for the mass production of metal parts. Hobsbawm (1962), Brown (1991), Horn, Rosenband, and Smith (2010) and Wrigley (2018) are key texts which cover this era of economic history, and we refer the reader to these sources for an extended discussion.

Empirical estimation of trends in real wage growth in this period are difficult and fraught with problems, although evidence suggests that real wage growth in England was close to zero between 1750 and 1813, subsequently rising to 1.2% per year (Crafts and Mills 1994). Hartwell (1961) found reasonable evidence that life expectancy in England increased slowly in the early nineteenth century and more rapidly after 1840. Hartwell also concluded that this improvement had more grounding in the improved economic and social environment, rather than strictly medical advances.

While the economic infrastructure and institutions were vastly transformed during the Industrial Revolution, Feinstein (1998) and Komlos and Snowdon (2005) remind us that the actual impacts on the standard of living for average workers was perhaps not as optimistic, at least during the early stages of the era, if other metrics are considered beyond per capita income. As Szreter and Mooney (1998) point out, child mortality among the working classes in industrial and urban sectors remained high until the mid-nineteenth century. Fogel (2004) emphasised that the great economic transformations in society during the Industrial Revolution did not substantially translate into improved nutrition and lower mortality rates for the working classes until the twentieth century.

4 The technological revolution: the second

The Second Industrial Revolution, or Technological Revolution, occurred from about 1850 to about 1920. Its defining features were the massive advancement of manufacturing and organised production capacity, as electricity, telecommunications, transportation, and the production line mobilised ideas, resources, and commerce. The era saw the widespread adoption and innovative integration of technologies throughout supply chains, which transformed production processes and commercial trade using electricity and better business management (Morison 1966). Due to its impact on economic growth and its clear regime shift away from the previous Malthusian dynamics, Galor (2005) and other authors refer to the period of economic history from the Technological Revolution to the present day as the "Sustained Growth Regime."

Increased productivity can be traced to several technological advances. These especially include the following: the development of the Bessemer process for the mass production of steel parts for construction and machinery; substantial railroad networks for the convenient transportation of people and commerce; the Suez canal and improved access to water-based trade routes with better, powered vessels to navigate them; the invention of the telegraph and telephone for rapid communication of information; the introduction of electrical devices (for example, controlled lighting) and the AC power sources to manage them; and the technology to support a petroleum industry, which generated fuel and an array of useful chemicals and other materials (Hull 1999). Of course, the Technological Revolution also witnessed the introduction of rubber, internal combustion engines, automobiles, and powered manned flight. Compared to the technological advances made in the Industrial Revolution, network effects and widespread adoption of technological applications in each industry during the Technological Revolution caused faster increases in living standards, as seen in Figure 2.1. In the latter years of the Technological Revolution, the domestic consumer market rose as an influential driver of new products, including durables, spurred on by dramatic population growth and rising incomes, especially in the United States.

It is also worth noting that, as with the Industrial Revolution, the Technological Revolution was still largely Eurocentric, in that the various European economies were arguably still leading the world in terms of measurably innovating and transforming their industries to make use of the latest technology and become more productive (Hartwell 1971). The word "capitalism" first entered a state of widespread use in the public and economic vocabulary in the 1860s. Many authors have pointed out that the various economic institutions (especially banking, governance, and the rule of law) in European society by this time were mature enough to support a largescale transition in the way that value was created and exchanged, especially in the British economy. Hobsbawm (1975, p. 15) went so far as to say that the "(British) industrial revolution had swallowed the (French) political revolution."

During the height of the Technological Revolution in 1889, the American economist David Wells wrote candidly of the numerous economic shifts which had upended old industries and presented many new opportunities and challenges. In his own words:

> The economic changes that have occurred during the last quarter of a century – or during the present generation of living men – have unquestionably been more important and varied than during any former corresponding period of the world's history. It would seem, indeed, as if the world, during all the years since the inception of civilization, has been working up on the line of equipment for industrial effort – inventing and perfecting tools and machinery, building workshops and factories, and devising instrumentalities for the easy intercommunication of persons and thoughts, and the cheap exchange of products and services; that this equipment having at last been made ready, the work of using it has, for the first time in our day and generation, fairly begun; and also that every community under prior or existing conditions of use and consumption, is becoming saturated, as it were, with

its results. As an immediate consequence the world has never seen anything comparable to the results of the recent system of transportation by land and water; never experienced in so short a time such an expansion of all that pertains to what is called "business" and has never before been able to accomplish so much in the way of production with a given amount of labor in a given time. Concurrently, or as the necessary sequence of these changes, has come a series of wide-spread and complex disturbances; manifesting themselves in great reductions of the cost of production and distribution and a consequent remarkable decline in the prices of nearly all staple commodities, in a radical change in the relative values of the precious metals, in the absolute destruction of large amounts of capital through new inventions and discoveries and in the impairment of even greater amounts through extensive reductions in the rates of interest and profits, in the discontent of labor and in an increasing antagonism of nations, incident to a greatly intensified industrial and commercial competition. Out of these changes will probably come further disturbances, which to many thoughtful and conservative minds seem full of menace of a mustering of the barbarians from within rather than as of old from without, for an attack on the whole present organization of society, and even the permanency of civilization itself.

(Wells 1889, p. v)

Many industries struggled to adapt to the rapid changes, and while per capita incomes were rising, there were severe social challenges associated with increasing urbanisation and the changing composition of workforce as many new jobs were created and old trades disappeared. Average wages may have been rising, but average housing conditions for workers were quite poor, and working conditions were mostly unregulated, leading to preventable injuries and poor health (Clark 2002). These urban issues caused by industrialisation were equally matched by issues in the countryside caused by persistent neglect as the centre of mass for the economy's engine shifted (Hopkins 2000, p. 93).

5 The digital revolution: the third

The Digital Revolution, or Third Industrial Revolution, found its roots in the post-war 1950s and, in the opinion of the authors, concluded in the mid-2000s when smartphones and multipurpose mobile computing devices first became widespread. The defining feature of the Digital Revolution was the mass production of microprocessors and various other electronic devices for computation, communication, and data storage. The rapid pace of growth in this sector drew significant attention from researchers (Chow 1967; Bresnahan 1986). In essence, the era saw the rise of computing power and storage capacity in accordance with Moore's law, along with new data transmission technologies. Some of the most economically valuable applications of this new technology included personal computers, the CD-ROM, the internet, automated teller machines, digital cameras, and cell phones (Garifova 2015).

Another glance at Figure 2.1 shows that during the Digital Revolution, per capita incomes skyrocketed at a pace far beyond that of the previous two industrial revolutions. Of course, there were also negative pollution externalities resulting from production processes which are not represented in per capita incomes (Bowers 2014). The aforementioned technological applications generated increased productivity in several ways (Jorgenson and Stiroh 2014). For instance, the ability to communicate instantly via email or while commuting with a cell phone meant that less idle time was wasted waiting for a response, and the cost of communicating fell, leading to quicker decisions and higher labour productivity. This included the technology to achieve cost-effective one-to-many communication via email, instead of the old one-to-one communication via phone or post. This scalability supported the growth of many businesses. It also enabled travellers to be more productive while away from the ordinary work environment (Wardman and Lyons 2016). Moreover, the commoditisation of knowledge through organised digital storage and retrieval systems, along with the means to search for, reproduce, and copy information as required, generated positive externalities leading to greater human capital resources and higher labour productivity (Jorgenson 2001). In addition, the heightened ability to process and interpret data enabled more accurate modelling to occur in a variety of industries, creating better preparedness for contingencies and less time and money wasted on avoidable mistakes. Another large contributor to the massive growth in output per capita stemmed from the general replacement of humans with computers for mundane administrative functions (Acemoglu et al. 2014). Not only were workers freed to spend their time solving higher-order problems and tasks, but their previous administrative tasks were completed with fewer costly errors, in less time. As Pabilonia and Zoghi (2005) point out, however, wages tended to rise only when workers were able to learn new skills to use the new and more efficient technology. Many former job roles had to be completely reimagined (Levy and Murnane 1996). Instant communication around the world helped make international outsourcing more affordable, enabling many smaller businesses to access and grow into the global marketplace (Litan and Rivlin 2001).

If the first and second industrial revolutions replaced animals with machines and better connected the world through the physical movement of people and products, the third industrial revolution replaced humans with computers and better connected the world through the digital movement of information. The Digital Revolution affected industries globally, even in less-developed economies. Nevertheless, the economies which grew the most rapidly had high existing levels of human capital, extensive fixed capital in the form of telecommunications infrastructure, and a large number of supporting products and services (Antonelli 2003). This is one reason why the United States arguably led the world through the Digital Revolution in terms of economic growth and innovative output (Cardona, Kretschmer, and Strobel 2013), in contrast to the previous two industrial revolutions which were led by European countries.

6 The Fourth Industrial Revolution

The Fourth Industrial Revolution (henceforth, 4IR) is the current period of economic transition since the mid-2000s, which is characterized by a fusion of new digital technologies, rooted in advances from the Digital Revolution, with technological applications in the physical and biological domains. This fusion is also known as "technology convergence" (Park 2017).

Klaus Schwab, the Founder and Executive Chairman of the World Economic Forum, is credited for bringing to the world's attention the importance of the 4IR, presenting a strong case that the characteristics of the transitions now facing economic institutions, industry and society at large are of a fundamentally different nature to those seen in the Digital Revolution. His seminal book, *The Fourth Industrial Revolution*, argues that the present industrial revolution exceeds the Digital Revolution as measured by (1) the velocity of technology convergence; (2) the breadth and depth of the institutional shifts reshaping our identity and *modus operandi*; and (3) the impact at the systems level not just within, but also across, industries and countries (Schwab 2016, p. 8).

Schwab goes onto list what he identifies as the most influential "technological mega-trends" of the 4IR, which underpin and drive the changes we are presently witnessing. In the physical category, he notes the role of autonomous vehicles, 3D printing, advanced robotics, and new materials for construction and design. In the digital category, he highlights the pervasive impact of the so-called (Industrial) Internet of Things (IoT/IIoT), blockchain applications, and various digital platforms designed for large numbers of users. In the biological category, Schwab emphasizes the rapid developments in synthetic biology, health maintenance, and the neurosciences. Many other technological trends of the 4IR are discussed in the sequel book, *Shaping the Future of the Fourth Industrial Revolution* (Schwab 2018).

In this book, we suggest that the latest generation digital platforms and IIoT systems based on evolving Internet technologies, the many creative blockchain use cases (beyond crypto-currency), and the applications of artificial intelligence which replace automation with "smartization" (Park 2017) are the three most important of all of these technological mega-trends in terms of their realised and potential impact on the economy and its institutions.

The following characterize some of the most noticeable economic impacts of the 4IR. Firstly, we have witnessed an exponential acceleration of the rate of innovation, disruption, and market penetration; for example, the world witnessed over a billion smartphones in use around the world within several years of the iPhone launch. We have also seen historically unprecedented returns to scale, where many digital businesses have marginal costs which now tend toward zero. The changing role of capital versus labour in the production process is crucial, as in many industries the return to capital is outpacing the returns to labour. We have also observed the creation of many unexpected new markets and ecosystems as technology lowers the cost of satisfying previously unmet needs of consumers, making new business models operationally viable (Dirican 2015). In some cases, these may represent lowered search costs in the marketplace. In other cases, the technology may work behind the scenes in a supportive capacity, freeing up the businesses to add a more human element to their goods and services.

The 4IR also comes with its fair share of challenges, such as rising economic inequality; the short-term destabilising effects of deinstitutionalisation, democratisation, and decentralisation; and a lingering uncertainty around the future of work and the future sources of economic growth (Caruso 2018). As global per capita incomes have risen rapidly in the last two decades, the formerly bimodal distribution of world incomes has become more unimodal (Ravallion 2016). It also raises some ongoing questions, such as: To what extent are countries' future economic fortunes dependent upon their past (Landes 1998)? Is sustained economic growth possible for the future (Saniee et al. 2017; Özak 2018)? The 4IR may be a great equaliser across economies in terms of measured averages, but the spread of wealth and income within economies is generally rising. There is also plenty of evidence to suggest that the 4IR, unlike its predecessor the Digital Revolution, is not predominantly being led by the United States' economy. Several other economies, especially China, are now generating technological innovation at a scale to rival the United States and possess a business ecosystem sufficiently mature to support global commercialisation.

With such challenges clearly in mind, Schwab writes that

> the Fourth Industrial Revolution is much more than just a description of technologically-driven change. . . [W]e need to deepen our understanding of the way that new technologies connect with one another and influence us in both subtle and obvious ways, reflecting and amplifying human values as we make decisions around investment, design, adoption and reinvention. It is difficult, if not impossible, to collaborate on investments, policies and collective action that positively affect the future unless we can appreciate the way that people and technologies interact. The overarching opportunity of the Fourth Industrial Revolution is therefore to look beyond technologies as either simple tools or inevitable forces, finding ways to give the greatest number of people the ability to positively impact their families, organizations and communities by influencing and guiding the systems that surround us and shape our lives. By systems, we mean the norms, rules, expectations, goals, institutions and incentives that guide our behaviour every day, as well as the infrastructure and flows of material and people that are fundamental to our economic, political and social lives.
>
> *(Schwab 2018, p. 6)*

Considering this wise commentary, this present book aspires to further explore a few of these behavioural and institutional aspects of the Fourth Industrial Revolution, as they relate to technological advances built upon the Internet, artificial intelligence, and the blockchain.

References

Acemoglu, Daron et al. 2014. "Return of the Solow Paradox? IT, Productivity, and Employment in US Manufacturing." *American Economic Review: Papers & Proceedings* 104(5): 394–399.

Aiyar, Shekhar, Carl Johan Dalgaard, and Omer Moav. 2008. "Technological Progress and Regress in Pre-Industrial Times." *Journal of Economic Growth* 13(2): 125–144.

Antonelli, Cristiano. 2003. "The Digital Divide: Understanding the Economics of New Information and Communication Technology in the Global Economy." *Information Economics and Policy* 15(2): 173–199.

Ashraf, Quamrul, and Oded Galor. 2011. "Dynamics and Stagnation in the Malthusian Epoch." *American Economic Review* 101(5): 2003–2041.

Baten, Joerg, and Jan Luiten Van Zanden. 2008. "Book Production and the Onset of Modern Economic Growth." *Journal of Economic Growth* 13(3): 217–235.

Berg, Maxine, and Pat Hudson. 1992. "Rehabilitating the Industrial Revolution." *The Economic History Review* 45(1): 24–50.

Berg, Peter, and Mark Staley. 2015. "Capital Substitution in an Industrial Revolution." *Canadian Journal of Economics* 48(5): 1975–2004.

Boserup, Ester. 1965. *The Conditions of Agricultural Growth.* Chicago, IL: Aldine Publishing.

Bowers, C. A. 2014. *The False Promises of the Digital Revolution: How Computers Transform Education, Work, and International Development in Ways That Are Ecologically Unsustainable.* Bern, Switzerland: Peter Lang Inc.

Bresnahan, Timothy F. 1986. "Measuring the Spillovers from Technical Advance: Mainframe Computers in Financial Services." *The American Economic Review* 76(4): 742–755.

Broadberry, S. et al. 2015. *British Economic Growth, 1270–1870.* Cambridge, MA: Cambridge University Press.

Brown, Richard. 1991. *Society and Economy in Modern Britain 1700–1850.* London: Routledge.

Cardona, M., T. Kretschmer, and T. Strobel. 2013. "ICT and Productivity: Conclusions from the Empirical Literature." *Information Economics and Policy* 25(3): 109–125.

Caruso, Loris. 2018. "Digital Innovation and the Fourth Industrial Revolution: Epochal Social Changes?" *AI and Society* 33(3): 379–392.

Chaney, Eric, and Richard Hornbeck. 2016. "Economic Dynamics in the Malthusian Era: Evidence from the 1609 Spanish Expulsion of the Moriscos." *Economic Journal* 126(594): 1404–1440.

Chatterjee, Shoumitro, and Tom Vogl. 2018. "Escaping Malthus: Economic Growth and Fertility Change in the Developing World." *American Economic Review* 108(6): 1440–1467.

Chow, Gregory C. 1967. "Technological Change and the Demand for Computers." *The American Economic Review* 57(5): 1117–1130.

Clark, Gregory. 2002. "Shelter from the Storm: Housing and the Industrial Revolution, 1550–1909." *The Journal of Economic History* 62(2): 489–511.

Crafts, N. F. R., and Terence C. Mills. 1994. "Trends in Real Wages in Britain, 1750–1913." *Explorations in Economic History* 31(2): 176–194.

Dalgaard, Carl Johan, and Holger Strulik. 2013. "The History Augmented Solow Model." *European Economic Review* 63: 134–149.

Dalgaard, Carl Johan, and Holger Strulik. 2016. "Physiology and Development: Why the West Is Taller Than the Rest." *Economic Journal* 126(598): 2292–2323.

Dirican, Cüneyt. 2015. "The Impacts of Robotics, Artificial Intelligence On Business and Economics." *Procedia – Social and Behavioral Sciences* 195: 564–573.

Doepke, Matthias. 2004. "Accounting for Fertility Decline During the Transition to Growth." *Journal of Economic Growth* 9(3): 347–383.

Feinstein, Charles H. 1998. "Pessimism Perpetuated: Real Wages and the Standard of Living in Britain during and after the Industrial Revolution." *Journal of Economic History* 58(3): 625–658.

Fogel, Robert William. 2004. *The Escape from Hunger and Premature Death, 1700–2100: Europe, America, and the Third World*. New York: Cambridge University Press.

Fouquet, Roger, and Stephen Broadberry. 2015. "Seven Centuries of European Economic Growth and Decline." *Journal of Economic Perspectives* 29(4): 227–244.

Galindev, Ragchaasuren. 2011. "Leisure Goods, Education Attainment and Fertility Choice." *Journal of Economic Growth* 16(2): 157–181.

Galor, Oded. 2005. "From Stagnation to Growth: Unified Growth Theory." Pp. 171–293 in *Handbook of Economic Growth*, edited by Philippe Aghion and Steven Durlauf. Amsterdam, Netherlands: Elsevier.

Galor, Oded. 2011. *Unified Growth Theory*. Princeton, NJ: Princeton University Press.

Galor, Oded, and David N. Weil. 2000. "Population, Technology, and Growth: From Malthusian Stagnation to the Demographic Transition and Beyond." *American Economic Review* 90(4): 806–828.

Garifova, L. F. 2015. "Infonomics and the Value of Information in the Digital Economy." *Procedia Economics and Finance* 23(October 2014): 738–743.

Gordon, Robert B. 1996. *American Iron, 1607–1900*. Baltimore: Johns Hopkins University Press.

Granger, Clive W. J. 1969. "Investigating Causal Relations by Econometric Models and Cross-Spectral Methods." *Econometrica* 37(3): 424–438.

Hansen, Gary D., and Edward C. Prescott. 2002. "Malthus to Solow." *The American Economic Review* 92(4): 1205–1217.

Hartwell, R. M. 1961. "The Rising Standard of Living in England, 1800–1850." *The Economic History Review* 13(3): 397–416.

Hartwell, R. M. 1971. *The Industrial Revolution and Economic Growth*. London: Routledge.

Hobsbawm, Eric. 1962. *The Age of Revolution: Europe 1789–1848*. London: Weidenfeld and Nicolson.

Hobsbawm, Eric. 1975. *The Age of Capital: 1848–1875*. London: Weidenfeld and Nicolson.

Hopkins, Eric. 2000. *Industrialisation and Society: A Social History, 1830–1951*. London: Routledge.

Horn, Jeff, Leonard N. Rosenband, and Merritt Roe Smith, eds. 2010. *Reconceptualizing the Industrial Revolution*. Cambridge, MA: MIT Press.

Hudson, Pat. 1992. *The Industrial Revolution*. London: Edward Arnold.

Hull, James. 1999. "The Second Industrial Revolution: The History of a Concept." *Storia Della Storiografia* 36(2): 81–90.

Inikori, Joseph E. 2002. *Africans and the Industrial Revolution in England: A Study in International Trade and Economic Development*. Cambridge, England: Cambridge University Press.

Jorgenson, Dale W. 2001. "Information Technology and the U.S. Economy." *The American Economic Review* 91(1): 1–32.

Jorgenson, Dale W., and Kevin J. Stiroh. 2014. "Productivity Growth: Current Recovery and Longer-Term Trends." *The American Economic Review* 89(2): 109–115.

Klemp, Marc, and Niels Framroze Møller. 2016. "Post-Malthusian Dynamics in Pre-Industrial Scandinavia." *Scandinavian Journal of Economics* 118(4): 841–867.

Komlos, John, and Brian Snowdon. 2005. "Measures of Progress and Other Tall Stories: From Income to Anthropometrics." *World Economics* 6(2): 87–136.

Kuznets, S. S. 1959. *Six Lectures on Economic Growth*. New York: Free Press

Lakwete, Angele. 2005. *Inventing the Cotton Gin: Machine and Myth in Antebellum America*. Baltimore: Johns Hopkins University Press.

Landes, David S. 1998. *The Wealth and Poverty of Nations: Why Some Are So Rich and Some So Poor*. New York: W. W. Norton & Co.

Landes, David S. 1969. *Unbound Prometheus: Technological Change and Industrial Development in Western Europe from 1750 to the Present*. Cambridge, England: Cambridge University Press.

Levy, Frank, and Richard J. Murnane. 1996. "With What Skills Are Computers a Complement?" *American Economic Review* 86(2): 258–262.

Litan, Robert E., and Alice M. Rivlin. 2001. "Projecting the Economic Impact of the Internet." *American Economic Review* 91(2): 313–317.

Madsen, Jakob B., James B. Ang, and Rajabrata Banerjee. 2010. "Four Centuries of British Economic Growth: The Roles of Technology and Population." *Journal of Economic Growth* 15(4): 263–290.

Madsen, Jakob B., and Fabrice Murtin. 2017. "British Economic Growth since 1270: The Role of Education." *Journal of Economic Growth* 22(3): 229–272.

Malthus, Thomas. 1798. "An Essay on the Principle of Population." 1–134.

Mantoux, Paul. 1928. *The Industrial Revolution in the Eighteenth Century*. New York: Evanston 1961; First English ed. 1928, first French ed. 1905.

Mokyr, Joel, ed. 1985. *The Economics of the Industrial Revolution*. London: George Allen & Unwin.

Møller, Niels Framroze, and Paul Sharp. 2014. "Malthus in Cointegration Space: Evidence of a Post-Malthusian Pre-Industrial England." *Journal of Economic Growth* 19(1): 105–140.

Morison, Elting E. 1966. *Men, Machines, and Modern Times*. Cambridge, MA: MIT Press.

Musson, Albert Edward, and Eric Robinson. 1989. *Science and Technology in the Industrial Revolution*. Taylor & Francis.

Nielsen, Ron W. 2016. "Unified Growth Theory Contradicted by the Mathematical Analysis of the Historical Growth of Human Population." *Journal of Economics and Political Economy* 3(2): 242–263.

Overton, Mark. 1996. *Agricultural Revolution in England: The Transformation of the Agrarian Economy 1500–1850*. Cambridge, MA: Cambridge University Press.

Özak, Ömer. 2018. "Distance to the Pre-Industrial Technological Frontier and Economic Development." *Journal of Economic Growth* 23.

Pabilonia, Sabrina Wulff, and Cindy Zoghi. 2005. "Returning to the Returns to Computer Use." *The American Economic Review* 95(2): 314–317.

Park, Hang Sik. 2017. "Technology Convergence, Open Innovation, and Dynamic Economy." *Journal of Open Innovation: Technology, Market, and Complexity* 3(1): 24.

Ravallion, Martin. 2016. "Are the World's Poorest Being Left behind?" *Journal of Economic Growth* 21(2): 139–164.

Rosenberg, Nathan. 1983. *Inside the Black Box: Technology and Economics*. Cambridge University Press.

Rostow, W. W. 1960. *The Stages of Economic Growth*. Cambridge University Press.

Saniee, Iraj, Sanjay Kamat, Subra Prakash, and Marcus Weldon. 2017. "Will Productivity Growth Return in the New Digital Era? An Analysis of the Potential Mipact on Productivity of the Fourth Industrial Revolution." *Bell Labs Technical Journal* 22(2).

Schwab, Klaus. 2016. *The Fourth Industrial Revolution*. Geneva: World Economic Forum.

Schwab, Klaus. 2018. *Shaping the Future of the Fourth Industrial Revolution*. Geneva: World Economic Forum.

Smith, Adam. 1776. *An Inquiry into the Nature and Causes of the Wealth of Nations.*

Strulik, Holger, Klaus Prettner, and Alexia Prskawetz. 2013. "The Past and Future of Knowledge-Based Growth." *Journal of Economic Growth* 18(4): 411–437.

Strulik, Holger, and Jacob Weisdorf. 2008. "Population, Food, and Knowledge: A Simple Unified Growth Theory." *Journal of Economic Growth* 13(3): 195–216.

Szreter, Simon, and Graham Mooney. 1998. "Urbanization, Mortality, and the Standard of Living Debate: New Estimates of the Expectation of Life at Birth in Nineteenth-Century British Cities." *Economic History Review* 51(1): 84–112.

Taylor, George Rogers. 1951. *The Transportation Revolution: 1815–1860.* Holt, Rinehart and Winston.

Thomas, R., and N. Dimsdale. 2017. "A Millennium of UK Data: Bank of England OBRA Dataset." www.bankofengland.co.uk/research/Pages/onebank/threecenturies.aspx.

Toynbee, Arnold. 1884. "Lectures on the Industrial Revolution."

Voigtländer, Nico, and Hans-Joachim Voth. 2013. "Gifts of Mars: Warfare and Europe's Early Rise to Riches." *Journal of Economic Perspectives* 27(4): 165–186.

Wardman, Mark, and Glenn Lyons. 2016. "The Digital Revolution and Worthwhile Use of Travel Time: Implications for Appraisal and Forecasting." *Transportation* 43(3): 507–530.

Wells, David A. 1889. *Recent Economic Changes and Their Effect on Production and Distribution of Wealth and Well-Being of Society.* New York: D. Appleton & Company.

Woodward, Donald. 1981. "Wage Rates and Living Standards in Pre-Industrial England." *Past & Present1* 91(1): 28–46.

Wrigley, E. Anthony. 2018. "Reconsidering the Industrial Revolution: England and Wales." *Journal of Interdisciplinary History* 49(1): 9–42.

3

THE *TELOS* OF INDUSTRIAL REVOLUTIONS

How what people value drives the adoption of new technologies

In this section, we introduce a useful framework to not only understand why technological applications were successfully adopted in the first three industrial revolutions, but also understand some of the fundamental human forces driving changes now and in the future through the Fourth Industrial Revolution.

Earlier it was mentioned that industrial revolutions occur when major systematic and industry-independent breakthrough applications of innovative technology permit new manifestations of essential economic institutions or marketplaces and shift the aggregate production possibilities frontier outward while permanently raising the standard of living. Now, at the end of the day, these applications of innovative technology will only have an impact on the economy if people, whether acting individually or within legally ordained groups (such as companies, government organisations, or nongovernmental organisations), decide to adopt and use them. This adoption decision is key because it represents an allocation of limited time and limited resources (such as money) towards procurement and implementation, in preference to alternative possible allocations.

In a free marketplace, rational economic agents only allocate time and resources towards those things which they perceive as sufficiently valuable – at least as valuable as the time and resources spent in procurement and consumption in order to realise the utility of the thing. Many thousands of pages have been devoted to studying choice theory and answering the question of what constitutes "rationality." We will not delve into this literature here beyond a few observations.

In the standard economic model, the rationality axioms are (1) *completeness*, where agents maintain a preference ordering across every pair of elements in their action set, and (2) *transitivity*, where agents have consistent preference orderings. The typical economic axioms which accompany these are (1) *monotonicity*, where more of a thing is generally preferred to less of it, and (2) *convexity*, where variety is generally preferred to monotony. Expected utility maximisation and Bayesian probability theory are used to extend this simplistic concept of rationality to more realistic decisions under an uncertainty of the outcomes (Simon 1955; Gomes 2011). Other extensions involving discounting and time preferences are relevant when the utility of the thing is not immediately realised or is realised over an extended period. Behavioural economic models tend to extend the idea of rationality to "the pursuit of perceived self-interest" in order to account for bounded rationality due to incomplete information or cognitive failures and the observation that agents tend to make decisions using heuristics rather than strictly optimising their payoffs (Baumeister 2001; Wilkinson and Klaes 2012, p. 8).

For this discussion, however, we are less interested in the mechanics of rationality and more interested in the derivation of value. We are less interested in choice theory and more interested in the underlying causes of preferences. Instead of asking "What do people prefer?" we must ask "What do people want?" and "What motivates people to act and pursue something?" This will help us to identify the general direction in which trends will move in the economy.

1 Means, ends, and value

A helpful, if not Aristotelian, approach to think about this question is in terms of means and ends. Most people, whether they consciously think about it or not, have some list of objectives, either tacit or explicit, which they are striving towards, either in the short-term, medium-term, or long-term. Several prominent recent authors, including Sen (1990), have raised similar points. Sen opined, "Rationality may be seen as demanding something other than just consistency of choices between different subset. It must, at least, demand cogent relations between aims and objectives actually entertained by the person and the choices that the person makes."

Now, most people desire to attain some sufficient measure of satisfaction or happiness, and the attainment of such may be considered the *ultimate end* or *final end* towards which people are striving. Indeed, in his *Nichomachean Ethics*, Aristotle argues that

> if there is only one final end, this will be the good of which we are in search; and if there are more than one, it will be the most final of these. Now we call an object pursued for its own sake more final than one pursued because of something else, and one which is never choosable because of another more final than those which are choosable because of it as well as for their own sakes; and that which is always choosable for its own sake and never because of something else we call final without any qualification. Well, happiness more than anything else is thought to be just such an end, because we always choose it for itself, and never for any other reason. It is different with honour, pleasure, intelligence and good qualities generally. We do choose them partly for themselves . . . but we choose them also for the sake of our happiness, in the belief that they will be instrumental in promoting it.
>
> *(Aristotle, 1097a, p. 30, 1097b, p. 5)*

With reference to this line of reasoning, we shall refer to those ends which are distinct from but tend to support the attainment of human satisfaction and happiness as *instrumental ends* or *penultimate ends*. These penultimate ends are those meaningful things in life which people generally consider to be desirable ends in themselves, but which also represent a means to obtain the ultimate end. One's ultimate end cannot be determined using economics. It does not matter for the purpose of this analysis what a person's ultimate end is, but only that nearly everyone is in agreement on the things which will make it easier for you to attain it.

Many authors of the last century, such as Maslow (1943, 1954), Galtung (1980), and Max-Neef (1991), have attempted to create a model for human motivation based on hierarchical categories of universal needs. Even in ancient times, Plato noted an implicit hierarchy of needs: "Now the first and chief of our needs is the provision of food for existence and life. The second is housing and the third is raiment and that sort of thing" (Plato, *Republic*, II, 369D). Translated into English, the German economist Ernst Engel stated in 1895 that "all living things are born with a number of needs, whose non-satisfaction leads to death. The human being is not an exception. Also in him works the urge to satisfy (these needs) with a natural power that can overcome strong constraints that either carry humans away from or lead them to victory." Several paragraphs later, Engel continued: "Needs are not of the same rank. At the top stand those needs whose satisfaction is key to physical sustenance: nourishment, clothing, housing, heating and lighting and health. Of a second order follow: intellectual and spiritual care, legal protection and public safety, public provisions and assistance." (Engel 1895, p. 8). This early work was significant because, as Chai and Moneta (2012) point out, Engel decided to analyse how household expenditure is distributed across consumer needs rather than across goods and services, the more typical approach. This approach was also noted by the economist Nicholas Georgescu-Roegen, who stated,

> There, we find that before anyone speaks of utility, of value or of how the individual behaves, one mentions needs, wants, uses, etc. These latter concepts are, it is true, far from being precisely defined, but so is utility or satisfaction, if we care to look into the matter. Lack of precise definition should not, however, disturb us in moral sciences, but improper concepts constructed by attributing to man faculties which he actually does not possess, should. And utility is such an improper concept, supported by other undefined concepts such as wants, uses, etc.
>
> *(Georgescu-Roegen 1954, p. 512)*

2 A hierarchy of value

Building upon these contributions, we now present a simple model of seven core penultimate ends across three levels which we have identified as useful for orientating ourselves among the torrent of new disruptive and transformative forces which are characteristic of industrial revolutions. These ends are neatly summarized in Figure 3.1, along with some examples of antepenultimate ends, which collectively act as a means to attaining the corresponding penultimate ends. This is not a hierarchy of needs but rather a technologically driven progressive freeing of time to devote to higher order activities. We all have finite energy and time, and

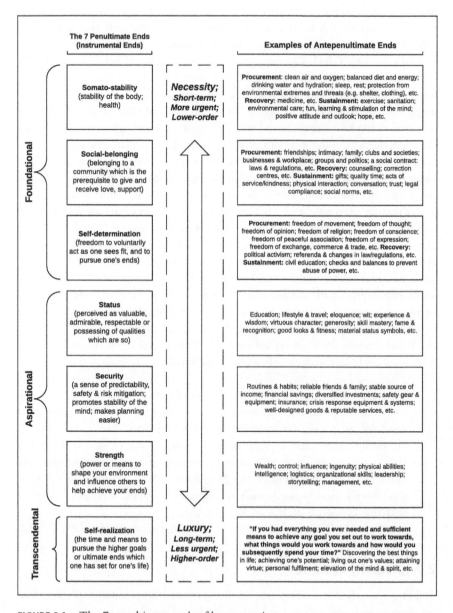

FIGURE 3.1 The 7 penultimate ends of human action.

The penultimate ends are those meaningful things in life which people generally consider to be desirable ends in themselves, but which also represent a means to obtain the ultimate end, generally understood to represent some sufficient measure of satisfaction, or happiness.

though often neglected in economic analysis, these are just as important as financial resources in peoples' resource allocation decisions.

People demand goods and services which help procure, recover, or sustain the antepenultimate ends. People gain utility from the attaining of these ends. It is our observation that almost every conceivable product or service that exists in the various economic marketplaces can be mapped to one or more of the antepenultimate ends. Even nonmarket goods and services such as air quality and noise can be mapped to these ends (Champ, Boyle, and Brown 2017). The goods and services associated with the lower-order ends tend to be treated as necessities, and those associated with the higher-order ends tend to be treated as luxuries. This approach yields a much fuller view of consumption utility than the standard model, which tends to treat goods and services as utility-providing items which ought to be consumed for their own sake. In our model, products and services do not simply provide utility to consumers (Ironmonger 1972); they help consumers to achieve their own ends.

Attainment of the higher-order ends generally requires some measure of attainment of the lower-order ends, but the reverse is not necessarily true. The lower-order ends are generally more fundamental and urgent, such that under conditions with less free time and fewer resources at their disposal, people will often choose to satisfy the three foundational ends at the expense of the higher-order ends. People may still prefer to be allocating time and resources to the higher-order ends, but the force of necessity prevails. This is in accordance with Engel's law (Chai and Moneta 2012, p. 655). This is not a new concept. Back in the 1840s, Banfield noted:

> The first proposition of the theory of consumption is that the satisfaction of every lower want in scale creates a desire of a higher character . . . The removal of a primary want commonly awakens the sense of more than one secondary privation: thus a full supply of ordinary food not only excites to the delicacy in eating, but awakens attention to clothing. The highest grade in the scale of wants, that of pleasure derived from the beauties of nature or art, is usually confined to men who are exempted from all the lower privations . . . It is the constancy of a relative value in objects of desire, and the fixed order of succession in which this value arises, that makes the satisfaction of our wants a matter of scientific calculation.
>
> *(Banfield 1845, pp. 11–21)*

Georgescu-Roegen (1954) refers to this concept as the Principle of the Subordination of Wants, in accordance with the work of Menger (1950).

2.1 Transcendental value

The higher-order, or transcendental, penultimate end in our model is *self-realization*. Self-realization represents the state of being in which you no longer need to be substantially concerned with allocating significant amounts of time to the first six penultimate ends beyond that required to protect and sustain them, giving you the ultimate freedom to pour time and resources into pursuing the higher objectives that you have set for your life, which you ultimately find most fulfilling. To illustrate, some people might suggest that self-realization can be most fully pursued when a person is financially free, possesses a loving and supportive family who loves them in return, has decent health, lives in a free society, is respected by the community, has plans for future contingencies, and has good relationships with other people who can help them achieve their objectives.

The exact nature of these objectives may differ from individual to individual, but could be determined by honestly answering the following question: "If you had everything you ever needed and sufficient means to achieve any goal you set out to work towards, what things would you work towards and how would you subsequently spend your time?" Self-realization cuts right to the question of "What do you really live for?" For some, this might be the cultivation of virtue, learning, or philanthropy, or an elevation of the mind and spirit, or the fulfilment of potential; for others, this might represent having enough time to enjoy the simple and good things in life simply because they are good. An individual's objectives with regard to self-realization will tend to be heavily reliant upon their moral philosophy, ethics, religion, and broader worldview.

2.2 Foundational value

The lower-order, or foundational, penultimate ends are *somato-stability*, *social-belonging*, and *self-determination*. By foundational we mean that without a sufficient measure of attainment of each of these three ends, it is near impossible to do much else to achieve your ultimate goals. In the absence of one of the foundational ends, there is a high probability that you will allocate most of your time, energy, and other resources towards efforts to procure or recover the end which is missing. The goods and services associated with attaining these foundational ends are typically subject to the saturation hypothesis, meaning that there tends to be an upper limit, known as the saturation level, to the allocation of resources put towards consuming them (Moneta and Chai 2014). As a caution to policymakers, Azgad-Tromer recently argued that the marketplaces for goods and services which satisfy these foundational penultimate ends are particularly vulnerable: "Markets of essentials tend toward failure of demand, due to consumers' bounded voluntariness and lower probability of informed choice. Accordingly, sellers in markets of essentials have higher incentives for collusion and lower incentives for price competition and for investment in product quality. Thus, the likelihood of market failure increases with the essentiality of the product: the more basic the underlying need, the higher the probability for market failure" (Azgad-Tromer 2015).

Somato-stability represents the state of being in which bodily systems and vital functions are operational and stable, such that one possesses physical well-being and the absence of serious disease or infirmity. This foundational end is desirable because its attainment is a prerequisite to attaining higher order objectives. Living is the prerequisite to living well. The antepenultimate ends which tend to help confer somato-stability include clean air and oxygen, a balanced diet, clean drinking water, quality sleep, protection from environmental extremes and threats, exercise, sanitation, environmental care, fun and mental stimulation, a positive attitude and outlook, and hope.

Social-belonging represents the state of being in which one identifies with and participates in communities of other people and feels accepted by the other members of the community. This foundational end is desirable because its attainment allows you to not only give and receive love, emotional support, and intellectual stimulation, but also possess the natural satisfaction that results from sharing experiences with other people whom you like (Scitovsky 1976, pp. 82–84). The antepenultimate ends which people tend to believe confer social-belonging are many and complex, but typically include personal bilateral friendships, physical interaction or intimacy, a healthy family dynamic, membership of clubs and societies, good relationships within businesses and within the workplace, a fair political system, a just social contract along with appropriate laws and regulations, counselling services, correction centres if necessary, gifts, quality time, generous acts of kindness, stimulating and honest conversation, and a sense of trust.

Self-determination represents the state of being in which one is free to voluntarily act as one sees fit, and to pursue one's own ends. This foundational end is desirable because its attainment allows you to work freely towards achieving your objectives. For instance, a person who lives in slavery, or under the purview of laws which overly restrict personal autonomy, will have great difficulty in working towards their ultimate goals. The antepenultimate ends which people tend to believe confer self-determination typically include rights such as freedom of movement, freedom of thought, freedom of opinion, freedom of religion, freedom of conscience, freedom of peaceful association, freedom of expression, and freedom of exchange, commerce, and trade in economic marketplaces. In some circumstances, the antepenultimate ends which support self-determination may include political activism and changes in the law or regulations, appropriate civil education, and checks and balances to prevent an abuse of power.

2.3 Aspirational value

The middle-order, or aspirational, penultimate ends in our model are *status*, *security*, and *strength*. All three of these aspirational penultimate ends require some measure of attainment of the three foundational penultimate ends.

Status represents the state of being in which you are perceived as valuable, admirable, and respectable, or possessing of qualities which are so. Your self-perception and the perception of you by others are both relevant. Status presupposes the existence of social-belonging, since status is derived from the possession of a good reputation among the other members of the communities in which you participate. Status is the aspirational end for the foundational end of social-belonging. The antepenultimate ends which people tend to believe confer status are many and varied, but typically include such things as a well-rounded education, a virtuous character, an interesting or fashionable lifestyle, luxury travel, a mastery of eloquence and wit, composure, experience and wisdom, the mastery of skills, fame and recognition, good looks and bodily fitness, and the possession of cultural status symbols.

Security represents the state of being in which you possess a sense of safety with regard to the uncertain future that lies before you, perhaps because you are confident in your provisions to mitigate risk or have sufficient experience to judge the predictability of events. Security is valued because it permits stability of the mind, freeing up mental resources and time to be allocated to higher order activities, which would otherwise be spent worrying and monitoring. Security is the aspirational end for the foundational end of somato-stability. The antepenultimate ends which people tend to believe confer security are many and varied, but typically include such things as routines and habits due to the experience and familiarity associated with following a procedure already tried and tested; reliable friends and family who you believe will help support you if the need arises; a stable source of income which allows you to plan for future investment and expenditure; financial savings which you plan to rely on in case of unexpected emergencies; diversified investments due to the mitigation of risk; safety gear and equipment for undertaking dangerous activities; insurance to protect against damage to valuable assets; crisis response equipment and systems to deal with emergency situations; and well-designed goods which you can trust will perform as desired or reputable services which you believe can be relied upon.

Strength represents the state of being in which you are able to influence your environment and the beings within it to help you achieve your objectives. This is desirable because when your environment facilitates the activities you undertake, and other people and beings come together to help you undertake them, the amount of personal time and energy you have to allocate in order to achieve the same results diminishes. Strength is the aspirational end for the foundational end of self-determination. The antepenultimate ends which people tend to believe confer strength are many and varied, but typically include such things as wealth, for the ability to hire people and purchase capital items; control and influence over the rules by which economic marketplaces and other social, political, or economic institutions operate; intelligence and ingenuity to find unique methods of attaining objectives despite specific obstacles; physical fitness, for the ability to shape your physical environment and defend yourself in combat; organizational and logistical management skills; and leadership skills and storytelling, for the ability to inspire and raise the level of emotional investment by others towards achieving a given objective.

3 Industrial revolutions promote higher-order values

Now, the model assumes that every person has a finite resource constraint which dictates an upper bound on their capacity to pursue the attainment of any of these ends (Strotz 1957). Instead of a typical budget constraint composed of pure monetary resources, however, it is more useful to consider a broader budget constraint which is composed of a fixed amount of time, along with a finite amount of financial resources and a finite amount of personal energy (which may comprise physical or mental energy as the situation requires). This reflects the observation that money is just one resource, which only has relevance in the context of economic marketplaces in which money is exchanged for a product or service. There are plenty of economic marketplaces, especially now in the Fourth Industrial Revolution, where the commodity exchanged is someone's attention, that is, their time. We will examine examples of this in more detail later in this book.

In many cases, the pursuit of the penultimate ends requires some measure of time, money, and energy to be allocated towards the effort. It is too simplistic to assume that economic agents compare substitute goods and services purely on price. In many cases, new products and services based on innovative technology achieve successful large-scale adoption in the marketplace not because of their price, but because of their convenience, enabling their consumer to save time or the unnecessary expenditure of energy in the pursuit of the same ends, compared to the products and services which they displace. With this additional time and energy at their disposal, people have an improved ability to allocate personal resources to the pursuit of higher-order ends. As Jevons (1924, p. 54) stated, "the satisfaction of a lower want . . . merely permits the higher want to manifest itself."

In accordance with the old adage, sometimes time really is money. Depending on how much their marginal utility of money decreases as they become better-off, they may convert some of their time and energy savings into increasing their financial resources through extra employment, which represents a net creation of value for the economy overall, raising average per capita incomes. For the pre-growth era of economic history, the representative agent allocated most of their time, money, and energy resources towards achieving the first three foundational penultimate ends. After taking care of the attainment of these ends, the average person did not have substantial amounts of time or other resources left to allocate towards higher order pursuits.

In the modern world, however, the average person is able to attain a sufficient measure of attainment of the foundational ends with the expenditure of significantly less time, energy, and money, leaving them much freer to be more productive and pursue the higher order aspirational and transcendental ends. Leisure time has also increased substantially, and society is better off overall. At a societal level, when sufficient numbers of the population are able to devote more time to higher order activities, as a result of fundamental shifts in the technological foundations for the economy, the civilisation rises, and the economy undergoes an industrial revolution.

References

Aristotle n.d., *The Nichomachean Ethics*, Penguin Classics, translated by JAK Thomson in 1953 and revised by Hugh Tredennick in 1976, London

Azgad-Tromer, S 2015, 'A Hierarchy of Markets: How Basic Needs Induce a Market Failure', *DePaul Business & Commercial Law Journal*, vol. 14, no. 1, pp. 1–47

Banfield, TC 1845, 'Four Lectures on the Organization of Industry'.

Baumeister, RF 2001, 'The Psychology of Irrationality: Why People Make Foolish, Self-Defeating Choices', in I Brocas & JD Carrillo (eds.), *The Psychology of Economic Decisions*, pp. 3–16, Oxford University Press, Oxford

Chai, A & Moneta, A 2012, 'Back to Engel? Some Evidence for the Hierarchy of Needs', *Journal of Evolutionary Economics*, vol. 22, no. 4, pp. 649–676

Champ, PA, Boyle, KJ, & Brown, TC (eds.) 2017, *The Economics of Non-Market Goods and Resources: A Primer on Nonmarket Valuation*, Springer, Netherlands

Engel, E 1895, 'Das Lebenskosten Belgischer Arbeiterfamilien früher und Jetzt', *Bulletin of the International Statistical Institute*, vol. 9, pp. 1–124

Galtung, J 1980, 'The Basic Needs Approach', in K Lederer (ed.), *Human Needs*, Oelgeschlager, Gunn and Hain, Cambridge

Georgescu-Roegen, N 1954, 'Choice, Expectations and Measurability', *The Quarterly Journal of Economics*, vol. 68, no. 4, pp. 503–534

Gomes, O 2011, 'The Hierarchy of Human Needs and their Social Valuation', *International Journal of Social Economics*, vol. 38, no. 3, pp. 237–259

Ironmonger, DS 1972, *New Commodities and Consumer Behaviour*, Cambridge University Press, Cambridge, England

Jevons, WS 1924, *The Theory of Political Economy*, 4th edn, Palgrave Macmillan, London

Maslow, AH 1943, 'A Theory of Human Motivation', *Psychological Review*, vol. 50, no. 4, pp. 370–396

Maslow, AH 1954, *Motivation and Personality*, Harper & Row Publishers, Inc., New York

Max-Neef, MA 1991, *Human Scale Development: Conception, Application and Further Reflections*, Apex Press, London

Menger, C 1950, *Principles of Economics*, Translated and edited by J Dingwall & BF Hoselitz, The Free Press, New York

Moneta, A & Chai, A 2014, 'The Evolution of Engel Curves and its Implications for Structural Change Theory', *Cambridge Journal of Economics*, vol. 38, no. 4, pp. 895–923

Plato n.d., *Republic*, Harvard University Press, 'Plato in Twelve Volumes' translated by Paul Shorey in 1969, Cambridge, MA

Scitovsky, T 1976, *The Joyless Economy*, Oxford University Press, New York

Sen, AK 1990, 'Rational Behavior', in J Eatwell, M Milgate, & P Newman (eds.), *The New Palgrave: Utility and Probability*, pp. 198–216, W. W. Norton & Co., New York

Simon, HA 1955, 'A Behavioral Model of Rational Choice', *The Quarterly Journal of Economics*, vol. 69, no. 1, p. 99

Strotz, RH 1957, 'The Empirical Implications of a Utility Tree', *Econometrica*, vol. 25, no. 2, pp. 269–280

Wilkinson, N & Klaes, M 2012, *An Introduction to Behavioral Economics*, 2nd edn, Palgrave Macmillan UK, London

4

THE "BRISBANE CLUB" MODEL

Mind, society, economy as complex evolving networks

What differentiates our contribution to the study of the Fourth Industrial Revolution from others is the mode of analysis it applies. We make use of a model of the economy which was specifically designed to account for the effects technology has at all levels of analysis: from the micro-scale of everyday life to the macro-scale of the socioeconomic system as a whole. With this model we can "place" the various mega-technologies of the Fourth Industrial Revolution within it and then project their likely interaction with the broader socioeconomic system.

This model was developed in the early twenty-first century at the University of Queensland through the contributions of Jason Potts, Kurt Dopfer, John Foster, and Stan Metcalfe as well as Ulrich Witt and Peter Earl in particular, hence it is known as the "Brisbane Club" model. This model conceives of the economy as a complex evolving system formed by individuals acting on the basis of their socio-economic environment and psychology, enabled by the technologies available to them. It incorporates elements of behavioural and psychological economics (Earl, 1983, 1984, 1986, 2017), institutional economics where it focusses on the rules governing socioeconomic interaction (Dopfer, Foster and Potts, 2004; Dopfer and Potts, 2008), and evolutionary economics (Metcalfe, 1998; Witt, 2008). It is also strongly influenced by the literature on complex systems and emergence within them (Potts, 2000; Foster, 2005; Foster and Metcalfe, 2012).

We will introduce the Brisbane Club model of socioeconomic systems at some length so that we may apply it in later chapters to analysing the mega-technologies of the Fourth Industrial Revolution. We will first introduce the argument that we can best understand socioeconomic evolution as a process of structural evolution in the formation of socioeconomic networks. We will then introduce the Brisbane Club model of how those networks form out of the interaction between individual psychologies and the socioeconomic environment, and then discuss the various factors influencing the evolution of those networks through the change of individual behaviour. We will then introduce the micro-meso-macro perspective by which we will switch between microscopic and macroscopic analysis of socioeconomic systems. We will finally summarise how we will use this model to analyse the various mega-technologies of the Fourth Industrial Revolution. For the interested reader, a technical appendix contains a sketch of the formal properties of this model.

1 Society and economy as complex evolving networks

The core proposition around which the Brisbane Club model of socioeconomic systems is built is that the economy is a complex evolving system formed by individuals acting on the basis of their psychology and socioeconomic environment enabled by technology. These systems are appropriately thought of as network structures where individuals form connections whenever they decide to transfer or exchange goods and services, mediums of exchange, or information. Anytime you interact with someone in a socioeconomic context, you form a connection in socioeconomic networks. Buy a cup of coffee, a connection comes into existence between you and the vendor. Exchange your labour for wages, a connection comes into existence between you and your employer. Strike a multi-million-dollar investment contract with another company, a connection comes into existence between yourself and your counterpart in that company.

That of course sounds like a natural way to model socioeconomic systems, but for various historical reasons, traditional economics is not "done" in this way. The tendency for economic analysis (as Philip Mirowski argued in 1989) is to imagine that the economy is something like an electromagnetic field, which is a complete network (all connections that can be made *are* made) where socioeconomic interactions are akin to electromagnetic flows settling down to an equilibrium. This perspective was immensely useful for understanding the interaction of price dynamics across many markets – changes in one market leading to changes in another and so on. The problem with it, however, as Jason Potts argued in his seminal *New Evolutionary Microeconomics (2000)* was that it is difficult to make sense of *structural* evolution with such a model. If a system is fully connected there aren't any new connections to be made. The alternative Potts offered was to recognise that the network structure of the economy is incomplete *and therefore* interesting: new connections can be made, existing connections can be transferred, and the structure of the economy can evolve.

Potts's argument was to stimulate a decade of thought at the University of Queensland under the leadership of Professor John Foster at the School of Economics. Various thinkers from across the world concentrated on the School, becoming the "Brisbane Club," and contributed elements to the view offered by its emerging model. This model integrated insights from psychological, institutional, and evolutionary economics, while keeping traditional analysis as a special case. To analyse the mega-technologies of the Fourth Industrial Revolution we will make use of the model as synthesised and formalised in two technical documents written by one of the present authors over the course of his doctoral research (Markey-Towler, 2016, 2018a).

New technologies manifest in this model by their effect on human behaviour and the way they thus cause socioeconomic systems to evolve in a structural manner. So, in order to prepare ourselves to apply the Brisbane Club model to analysing the mega-technologies of the Fourth Industrial Revolution, we need first to understand how socioeconomic systems emerge from human behaviour, how human behaviour is determined, and how human behaviour evolves so as to cause the system to evolve. We can then analyse the effects of the mega-technologies by considering their nature and how that nature interacts with human action to cause behaviour and socioeconomic systems to evolve.

2 Formation of socioeconomic systems: environment, mind, and socioeconomy

Socioeconomies are complex evolving network structures formed by the behaviour of individuals acting on the basis of their psychology and socioeconomic environment enabled by technology. To understand their formation, thus their evolution, we need to understand how human psychology interacts with the socioeconomic environment to determine behaviour. Such a perspective as allows us to understand how socioeconomic structure emerges from human behaviour was contributed to the Brisbane Club by Peter Earl in particular.

The core proposition of the Brisbane Club model of psychology, which is at the core of its model of socioeconomic systems, is that the mind, much like the brain from which it emerges, is a network structure. The model built on this proposition draws, in particular, on the neuropsychological perspective offered by Friedrich Hayek (1952), the philosophical perspective of Kenneth Boulding (1956), and Kelly (1963), but also the cognitivist perspective offered by Herbert Simon (1968). The nodes in mental networks represent objects and events that exist in our environment and higher order categorisations thereof – people, goods, services, money, their attributes, actions, speech, needs, wants. The connections within these networks represent our knowledge of the world, our "worldview" or "personal construction" of reality, in the form of the relationships we construe between objects and events in the environment and higher-order categorisations of them. Mental networks take on the aspect of classificatory schema (Piaget, 1923; Luria, 1973; Hayek, 1952) as well as cognitive systems for analysing the relation of such categorisations (Newell, 1990) and expectations of the course of events such as are categorised thereby (Kelly, 1963). They are in constant state of evolution through the incorporation of new connections, the strengthening of those which exist by their use and the fading of those which aren't used (Edelman, 1987). The psychological process which transforms the socioeconomic environment into behaviour is constrained to operate within this network, and operates upon it to cause its evolution.

The socioeconomic environment, which is both external *and* internal to the individual (in the style of Simon, 1956) contains information (in the Shannonian, 1948a, 1948b sense) which must be transformed into *percepts* of the objects and events and classifications thereof in the environment. This is the role of *perception*, which transforms information in any given environment into percepts of the objects and events in the environment along with classifications thereof. Perception, we might say, provides us with the interface between the world and our personal knowledge of it (Merleau-Ponty, 1945, 1948; Polanyi, 1958).

The process of *analysis* connects these impressions of sense-data together on the basis of the sets of connections between them contained in mental networks to present an understanding of the relations between objects and events in the environment and classifications thereof. From the mental "map" of the world contained in our mental networks emerges a "model" of any given environment (Hayek, 1952). The process of analysis serves to categorise and classify objects in the environment based on the schema built up by our experiences of their relationships manifest in our mental networks (Piaget, 1923; Luria, 1973; Hayek, 1952). But the process of analysis also connects these categorisations and classifications together in order to present us with an understanding of their relation. These can be interpreted in either of two ways, reality of course being a mixture between them. In the first, intuitive instance, we can imagine the connections formed as part of analysis to be our construction of the expected course of future events (Kelly, 1963) – a form of *reasoning* (Elster, 2009) and forming *expectations* (Shackle, 1969, 1972). In the second instance, we can imagine the connections formed in the process of analysis to be a cognitive processing based on algorithmic rules manifest in our mental networks (Newell, 1990; Simon, 1968) which relate hierarchical classifications and categorisations of objects and events in the environment (Pinker, 1999). Of course, much of this process takes place at a subconscious level such that the conscious mind is presented with a "feeling" rather than an explicit set of judgments, though it of course may rise to the conscious level of the higher cortical functions (Luria, 1973). As a result of perception and analysis, the individual is presented with a set of connections between objects and events in the environment and classifications of the goods, services, mediums of exchange, people, and actions within it, but also, most importantly, between such classifications and the *motivational* complexes in the internal environment.

Contained within our analysis of the environment is our understanding of the *implications* of various potential courses of action available to us, or (at a subconscious level) the *predicates* for engaging in certain behaviours. The relationship established in these sets of connections between the course of action and our motivational complexes creates an aesthetics, a "feel" which allows us to establish preferences between the various sets of expected outcomes. Only certain of the courses of action which are associated with these expected outcomes however are actually contained within the set of those which an individual is *capable* of engaging in given the current state of technology (Sen, 1999). A useful theory of *decision* then is that an individual engages in *that feasible course of action associated with the most preferable expected outcomes out of all feasible courses of action*. This is, of course, on the face of it, a very similar theory to the theory of rational choice. This is actually a *strength* of the present theory for it maintains the kernel truth of rational choice theory while placing that truth in the context of an overall psychological process. Behaviour arises out of a psychological process, and indeed, if preferences are decided by the operation of a behavioural *rule* rather than the outcomes of a process of reasoning, we could say that behaviour is guided by rules as much as by rational choice.

From the behaviour which thus arises socioeconomic systems form. Where the behaviour of any given individual includes some form of interaction with another, that behaviour brings a socioeconomic connection into existence. So if the individual chooses to buy or sell some good or service, they create a connection with their counterpart. If they choose to interact in any way with some other individual, they create a connection with that other individual. As we observe the behaviour of more and more individuals in their socioeconomic environment, we observe the formation of socioeconomic systems as complex network structures. This gives us the static perspective of the Brisbane Club model, and it is a model which is essentially similar to that offered by Friedrich Hayek (1945, 1988) of the economy as a system which coordinates knowledge, but with a modern psychological foundation. The personal knowledge (Polanyi, 1958) of individuals which is expressed in their mental networks is applied by the process of analysis to the individual's perception of the environment and gives rise to their behaviour, and thus the structure of socioeconomic network systems.

3 Evolution of socioeconomic systems: changing environments, changing minds, changing technologies

In the Brisbane Club model, socioeconomic systems are formed by the behaviour of individuals acting on the basis of their psychology and socioeconomic environment enabled by technology as we have seen. Their structure, however, is incomplete as Jason Potts (2000) argued, which Earl and Wakeley (2010) argued is the natural outcome of the capability, cognitive, and psychological constraints imposed by the psychological process, so there is scope for their evolution. Socioeconomic connections are formed as a result of individual behaviour changing in response to the socioeconomic environment. So when an individual begins to interact with someone they had hitherto not interacted with, a new connection is created as a result of the changed behaviour – either completely or as a result of the transfer of an existing connection. If you are the logistics manager for a manufacturer and you change your choice of suppliers, you will transfer your existing connections to the new supplier and cause the economic system to evolve. If you are an entrepreneur and get your first customer for your startup, you will cause a new connection to come into existence and cause the economic system to evolve and grow.

There are various points in the psychological process at which factors in the environment and the mind itself may cause behaviour to change and thus cause behaviour to change. The study of these points in the psychological process has been the particular project of one of the present authors (Markey-Towler, 2017, 2018a, 2018b, 2018c), drawing substantially on the work of Peter Earl (2017), in particular studying the evolution of behaviour in complex socioeconomic systems.

We can put these points into three groups: the role of incentives and technology, the role of mental evolution, and the role of "framing." The first group has traditionally been the province of economics, the second has traditionally been the province of developmental psychology, and the third has traditionally been the province of behavioural economics. Technology, however, is not limited to having only a direct influence on individual behaviour; as we will see when applying this system to analysing the mega-technologies, it impacts on each and every step of the psychological process.

3.1 Substitutes and complements: incentives and technology

Traditionally, economic theory has studied behaviour as governed by what technologies are available to extend the range of human capability (Lawson, 2010), thus the "feasible set" (Becker, 1962) and the rival incentive structures available as a result of that capability (Friedman, 1962; Marshall, 1890). These traditional dynamics in behavioural change are preserved in the present theory, as they ought to be. Incentives and technology gain their force over behaviour through the phenomena of substitutability and complementarity in particular.

A state of substitutability exists if we can find a particular incentive structure associated with a given course of action such that it obtains equivalent preferability with another. To put it in different terms, a state of substitutability exists when we could take one action, substitute another for it, and obtain expected outcomes of roughly equivalent preferability. If a state of substitutability exists, then we may observe a change of behaviour as long as the incentives associated with a non-selected course of action improve to a point where they cause the implications of that action to become more preferable than those associated with the currently adopted behaviour. Obviously such behaviour change will be observed most commonly when incentive structures are changing as a result of prices (Friedman, 1962). Typically, if the price of some new product is lowered to a point below that associated with the state of substitutability then we will observe a change of behaviour whereby the now relatively inexpensive new product is substituted for the old. We may, alternatively, observe such a change of behaviour when incentive structures are changing as a result of product attributes (Ironmonger, 1972; Lancaster, 1966a, 1966b), so that as the attributes of some new product – for instance, an internet browser – improve to a point beyond that associated with the state of substitutability, we will observe a change of behaviour. Substitution is not limited to transferring connections, though; it may be the case that new connections are brought into existence when the incentive structures associated with some new good or service exceed the point at which they create a state of substitutability between doing *nothing* and obtaining that good or service, thereby creating a new connection.

A state of substitutability might *not* exist, however, at which point we need to consider other means by which behavioural change might be brought about. The existence of a state of substitutability can be undermined for a number of reasons, most obviously by the existence of *needs* as distinct from wants. Ironmonger (1972) provided a model which showed how until needs can be met by some course of action, it cannot be considered as a viable course of action to be engaged in. As Blatt (1979) put it somewhat dramatically to make a point, it is rather difficult to imagine that any conceivable state of substitutability could exist between some course of action in everyday life and one with a degree of certainty to lead to being hanged on the gallows. But the operation of simple cognitive rules in our psyche may also undermine the existence of a state of substitutability insofar as they impose *requirements* which must be met by any given course of action before it can even be considered as a viable course of action to be engaged in. If this is the case, we may need technology to improve the outcomes which may be associated with a given course of action before it can be considered as a viable course of action. For instance, a state of substitutability between an airline with a poor safety record and one with a good safety record can only exist in the minds of so many consumers until its organisational and physical technology improves sufficiently to establish its preferability. Technology plays a "facilitating" role here in making the existence of a state of substitutability more feasible, but it can also play an "expansionary" role in the way it may interact with the set of capabilities and the realisation of *complementarities*.

Complementarities are the contrary of substitutabilities insofar as they concern not the substitution of one course of action for another, but the taking of them together. Complementarities exist between two actions if, when taken *together* in a particular course of action, they lead to better outcomes than if they are taken in isolation. Complementarities can be extremely important for determining behaviour insofar as the capacity for realising them may make a course of action more preferable than otherwise. It is in this way that technology has an "expansionary" effect on behaviour insofar as it may expand human capability (Lawson, 2010) to the extent that it makes some action feasible, and the realisation of complementarities possible, where they hitherto had not been. If technology expands the range of human capability to include some action which is complementary with others in a certain course of action, then it may cause that course of action to become *the* most preferable, and a change of behaviour results. This is particularly important in the context of, for instance, platform technologies which facilitate interaction. Platforms may make the formation of entirely new relationships feasible which hitherto had not been, and thus the adoption of that platform is complementary with those relationships.

Now if a state of substitutability does not exist, and complementarities are not particularly important, then we need to understand behavioural change as something more than the result of changing incentives or technology. If technology has expanded the range of human capability already, and incentives are not changing greatly, then behavioural change must be the result of something else – the interaction of the individual, and specifically their mind, with their environment. This leads us into the realm first of developmental psychology and then behavioural economics.

3.2 Creativity, experimentation, play, and narratives in mental evolution

At the most basic level, before some new behaviour can be realised, the knowledge of *how* and *why* to engage in it must be contained within mental networks in order for the individual to engage in it. If it were not contained therein there would be no basis for analysis which includes the implications of that action. This is especially important in the context of understanding technology as technology will often make things possible which had not even been thought of before. So if a change of behaviour is to emerge and cause the socioeconomic system to evolve, it may often be necessary for the knowledge of *how* and *why* to engage in it to be incorporated into the mind first (Markey-Towler, 2018c).

It is well known that our minds are not a "blank slate" – we are born with certain innate structures in our mental networks (Pinker, 2002). However, we are not limited to this innate structure; our minds can grow by the incorporation of new connections into the mind, a process we call "development," whereby schema for classifying, categorising, and understanding the world grow (Piaget, 1923). The origins of such connections are three. In the first instance, we must recognise the possibility that such connections may be created *ex nihilio* as a result of deep creativity, forming a "bisociation," which Arthur Koestler (1964) famously called "the act of creation." However, apparent connections between objects and events in the environment may also present themselves to the senses and thereby be *perceived*. Broadly speaking, there are two particularly important means, aside from simple interpersonal communication, by which such connections may present themselves to the senses: experimentation and play. By experimentation we mean conscious actions which cause new information to be present in the environment which presents new connections to the individual. John Dewey (1910), among others, identified this as a source of new connections which might be incorporated into the mind in the process of learning. By play we mean those activities which are engaged in for the sake of it which happen to cause new information to be presented to the senses – which Piaget (1923), among others, identified as a particularly important source of new connections especially in childhood.

Connections presented to the mind are not the same as connections incorporated into the mind, however, and there are certain conditions which govern the likelihood they will be so incorporated. From these we can derive a set of five further conditions which govern the likelihood that an *idea* – a set of connections – will be incorporated into the mind. These conditions can be shown (see Markey-Towler, 2018a) to map pretty well onto the conditions identified by Chip and Dan Heath in their long research program into what makes an idea "stick" (Heath and Heath, 2007). The idea must be relatively simple in the sense that it must not contain many connections. It must, to the greatest extent possible, be made up of connections already contained within the mind. It must connect objects and events with a strong hold over attention. It must build at the periphery of mental networks rather than their "core." And it must be as least dissonant – contradictory to – ideas applied in that environment as possible. To put it another way, it must be simple, connect ideas with a strong hold on the individual's attention, and build on the periphery of mental networks without contradicting them. It is for this reason that *narratives* are so important for understanding socioeconomic behaviour (Shiller, 2017). They spread ideas about how and why to adopt new forms of behaviour and new forms of enabling technology (Markey-Towler, 2018c). It is absolutely no accident then, that the archetypal tech company – Apple – legendarily owes its success to its greatest CEO, Steve Jobs, who was a famous storyteller.

Now knowledge of how and why to act in a new way, enabled for instance by a new technology, may be incorporated into the mind by this process, but behavioural change may only be realised if that knowledge is actually *applied* in the process of analysis so as to guide behaviour toward its new form. This leads us now into the realm of behavioural economics. For whether knowledge is applied in the process of analysis and in such a way as to guide behaviour toward a new form depends on how the environment is *framed* relative to the environment.

3.3 Salience, chains, and anchoring: framing the environment

What knowledge manifest in our mental networks is "brought to mind" in the process of analysis depends on what objects, events, and classifications thereof are called to mind by that process. This depends, of course, on the way information is transformed into percepts of objects and events in the environment. This depends on two phenomena we call "salience" and "chains." The effect of those percepts on behaviour is then obtained by their effect on preferences, which depends on a further phenomenon we call "anchoring."

The totality of the information which exists in our environment is not mapped to percepts of objects and events within it, only a small fraction. We only notice what is noticeable. We call this phenomenon "salience" – only that information which corresponds to objects and events which makes a sufficient impression on the sensory organs relative to the environment is mapped to percepts of those objects and events. This has the effect of "focussing" our attention on the most salient objects and events in our environment. Hence, we tend to notice more extreme and unusual events in the environment relative to common ones, we tend to notice gaudy and loud advertisements, we tend to be dominated by our emotions rather than thoughts about the future, and so on.

We also do not perceive only the base sense-data of our environment. We also perceive higher-order categorisations and classifications thereof. The phenomenon by which this is brought about we call "chains," and is underlain by the way neurons excite one another by the passage of charge along synaptic networks. If a set of anterior percepts are perceived which are sufficiently strongly connected to a posterior set of percepts in mental networks, then the latter will be perceived as well. So the phenomenon of chains means that our understanding of reality affects the way we *observe* reality. This, of course, is one way that our personality – the tendencies within the way we construe events – manifests in the world, as our perception is contingent on the personality which manifests in our mental networks. It is also how it comes to be that we judge different objects and events to have such a degree of similarity that we can represent them to be members of the same category.

So what percepts come to mind, and thus the judgement we form of our environment based on our analysis, depends on the way the environment is framed so as for certain objects and events to have a greater impact on our sensory organs relative to the environment and the classification schema built around them in mental networks. But the framing of the environment does not in itself change behaviour; it must have an effect on the preferability of the various expected outcomes the individual believes will arise. This effect arises from the phenomenon we call "anchoring."

The great psychologist George Kelly (1963) taught that nothing can be made sense of except *relative* to some other thing. We cannot, for instance, really make sense of our income or wealth except insofar as we know what it is worth relative to the goods and services we might buy it with. Any object or event thus needs to be related to axes, or "anchored" to an "anchor" by which it may be classified and a relationship thereby established. Anchors are extremely important, for networks are rarely modular and often contingent, so the presence of an anchor in perception may have a significant effect on the overall judgment formed of the environment in the process of analysis. Where they have a sufficient effect as to change the preferability of the expected outcomes to follow upon some course of action, we say that that anchor is *non-inert*. A *positive* non-inert anchor with respect to a particular course of action, when present in perception, *increases* the preferability of its expected outcomes, while a negative non-inert anchor with respect to a particular course of action, when present in perception, *decreases* the preferability of its expected outcomes. Obviously then, we may imagine that the presence of anchors in perception, and thus anchoring relations in analysis, may be decisive for behaviour. For instance, the presence of the anchor that is peer consumption levels may give rise to "conspicuous consumption" for by establishing consumption *relative* to peer consumption, it may make a greater consumption more preferable than it would otherwise have been.

3.4 Summary: evolution of socioeconomic systems at the micro-level

The Brisbane Club model views socioeconomic systems as complex *evolving* systems, where the connective structure of the system is changing and evolving as individual behaviour changes in response to the environment, changing technology, and changing psychology. It offers a more or less coherent perspective on how individual behaviour changes, and thus how socioeconomic systems evolve at a micro-scale by the creation of new connections or the transfer of existing ones. Broadly speaking, we have established that behaviour changes due to the role of incentives and technology, the role of mental evolution, and the role of "framing."

In the first instance, socioeconomic systems may evolve as incentives within them change, causing individuals to substitute between existing modes of behaviour and new modes of behaviour – such as that which would constitute the adoption of a new technology – as long as incentives are sufficient to do so. If there is no incentive structure under which such substitution may be obtained, then technological change may be required so as for necessities and requisites to be met. Technology may also cause socioeconomic systems to evolve in a more direct manner by expanding the range of human capability and making it possible to realise complementarities between various elements of behaviour.

If incentives are not particularly relevant, and technology has already made the realisation of complementarities feasible, behavioural change is brought about by the development and application of personal knowledge. New ideas about how and why to behave in a new manner – such as adopting a new technology – must be developed by creativity, experimentation, and play, and then incorporated into the mind. Those ideas which are simple, connect objects and events with a powerful hold on the individual's attention, and build on the periphery of existing mental networks without contradicting them greatly are more likely to be incorporated. The environment must then be framed so as for that knowledge to be applied to perception of the environment in the process of analysis in such a way as for new modes of behaviour to be selected. This requires that the information which corresponds to positive non-inert anchors for new modes of behaviour, or information that corresponds to perceptual antecedents thereof which are strongly connected to them, to be placed and presented in such a way as to have a significant impression on the sensory organs, and the opposite for negative non-inert anchors.

As behaviour changes from existing to new modes through the role of incentives and technology, the role of mental evolution, and the role of "framing," we observe the emergence of new connections in socioeconomic systems at the micro-scale. So in order to understand the impacts of the mega-technologies of the Fourth Industrial Revolution, we must understand the interaction of that technology with the expansion of human capabilities in its own right. But we must also understand the interactions of that technology with the various elements of the psychological process which give rise to changes in behaviour.

4 Micro-meso-macro: new ways of doing things cause disruption, then re-coordination

The Brisbane Club model of socioeconomic systems is what we call "methodologically individualist." It takes the individual human being as the fundamental unit of socioeconomic analysis and builds a perspective from this basis (Hodgson, 2007). There are limitations to a strictly individualist methodology, however, as any "higher level" analysis of large parts of the system is difficult with a model which does not abstract away from individual idiosyncrasies. This is, of course, the reason that any economics needs some form of a "representative agent" in order to analyse the functioning of socioeconomic systems at any higher level of analysis.

The singular contribution of Kurt Dopfer, John Foster and Jason Potts (2004) to the Brisbane Club model was to provide a means for doing so in the form of the micro–meso–macro framework.

As we broaden our perspective on socioeconomic systems from the level of the individual to take in groups of greater and greater size, we can begin to observe certain regularities in the way individuals interact with their socioeconomic environment. What we are observing in these regularities is the operation of what Dopfer, Foster and Potts (2004) called the "meso-rule." A meso-rule is a cognitive structure for interpreting how and why to act in a particular socioeconomic environment which has sufficient regularity as to allow us to define a corresponding "meso-population" of individuals who act according to the dictates of that rule without loss to our analysis. At the macroeconomic level, we therefore see the socioeconomic system as a network between various meso-populations of individuals interacting according to a particular rule structure. These rules ought to be defined pragmatically for the purposes of analysis and can be both technical rules (which might define, say, an industry as a meso-population by its production technology) or psychological rules (which might define, say, a particular class of consumer as a meso-population by the commonalities in their consumption behaviour).

Meso-rules are *emergent* in the sense that they spread as the result of individual action and thus come to cause the coordination of socioeconomic structures. They are *originated*, ultimately, through creativity – a new technology is developed along with new knowledge of how and why to use it – and then they *diffuse* as the knowledge they manifest is spread from individual to individual and selected as they incorporated into the mind. So they rely on the very structure of socioeconomic networks that they coordinate to spread, as individuals communicate with each other through action and word. We observe certain regularities in their diffusion (Dopfer, Foster and Potts, 2004; Dopfer and Potts, 2008), which allows us to theorise the process by which a new form of behaviour – such as the adoption of a technology – emerges, and the effect it has on the socioeconomic system as a whole.

In the beginning, the technical "how" and psychological "why" knowledge for a new form of behaviour – such as the adoption of a technology – is created by some individual and applied. That knowledge is communicated by that individual through action and word to other individuals in their network who either incorporate it into their mind and adopt the behaviour themselves (if the microeconomic conditions for doing so apply) or they do not. If the former is the case, the idea begins to spread and becomes a candidate meso-rule guiding thought and action. As this occurs, it disrupts the overall system through the transfer of connections by the change from old modes of behaviour to new modes of behaviour. As the meso-rule continues to diffuse, and the meso-population grows, and the new form of behaviour such as the adoption of a new technology is increasingly adopted, we observe the gradual re-coordination of the overall system as more and more connections are made, and the meso-population is integrated into the system as a whole. The success or failure of this process at each step depends on the degree to which the new form of behaviour satisfies the micro-level requirements for behavioural change we have established above.

5 Summary: applying the Brisbane Club model to the mega-technologies of the Fourth Industrial Revolution

Our contribution adopts the Brisbane Club model of socioeconomic systems in order to analyse the mega-technologies of the Fourth Industrial Revolution – indeed this is what differentiates our analysis. The Brisbane Club model offers a perspective on socioeconomic systems as complex evolving networks formed by individuals acting on the basis of their psychology and socioeconomic environment. It was specifically designed to allow us to analyse the effects of technology on the socioeconomic system and incorporates insights from behavioural-psychological, institutional, and evolutionary economics.

The Brisbane Club model starts with the proposition that the economy is a complex evolving system formed by individuals acting on the basis of their psychology and socioeconomic environment, and places a model of the mind as a network structure within which and upon which the psychological process operates at the core of the socioeconomic system. Perception transforms information in the socioeconomic environment of the individual into percepts of the objects and events contained within that environment and classifications thereof. The process of analysis connects those percepts together to construe the relationship between objects and events and classifications thereof in the environment. This provides the basis for decision, which is guided by the preferences established by the knowledge of how and why to act in certain ways so that the individual chooses that feasible course of action associated with the most preferable implications out of all feasible alternatives. The mental networks within which this process operates are subject to continual evolution through the addition of new connections and the fading of old connections.

Socioeconomic networks form out of the behaviour of individuals within them where they interact and evolve as their behaviour does. Individual behaviour evolves wherever incentives are changing to make new modes of behaviour more attractive, or technology expands the range of human capability to make the realisation of complementarities feasible. Given a set of incentives and technology, behaviour evolves further where new knowledge about how and why to act in new ways is incorporated into the mind and applied to guide behaviour. New ideas are incorporated into the mind to become knowledge the simpler they are, the more the objects and events they connect have a hold on individual attention, and the greater the extent to which they build on existing mental networks at their periphery without contracting them. That new knowledge is *applied* the greater the extent to which the information corresponding to the elements of it, or perceptual antecedents thereto, are placed and presented in the environment so as to have a greater impression on the sensory organs. The greater the extent positive anchors exist within that knowledge, the greater the likelihood the new mode of behaviour will be adopted.

At the macroscopic level, the adoption of new modes of behaviour is reflected in the emergence of a meso-rule, which serves to define a meso-population of people whose thoughts and actions are guided by that rule. As the rule is adopted through its diffusion, it causes disruption initially as new modes of behaviour are adopted which cause new connections to be created. As its diffusion continues, however, and the meso-population which behaves according to the meso-rule grows, the economic system re-coordinates and integrates that meso-population into the overall socioeconomic system. Where the new behaviour constitutes the adoption of a new technology, the diffusion of a meso-rule is the process whereby a new technology diffuses and affects the overall structure of the socioeconomic system – first bringing disruption, then re-coordination.

We will use this perspective to analyse the mega-technologies of the Fourth Industrial Revolution throughout the rest of this book. In each case, we will consider first the nature of the technology, and then establish its relation to various aspects of the psychological process – role of incentives and technology, the role of mental evolution, and the role of "framing." Establishing this relationship will allow us to establish the relationship between the technology and behaviour, and this will allow us to establish the likely effect the technologies of the Fourth Industrial Revolution will have on our socioeconomic systems. With this analysis of the likely effects of the mega-technologies of the Fourth Industrial Revolution, we will be better able to formulate an understanding of where it presents opportunities to be seized, and problems to be mitigated.

Technical appendix

For the sake of simplicity, we will focus only on the formation of *economic* networks in this appendix, but a roughly equivalent formalism applies to the formation of social networks as well. The "Brisbane Club" model starts from the proposition that economies are complex evolving systems formed by individuals acting on the basis of their psychology and socioeconomic environment. From this proposition a model of economies as evolving networks formed by individual interactions may be constructed, and various technologies "released" into it once their effects are established. Drawing on the technical document provided by Markey-Towler (2016), we begin by defining the economy as a network consisting of a set of individuals N and a set of connections $g(N)$ between them

$$E = \{N\, g(N)\}.$$

A connection $ij \in g(N)$ within the economy we say consists of transfers of goods and services x_{ij} and mediums of exchange m_{ij}. between i and j, so that $\left[ij \in g(N)\right] = \left[x_{ij}\, m_{ij}\right]$. These connections are formed by individuals acting on the basis of their psychology and socioeconomic environment, so we require a model of the mind and psychological process to understand the formation and evolution of economic networks. Such a model is provided by Markey-Towler (2018a).

The mind of individual i is defined as a network μ_i where nodes H_i consist of representations of objects and events in the environment as well as higher-order categorisations and abstractions thereon, and connections $g_i(H_i)$ which represent connections between these objects, events, and abstractions there from that the individual construes to exist. Hence we have

$$\mu_i = \{H_i, g_i(H_i)\}.$$

The psychological process operates within and upon this network structure to transform information in the socioeconomic environment v_{N_i} into the behaviour which causes economic networks to form. That process consists of three parts: perception, analysis, and decision.

Perception $\rho_i : 2^V \rightarrow 2^H \cup 2^R$ is a mapping which transforms information $v_{N_i} \subset V$ contained within the space of all possible information V that exists in the "neighbourhood" N_i of the individual i to subsets $H'_i \subset H_i$ of the set of representations of objects and events and higher-order categorisations of them in the environment, as well as subsets $\{R_{hh'}\}$ of apparent relationships between them presented by that environment. We say that the information v_N constitutes the individual's "environment," both internal and external (Simon, 1956). So upon encountering a particular socioeconomic environment v_{N_i} we have

$$\rho_i(v_{N_i}) = \{H'_i, \{R_{hh'}\}\}$$

Perception thus presents a set of *percepts* of objects and events in the environment to the mind of the individual. The process of analysis then operates on the set of percepts H'_i to extract a set $g_i(H'_i)$ of connections between them from the overall set of connections $g_i(H_i)$ contained within mental networks μ_i. The process of analysis therefore presents a set of connections defined as a subset

$$g(H') = \{R_{hh'} \in g(H) : h, h' \in H'\} \subset g(H)$$

We say that this process is one by which a "model" of the environment is extracted from the "map" of the world the individual contains within their mental networks (Hayek, 1952). This process is analogous to the output of the cognitive process of forming judgment (Newell, 1990), or the process of thought which leads to the formation of expectations of future events based on personal constructs (Kelly, 1963). The basis for this process – the set of connections $g_i(H_i)$ – is in constant evolution. The evolution of mental networks is subject to four laws: three concerning the incorporation of new connections into the network and one concerning their decay. They are more formally complex than is necessary to state here, but they state that the likelihood any new connection is incorporated into the mind increases if that connection is present within the set of apparent relations perceived in the environment, if that connection would occupy a less "central" position in mental networks, and if it contradicts less of the individual's mindset at that time. The final condition concerning the decay of mental networks reflects Edelman's (1987) "neural Darwinism," stating that connections decay toward a state where they are no longer included in mental networks unless they are regularly used.

An individual may choose between various actions $a_i \in 2^A$ contained within a space of potential actions $A \supset A'$. It is not necessary for our purposes to define A', it is sufficient to restrict it to be contained within elicited states of mind $\{H' g(H')\} \supset A'$. The *implications* of various actions, or their *expected outcomes* are those connections which follow in $g_i(H'_i)$ upon the various courses of action in chains g_a defined as follows

$$g_{a_i} = \left\{ R_{hh'} : hh' \subset \{h_k h_{k+1}\}_{k=0}^K \subset g_i(H'_i) \& h_0 \in a_i \right\}$$

This definition can be generalised so as for g_{a_i} to be the "behavioural predicates" for a rather than the implications of a_i. The existence of motivational complexes within the mind imply the existence of an aesthetics within $g_i(H_i)$, which implies the existence of a preference ordering $\succeq \circ 2^{g_i(H'_i)}$ on subsets of $g_i(H_i)$ such that $g \succeq g'$ may be read "g is at least as preferable as g'" in the standard manner. A useful theory of behaviour now be posited using this preference: that an individual selects that action a_i^* out of a feasible set $B_i \subset 2^A$ which is associated with the most preferable implications when compared with all other feasible actions

$$a_i^* = \left\{ a_i \in B_i : g_{a_i} \succ g'_{a_i} \ \forall \ a'_i \in B_i \right\}$$

This may be derived also from the Socratic axiom. Now this bears a resemblance, of course, to standard rational agent theory, but it has the important caveat that individuals do what they *think* is best *given* the outputs of a psychological process. Behaviour is thus contingent on the way an individual's psychology interacts with their environment in a number of ways (see chapters 5 through 7 of Markey-Towler, 2018a). Further, the feasible set B_i is to be understood as a *capabilities* set rather than a simple feasible set following Sen (1999), and so behaviour is contingent upon the state of technology which enables action as well as psychology.

We say that such behaviour on the part of i as contains transfers of goods and services x_{ij} and mediums of exchange m_{ij} between i and j creates an economic connection between them, $ij \in g(N)$. That is

$$ij \in g(I) \Leftrightarrow a_i^* \supset [x_{ij} \ m_{ij}] \neq \varnothing$$

As we observe behaviour across the population $i \in N$, we observe the formation of economic networks wherever an individual i decides to transfer some goods and services or mediums of exchange. Collecting these together, we can define the set of connections $g(N) \in E$ which will form economic networks

$$g(N) = \left\{ \left[x_{ij} \, m_{ij} \right] : a_i^* \supset \left[x_{ij} \, m_{ij} \right] \neq \varnothing \right\}_{i \in N}$$

Now we would like, further, to distinguish a particular form of economic connection defined by its mutuality of exchange. This is a *market* exchange whereby i transfers some good or service x_{ij} to j and j transfers some medium of exchange m_{ji} to i mediated by a price p_{ij} that i charges to j, such that $m_{ji} = p_{ij} x_{ij}$. We could say that the market system $M = \left\{ N \, g_M(N) \right\}$ emerges from the economic system and contains special cases of the connections within it which are defined by the mutuality of exchange between two individuals, hence

$$ij \in g_M \Leftrightarrow a_i^* \cap a_j^* \supset \left\{ m_{ij} = p_{ji} x_{ji} \right\}$$

Again, as we observe behaviour across the population $i \in N$, we observe the formation of networks of market interactions wherever i decides to exchange some good or service x_{ij} to j in return for some medium of exchange m_{ji}, and vice versa for j. Collecting these together, we can define the set of connections $g_M(N) \in M$ which will form market networks

$$g_M(N) = \left\{ \left\{ \left\{ m_{ij} = p_{ji} x_{ji} \right\} : a_i^* \cap a_j^* \supset \left\{ m_{ij} = p_{ji} x_{ji} \right\} \right\}_{j \in N} \right\}_{i \in N}$$

Obviously, we will observe the evolution of the structure of the socioeconomic system, and the market system that emerges from it, wherever we see a change of behaviour a_i on the part of individuals i within it. A new connection is created when we observe a change of behaviour

$$a_i^* \not\supset x_{ij} \rightarrow a_i^* \supset x_{ij}$$

The connection $ij \in g(N)$ thus created will be an entirely new connection as long as there is no corresponding change of behaviour

$$a_i^* \supset x_{ik} \rightarrow a_i^* \not\supset x_{ik}.$$

If we consider the psychological process from whence a_i^* emerges, we can readily observe the necessities for such a change of behaviour. For the purposes of sketching these we will drop the subscript denoting the individual i when considering the elements of their psyche.

In the first instance, if we were only to change some particular aspect of the incentive structure in an otherwise fixed environment v_N, say some cost or benefit $\delta \subset H'$ which is connected to other objects and events within the implications of some course of action $R_{\delta h} \in g_a$. We say that a state of substitutability exists if there exists some cost or benefit at which point the implications $g_a \subset g(H')$ of a and the implications $g_{a'} \subset g(H')$ of a' become equivalently preferable, that is

$$\exists \bar{\delta} : g_a \sim g_{a'}$$

Obviouslyz enough, we could imagine that if we had a sequence of such costs and benefits, and initially $g_{a'}$ was *not* as preferable as g_a, we could change the cost/benefit δ to such a point as exceeds the point of substitutability and causes g_a to become *more* preferable than g_a. This, of course, could be decisive for behaviour being decided for a' rather than a. Breaks in the "chain of substitutability" as it can be known, such that a state of substitutability does *not* exist, may arise from the existence of *needs* which are not satisfied (Ironmonger, 1972) as well as the operation of simple behavioural rules which impose *requirements* on the psyche which must be met before certain courses of action will even be considered (Simon, 1968).

Now some course of action a might very well consist of a *range* of different actions $\alpha \subset a$. It may be the case that various of these behaviours are *complementary*, in the sense that two actions α, α' could, if taken *together* lead to better expected outcomes than if α' were not taken. That is to say, if a complementarity exists between two actions α and α' in a course of action a then

$$g_{a \supset \alpha, \alpha'} \succ g_{a \setminus \alpha'}$$

Now obviously enough again, we could imagine that the state of technology might be such that α' is presently infeasible – we have (roughly) that $\alpha' \notin B$ – and so of necessity so too is $a \supset \alpha, \alpha'$ (that is, $B \not\supset a \supset a, \alpha'$, only $a \setminus \alpha'$ is feasible). Now if $\alpha' \in B$, and thus $B \supset a \supset a, \alpha'$ we could well imagine that this might be decisive for deciding behaviour for a rather than some a' because of the improvement in the preferability of the implications a' thus brought about. This extension of human capabilities, roughly speaking, from a state where $\alpha' \notin B$ to a state where $\alpha' \in B$ is what is brought about by the improvement of technology (Lawson, 2010), and is the most direct effect of any technology on the economic system.

At a deep, basic level, we can see that *knowledge* of how and why to act in a certain way, the implications g_a, must be incorporated into the mind before any behaviour a can be engaged in. This may occur through the addition of new connections $R_{hh'} \in g(H)$ into mental networks, which will then fade over time unless refreshed. These connections may be *created* by an "act of creation" *a la* Koestler (1964), or they may be *perceived* as apparent relations between objects and events in the environment. Once presented to the mind, they must be incorporated into the mind. The laws governing this are sufficiently formally complex as to be unnecessary to state here, but we may state them informally. Any connection is more likely to be incorporated into the mind if it is in fact *perceived*, if it would take a *less* central place in mental networks, and if it would *contradict* less of the existing mindset.

Knowledge of how and why to adopt a certain form of behaviour must obviously be applied as part of the process of analysis, and be of such a form as to guide behaviour in that way. This depends on the way the environment is framed relative to the properties of salience, chains, and anchoring in the psychological process. Salience exists if the perception of some percept h is contingent upon the salience $\sigma(v')$ of the information $v' : \rho(v') = h$ corresponding to it, where $\sigma(\cdot)$ is a metric which reflects the overall impression of that information on the sensory organs. Some percept h will be perceived if and only if the salience $\sigma(v')$ of the information $v' : \rho(v') = h$ corresponding to it is sufficiently large (a constant $\bar{\sigma}$) with respect to the salience of the overall environment $\sigma(v_N)$. That is,

$$h \in \rho(v' \subset v_N) \Leftrightarrow \sigma(v') - \sigma(v_N) \geq \bar{\sigma}$$

Chains exist wherever some percept h is connected to another h' by a sufficiently strong connection $R_{hh'} \in g(H)$ in mental networks. If the "strength" of some connection $R_{hh'}$ can be represented by a metric $s(R_{hh'})$ which is commensurate with the salience metric $\sigma(\cdot)$ then $s(R_{hh'})$ being sufficiently large (a constant $\bar{s}$) relative to the salience of the environment $\sigma(v_N)$ means that the perception of h may cause the perception of h'. That is,

$$h \in H' \,\&\, \exists R_{hh'} \in g(H) : s(R_{hh'}) - \sigma(v_N) \geq \bar{s} \Rightarrow h' \in H'$$

This may be generalised to pertain to groups $\{h\}$ of anterior percepts.

Percepts gain their influence over behaviour insofar as they are anchors. An anchor is a concept, $\bar{\delta} \in H$, which becomes related to other percepts through an anchoring relation $R_{h\bar{\delta}}$ or $R_{\bar{\delta}h}$. *Other* relations may be contingent upon the presence of this anchoring relation within the outcome of the process of analysis $R_{hh'} = \{\,|\,R_{\bar{\delta}h} \in g(H')\}$. An anchor is *non-inert* if its perception $\bar{\delta} \in \rho(v_N)$ impacts the preferability of the implications $g_a \subset g(H')$ of some action a. That is

$$g_a \subset g(\rho(v_N) \supset \bar{\delta}) \succ g'_a \subset g(\rho(v'_N)\bar{\delta})$$

should the anchor be *positive* non-inert, and vice versa should the anchor be *negative* non-inert. Thus we can imagine that the framing of the environment so as for negative non-inert anchors with respect to some behaviour a to be suppressed by salience and chains in perception, and positive non-inert anchors perceived, and vice versa for some other behaviour a', may be decisive for behaviour.

Now in order to analyse socioeconomic systems at a more macroscopic scale, we require a criterion for defining groups which can be analysed *as* a group. A cognitive rule is a structure $r \subset g_i(H_i)$ contained within mental networks. Where rules have a certain degree of commonality we might define a "meso" rule r_m, and a corresponding "meso" population $P_m \subset N$ of individuals who have an approximately similar rule contained within their mental networks. That is,

$$P_m = \{i \in N : \exists r \subset g_i(H_i) \,\&\, r \sim r_m\}$$

We can analyse the behaviour of the meso-population P_M *as* that population acting out the rule r_m in its behaviour. We observe the emergence of this behaviour, and thus this population, as a result of the diffusion of the rule r_m across the population N, and the gradual emergence of connections between it and the rest of the population which constitute the re-coordination of economic network systems disrupted by its emergence.

References

Becker, Gary, (1962) "Irrational behaviour and economic theory", *Journal of Political Economy*, 70(1), pp. 1–13

Blatt, John M., (1979) "The utility of being hanged on the gallows", *Journal of Post Keynesian Economics*, 2(2), pp. 231–239

Boulding, Kenneth, (1956) *The Image*, University of Michigan Press, Ann Arbor

Dewey, John, (1910) *How We Think*, D.C. Heath and Co., Lexington

Dopfer, Kurt, Foster, John and Potts, Jason, (2004) "Micro-meso-macro", *Journal of Evolutionary Economics*, 14(3), pp. 263–279

Dopfer, Kurt and Potts, Jason, (2008) *The General Theory of Economic Evolution*, Routledge, London.

Earl, Peter, (1983) *The Economic Imagination*, Harvester Wheatsheaf, Brighton

Earl, Peter, (1984) *The Corporate Imagination*, Harvester Wheatsheaf, Brighton

Earl, Peter, (1986a) *Lifestyle Economics*, Harvester Wheatsheaf, Brighton

Earl, Peter, (2017) "Lifestyle changes and the lifestyle selection process", *Journal of Bioeconomics*, 19(1), pp. 97–114

Earl, Peter and Wakeley, Tim, (2010) "Alternative perspectives on connections in economic systems", *Journal of Evolutionary Economics*, 20(2), pp. 163–183

Edelman, Gerald, (1987) *Neural Darwinism*, Basic Books, New York

Elster, Jon, (2009) *Reason and Rationality*, Princeton University Press, Princeton

Foster, John, (2005) "From simplistic to complex systems in economics", *Cambridge Journal of Economics*, 29(6), pp. 873–892

Foster, John and Metcalfe, Stanley, (2012) "Economic emergence: An evolutionary economic perspective", *Journal of Economic Behavior and Organization*, 82(2), pp. 420–432

Friedman, Milton, (1962) *Price Theory*, Aldine, Chicago

Hayek, Friedrich, (1945) "The use of knowledge in society", *American Economic Review*, 25(4), pp. 519–530

Hayek, Friedrich, (1952) *The Sensory Order*, University of Chicago Press, Chicago

Hayek, Friedrich, (1988) *The Fatal Conceit*, University of Chicago Press, Chicago

Heath, Chip and Heath, Dan, (2007) *Made to Stick*, Random House, New York

Hodgson, Geoffrey, (2007) "Meanings of methodological individualism", *Journal of Economic Methodology*, 14(2), pp. 211–226.

Ironmonger, Duncan S., (1972) *New Commodities and Consumer Behaviour*, Cambridge University Press, Cambridge

Kelly, George A., (1963) *A Theory of Personality*, W. W. Norton & Co., New York

Koestler, Arthur, (1964) *The Act of Creation*, Picador, London

Lancaster, Kelvin, (1966a) "Change and innovation in the technology of consumption", *American Economic Review*, 56(1/2), pp. 14–23

Lancaster, Kelvin, (1966b) "A new approach to consumer theory". *Journal of Political Economy*, 74(2), pp. 132–157

Lawson, Clive, (2010) "Technology and the extension of human capabilites", *Journal for the Theory of Social Behaviour*, 40(2), pp. 207–223

Luria, Aleksandr, (1973) *The Working Brain*, Basic Books, New York

Markey-Towler, Brendan, (2016) *Foundations for Economic Analysis*, PhD Thesis, School of Economics, University of Queensland

Markey-Towler, Brendan, (2017a) "How to win customers and influence people: Ameliorating the barriers to inducing behavioural change", *Journal of Behavioral Economics for Policy*, 1(Special Issue: Behavioral Policy and its Stakeholders), pp. 27–32

Markey-Towler, Brendan, (2018a) *An Architecture of the Mind*, Routledge, London

Markey-Towler, Brendan, (2018b) "Salience, chains and anchoring: Reducing complexity and enhancing the practicality of behavioural economics", *Journal of Behavioral Economics for Policy*, 2(1), pp. 83–90

Markey-Towler, Brendan, (2018c) "A formal psychological theory for evolutionary economics", *Journal of Evolutionary Economics*, 28(4), pp. 691–725

Marshall, Alfred, (1890) *Principles of Economics*, 4th Edition, Macmillan and Co., London

Merleau-Ponty, Maurice, (1945) *The Phenomenology of Perception*, Routledge, London

Merleau-Ponty, Maurice, (1948) *The World of Perception*, Routledge, London

Metcalfe, Stanley, (1998) *Evolutionary Economics and Creative Change*, Routledge, London

Mirowski, Philip, (1989) *More Heat than Light*, Cambridge University Press, Cambridge

Newell, Alan, (1990) *Unified Theories of Cognition*, Harvard University Press, Cambridge, MA

Piaget, Jean, (1923) *The Language and Thought of the Child*, Routledge, London

Pinker, Steven, (1999) *How the Mind Works*, Penguin, London

Pinker, Steven, (2002) *The Blank Slate*, Penguin, London

Polanyi, Karl, (1958) *Personal Knowledge*, University of Chicago Press, Chicago

Potts, Jason, (2000) *The New Evolutionary Microeconomics*, Edward Elgar, Cheltenham

Sen, Amartya, (1999) *Commodities and Capabilities*, Oxford University Press, Oxford

Shackle, George L. S., (1969) *Decision, Order and Time*, Cambridge University Press, Cambridge

Shackle, George L. S., (1972) *Epistemics and Economics*, Transaction Publishers, Piscataway

Shannon, Claude, (1948a) "A mathematical theory of communication", *Bell Systems Technical Journal*, 27(3), pp. 379–423

Shannon, Claude, (1948b) "A mathematical theory of communication", *Bell Systems Technical Journal*, 27(4), pp. 623–666

Shiller, Robert, (2017) "Narrative economics", *American Economic Review*, 107(4), pp. 967–1004

Simon, Herbert A., (1956) "Rational choice and the structure of the environment", *Psychological Review*, 63(2), pp. 129–138

Simon, Herbert A., (1968) *Sciences of the Artificial*, MIT Press, Cambridge, MA

Witt, Ulrich, (2008) "What is specific about evolutionary economics?", *Journal of Evolutionary Economics*, 18(5), pp. 547–575

PART II

Internet

Hyper-competition, hyper-growth,
and the struggle for attention
in global markets

5

GLOBAL MARKETS AND THE STRUGGLE FOR ATTENTION

Communication and platforms in the rapidly-evolving internet age

Though it has become ubiquitous in everyday life across the developed world, the impacts of the first of the three mega-technologies of the Fourth Industrial Revolution – the internet – on socioeconomic systems are still making themselves felt through its diffusion. In many ways it provides the most basic infrastructure for the Fourth Industrial Revolution in the sense that artificial intelligence equipped with machine learning is made far more potent when using the data generated by it, and blockchain is enabled by it. It will continue to present new opportunities and challenges for individuals seeking to make their way in the global economy as it evolves and grows and diffuses.

In this chapter we will apply the Brisbane Club model to analysing the likely effects of the mega-technology of the internet and the economic infrastructure it constitutes on the socioeconomic system. Ha-Joon Chang (2010) has famously said that the internet has had less impact on the global economy than the washing machine – and this may be true in terms of productivity gains. However, we will see that in terms of the new connective structures that may be realised within socioeconomic systems with it, the global opportunities it creates, the challenges it poses in terms of competition, and the struggle for attention it creates, it is most certainly a profound technology.

We will begin by considering what exactly the internet *is* and what capabilities for human action it creates. We will then use this to establish the relationship between the technology and the psychological process to assess how it is likely to cause a change of behaviour from old modes to new modes of behaviour which are enabled by it. This can be used to assess the opportunities the internet presents, but we will also establish how the technology presents challenges through its interaction with the psychological process. This in hand, we can step back from the micro-scale dynamics facilitated by the technology to analyse how specifically the internet is likely to continue to disrupt the broader socioeconomic system and how the system will re-coordinate around the meso-populations it will create.

1 The internet: a remarkable data-transfer technology

Asking "what is the internet" is a little like the proverbial fish asking "what is water"; it is such an ubiquitous aspect of life in the modern economy. But if we understand what exactly the technology is and what it allows us to do, we will be better able to understand its relationship with various aspects of the psychological process, and thus the potential it brings for behavioural change at the micro-scale and socioeconomic evolution at the macro-scale. Probably one of the best ways to do this is to consider how it emerged in history as a solution to a particular problem (see Brugger, 2010) which then opened a range of other possibilities.

The first computers were closed systems – unit, integral, unconnected to any others. They could only process information programmed into them by human beings, using the processing algorithms programmed into them by human beings, and using only their own hardware. They were essentially large pocket calculators. Soon after they were built, however, the question arose as to whether they might be connected to one another so as to transfer information and programs from computer to computer, and distribute tasks among them. In the late 1960s the ARPANET was constructed, which first connected computers at UCLA and Stanford, then UC Santa Barbara and the University of Utah, allowing them to transfer information – "data packets" – from computer to computer directly and distribute computational tasks (Leiner et al., 1999). This was followed by an increasing number of variations and improvements on the underlying transfer protocol within the computers themselves, as well as variations and improvements on the physical infrastructure upon which that transfer protocol operated. A major breakthrough occurred when the "modem" was invented, which allowed transfer protocols to operate on existing telecommunications infrastructure by transforming data packets into sound. Thus was the "dial-up" internet born, in which one might use one's modem to execute transfer protocols over the telephone networks – literally using the phone lines to send requests for data packets to be transferred from one computer to another over the internet and then to transfer them.

The second major breakthrough, which created the internet as we now know it, was achieved by Tim Berners-Lee at the famous CERN, who wanted to devise a more ergonomic way to request the transfer of data packets and execute a transfer protocol between computers than laborious coding. To this end, Berners-Lee invented the "Hypertext Transfer Protocol" – http – which embedded a subroutine containing a transfer protocol within a protocol contained within a data packet which would be executed by the click of a mouse on a particular body of text – a "hypertext" – upon the screen of a computer (Hafner, 1998; Berners-Lee, 2000). Berners-Lee's invention gave rise to what we now call the World Wide Web: a network of computers within the internet storing data which might be transferred upon a request executed by a hypertext transfer protocol. This is the portion of the network which soon became accessible to non-specialists with the advent of search engines – the most famous of course being Google – which build a searchable index of data packets which might be transferred over the internet by simply executing all the hypertext protocols embedded within each data packet and repeating (Schmidt, Rosenberg and Eagle, 2014). Those data packets we know now as "sites," and the hypertexts which execute requests to transfer them we know as "links." When they are transferred to our computer for us to view, we "visit" them.

To this day, the World Wide Web contains only a fraction of the data packets which exist in the internet. A vast array of "sites" (data packets) which cannot be transferred by hypertext protocol and which are therefore not accessible by using search engines exist in the "deep web" (Sherman and Price, 2001). For instance, your email login exists in the World Wide Web, but your emails exist in the "deep web" where they can only be accessed by a specific transfer protocol. A further array of "sites" exist in the "dark web" where they can only be transferred with specific authorisations and software (Bartlett, 2014).

Originally, of course, the internet could only transfer a few packets at a time, being limited by the existing telephone networks, which provided the initial infrastructure for the large-scale internet. Both authors can still remember a time in the late 1990s when you could only use the internet when you were sure not to get a phone call because you could not use both modem and telephone at the same time! The internet in that era was an internet largely made up of data packets containing only lines of text, maybe an image or two. Two further inventions were necessary to give us the modern internet as we know it. The advent of broadband infrastructure vastly expanded the amount of data which could be transferred over the infrastructure, and so more complex data packets could be transferred – not only lines of text, but pictures and sounds, then videos of increasing sophistication, then music recordings of increasing sophistication, and eventually voice and video telecommunications in real time. The advent of wireless modem technology allowed data packets to be transferred over the air, freeing the computer from the physical infrastructure which supports the internet, and allowing it to be accessed using mobile devices such as laptops and smartphones. Of course, the evolving internet technology became cheaper and cheaper to use as the price of modems and computers decreased with economies of scale.

Hence the modern web evolved to be a vast network of computers storing data which might be transferred upon request by the execution of a transfer protocol. It allows for the sharing of vast amounts of data between people almost instantaneously at effectively zero marginal cost, and thus facilitates communication and social networks to arise which were hitherto unimaginable (Barney, 2004; Cantoni and Tardini, 2006; Castells, 2009). Any two persons anywhere on the planet (or, increasingly, off-planet too) can communicate virtually any kind of information almost instantaneously and effectively at zero cost if they have access to a computer connected to the internet.

Now what transformed the internet radically enough for it to become a core technology not only of the third industrial revolution, but also of the fourth, was the rise of the mobile device connected to the internet, and in particular the smartphone. In the third industrial revolution, the internet allowed instantaneous and effectively zero cost communication, but only once you had interfaced with a relatively stationary access point such as a personal computer, much in the same way as you would have to use a landline telephone. In the transition to the Fourth Industrial Revolution, internet access points became embedded within mobile devices – smartphones – which could be accessed readily and conveniently at any time and in any space. With the rise of the smartphone, the internet of the Fourth Industrial Revolution comes to you, so to speak, rather than you having to come to it. The internet of the Fourth Industrial Revolution then becomes ubiquitous and pervasive in everyday life, not just a convenient network to be accessed when necessary. The technology ceases to become a network to connect to and to adapt economic activity to using, and becomes a ubiquitous infrastructure on which to build economic systems.

The internet in this new form, of course, provides the infrastructure for many of the information technologies which we have observed in the early twenty-first century. Interpersonal communication for commercial purposes was of course one of the very first uses of email, but as the internet progressed, it made possible the communication of vast amounts of data about oneself and one's life events with others possible, even to the extent even that one might use it to keep a video log – a "vlog" – of everyday life. Thus it became the infrastructure necessary for the emergence of social media (Boyd and Ellison, 2007; Shirky, 2008; Kirkpatrick, 2011; Obar and Wildman, 2015) – the Facebooks, Twitters, Instagrams, and YouTubes which have become such an integral part of life in developed economies. Naturally, of course, the possibility of communicating information on the scale allowed by the internet made possible markets between entirely new groups of counterparties who could now discover opportunities for exchange – giving rise to the "platform revolution" about which Parker, van Asltyne and Choudary (2016) have written. Such commercial platforms, interestingly, are as integral to modern life as social media platforms – one has to travel a long way to discover people who have not heard of eBay, Amazon, or Uber. The vast amounts of data generated as a side effect of these activities in these platforms by individuals communicating is what has contributed to the rise of Big Data, which allows us (especially insofar as it can provide data for artificial intelligences endowed with machine learning) to infer patterns and trends in behaviour at the population level on a scale never hitherto possible (Clegg, 2017). The possibility for sharing not just basic data packets but entire programs has allowed for individuals to obtain algorithms for solving problems, from keeping data on exercise to lodging payslips more effectively or even amusing oneself, by downloading them as "apps" (Brown, 2014). The internet provides (rather obviously) the infrastructure for the Internet of Things, which, by embedding computers connected to the internet within any kind of appliance or machine and able to access real-time data, makes new efficiencies possible, from the electrical "smart grid" to the humble home appliance (Belk, 2016; Vedomske and Myers, 2016). The Internet of Things is already progressing to such a stage that orders for groceries may be automatically dispatched from a smart fridge. The internet is even beginning to make it more feasible to implement augmented reality by using the internet to transfer the data to the device, which will overlay computer generated objects and events into the physical environment (Lin, 2017; Peng, 2016; Sundstrom, 2015; Azuma, 1997; Azuma et al., 2001).

Note that although the technology offers profound capabilities in this sense, it also presents challenges, for the execution of a transfer protocol might transfer data packets between computers and fulfil a request made of the computer which an individual who stores data on that computer might not grant themselves. The transfer protocols within the internet make the undesired transfer of data feasible as well as desired transfers of data. In other words, the internet makes a profound new form of information communication technology available, but it also makes a profound form of "hacking" possible, with significant commercial and political consequences (Jordan, 2008; Coleman, 2014). This, of course, is the province of cybersecurity (Schatz, Bashroush and Wall, 2017), where the better design of transfer protocols is pursued so as to better prevent data packets stored on computers from being transferred over the deep web without the assent of the persons who own that data.

Thus in itself the internet presents challenges to be risen to and problems to be mitigated – a world with internet is a world in which data can be subject to undesirable transfer. But it is also a world in which data can be subject to desirable transfer, and the communicative potential this creates is to what we now turn to study the relationship between the internet and the psychological process. With this relationship in hand, we can understand how the internet is likely to affect socioeconomic systems through behavioural change at the micro-scale to new modes of behaviour enabled by the technology, assess the opportunities and challenges this presents, and then assess the disruption and re-coordination it may cause at the macro-scale.

2 Why the internet matters: platforms for socioeconomic interaction on a global scale

We have seen that the internet is a network of computers storing vast amounts of data which may be transferred upon request by the execution of a transfer protocol from one device to another, and allows communication at effectively zero marginal cost, almost instantaneously between any two individuals with access to it. This is particularly relevant for the evolution of socioeconomic systems insofar as it interacts with behaviour through expanding the range of human capabilities in what economists (Stigler, 1961) and psychologists call *search* (Simon, 1956). The internet offers communication capabilities and platforms, which presents opportunities to develop markets on a global scale hitherto impossible, but can also pose challenges in terms of introducing hyper-competition in those markets.

In the most basic sense, by allowing for information transfer and communication at effectively zero cost almost instantaneously between any two individuals, the internet significantly increases the capabilities of the individual to discover opportunities for exchange. Especially through the possibilities offered by search engines, it is in principle possible for any two individuals with an internet connection to discover one another and communicate opportunities for exchange simply by the one storing data (creating a website in the World Wide Web) which is indexed by search engines. A great deal of commerce is presently and will be realised as a result of this possibility alone, but it has been extended by the advent of *platforms* (Parker, van Alstyne and Choudary 2016), which are centralised databases for storing data on potential exchanges that can be searched readily for that express purpose. The old *agora* has been recreated in the form of eBay, Amazon, Uber, Foodora, and Gumtree. But it now is not limited to a physical space – any two individuals with access to the internet anywhere can effectively instantaneously and at zero cost communicate and discover opportunities for exchange as if they were meeting in a market square.

So the effect of the internet is to vastly expand the range of human capability for forming exchanges without incurring substantial costs. It has now become possible in everyday life to discover opportunities to obtain goods and services in truly global markets – as opportunities for exchange are possible to discover between *any* two individuals *anywhere* at effectively zero cost. Obviously this presents unmitigatedly good opportunities for buyers of goods and services as they are profoundly more able to discover goods and services which are more preferable to them specifically. The internet presents the possibility for behavioural change between old modes of behaviour, which were more limited to obtaining goods and services in geographically localised markets, to new modes of behaviour where goods and services may be obtained in truly global markets. By expanding the range of human capabilities in search, and the ability to discover opportunities for economic exchange, the internet provides platforms for new, truly global market structures to emerge.

Now the internet creates this *possibility*, but it does not mean that we *will* observe behavioural change between these modes of behaviour. Two potential outcomes are possible for individuals as internet-based platforms for market interaction emerge on a global scale. There are opportunities for obtaining hyper-growth in hyper-large markets, but there are also challenges posed by the potential for hyper-competition in those markets. Which of these two outcomes are realised depends on whether states of substitutability exist for the goods and services one is offering in internet-enabled market platforms.

Where a particular good or service is currently being offered for which a state of substitutability exists with respect to other goods or services, the effect of the internet is to make it all the more likely that those other goods and services are going to be discovered, and opportunities to obtain them presented. If the seller of those goods and services can provide a mix of costs/benefits which exceeds that point of substitutability (i.e., offer the right incentive structure given prices and product attributes), then the individual will change their behaviour to obtain them. The sheer scale of the markets implemented on internet-enabled platforms, again, makes it highly likely that such a seller can be found. So the internet introduces a degree of hyper-competition for those who offer goods and services for which substitutes are available. We could put this in terms of Michael Porter's (1979, 1980) five competitive forces. Because the internet significantly expands the scale of markets and thus makes substitutes more available, it increases the power of buyers of particular products and the power of suppliers of particular products, it increases both intra- and inter-industry competition, and it makes it more likely that new entrants will emerge. That is to say, the effect of the internet is to amplify all five competitive forces across all markets. This is a significant challenge presented by the internet – where one is offering a good or service for which substitutes are available, providing a fairly good mix of costs and benefits through prices and product attributes will not be enough; one must provide one of *the best* mixes *worldwide*.

On the other hand, where a particular good or service is currently being offered for which no state of substitutability exists with respect to other goods or services, the seller of those goods and services is relatively inoculated from the challenges posed by internet-enabled hyper-competition. Indeed, the effect of the internet is to introduce opportunities to expand into global markets by making it more possible to discover potential buyers for those goods and services. Provided that seller of those goods and services can produce them and transport them at a sufficiently low cost as for obtaining them to be within the set of capabilities for a market of buyers for whom the good or service is desirable, the seller of a good or service can occupy a "niche" in markets on a global scale. The lack of available substitutes for those goods and services will mean that they are inoculated from competition in this niche, and the limit of the extent to which they can extend their business is the minimum of the size of the market to which they might sell, or the size of production which yields zero marginal profits. Obviously this presents a profound opportunity for such sellers of goods and services. The effect of the internet is to introduce an opportunity for hyper-growth and a global market where one is offering a good or service for which no substitutes are available, and one that can be seized as long as production capabilities allow.

What is particularly interesting about the mega-technology of the internet in the Fourth Industrial Revolution is that these competitive dynamics affect the very *platforms* on which socioeconomic interaction occurs. Brynjolfsson and McAfee (2017) drew particular attention to this phenomenon, albeit in a different terminology: it is now common for platforms for socioeconomic interaction to be products in and of themselves. The *agora* of the internet age is itself a product to which access can be bought and sold. We have discovered that these platforms are particularly subject to the competitive dynamics we have discussed as they, in a sense, exist in a global meta-marketplace for markets. Where they offer a platform for which no substitutes exist, they have the potential for hyper-growth as they become *the* platform for particular forms of global commerce. Where they offer a platform for which substitutes *do* exist, they are subject to hyper-competitive forces as they compete for adoption in a global meta-marketplace. Indeed, these dynamics are amplified for platforms in this meta-market as the expected outcomes from

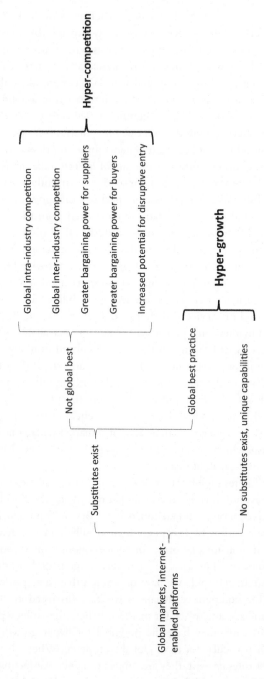

FIGURE 5.1 Global markets and competitive forces.

The effect of the internet is to create truly global markets, and this creates potential for hyper-growth of value-creating networks of exchange if a product represents global best practice or unique capabilities, or the amplifying of all of Porter's five competitive forces if this is not the case.

adopting them are determined by "network effects" – the more they have already been adopted, the better the expected outcomes of adopting them are.

In establishing these opportunities and challenges presented by the internet in the Fourth Industrial Revolution, we have taken as given that opportunities for exchange *will* be discovered by search activities on the part of buyers and sellers in truly global markets. However, the relative availability of information for discovery through search does not guarantee that it will be discovered, but it still further does not guarantee that that information will be *perceived*. So where there are challenges introduced by hyper-competition enabled by the internet, we must also consider whether those challenges are mitigated by the possibility that the internet does not guarantee that competition will be discovered through search. Similarly, where there are opportunities introduced by the hyper-growth enabled by the internet, we must also consider whether those opportunities will be countervailed by the possibility that the internet does not guarantee that opportunities for exchange on a global scale will be discovered through search.

3 The struggle for attention in the internet: cognitive constraints in a sea of information

It is something of a truism of human behaviour that we only notice what is noticeable. But the fact corresponding to this truism exists for good evolutionary reasons. There is vastly more information in the environment than we are cognitively capable of processing. The great economist Ronald Heiner (1983, 1985) pointed out that this leads to what we might call a "competence-difficulty" gap in psychological processing which, were we to seek to bridge it, would cause us to be paralysed and unable to make any decision at all, let alone the right one. What we *must* do in order for us to be able to function at all is to filter vast amounts of information in the socioeconomic environment in perception so as to focus on the most important, most *salient* aspects of the environment for our decision-making. Our attention must be focused to those aspects of the environment.

We have already seen how salience plays a role in socioeconomic systems within the Brisbane Club model. Objects and events in the environment are only perceived if they are placed and presented in the environment in such a way as has a sufficiently strong impression on the sensory organs. So in order for any course of action to be possible, information corresponding to the elements of the knowledge of how and why to engage in it must first be placed and presented in the environment in such a way as to make a sufficient impression on the sensory organs. If that information is not so placed and presented in the environment, further considerations of substitutability and competition are moot, for the knowledge of *how*, let alone *why* to act in a particular way is not present to guide the individual in their decision-making.

This is a problem which is particularly important in the Fourth Industrial Revolution, for the core mega-technology of the internet is, by its nature, a technology which enables communicating information in a way and allowing individuals to discover new information through search that was hitherto impossible. The outcomes of that search are constrained not only by the algorithmic structure of search engines and platforms and the way these interact with the costs and benefits of further search by buyer or seller (Stigler, 1961), but also by the cognitive constraints of individuals. The internet creates the possibility that search can be rationalised by individuals to the point that the information corresponding to new information is placed and presented in their environment and thus discovered. But it does not create the *certainty* that that information will actually be perceived due to the salience property focusing attention and causing much information in the environment to be filtered out in perception.

As the internet is, by its nature, a technology with global reach, the challenge of having opportunities for exchange being discovered *and* perceived by search is not a small one. A global market of sellers will be seeking to broadcast opportunities for exchange with any given buyer, which makes it very difficult in principle for any one seller to be able to place and present information in the environment which makes a sufficiently strong impression on the sensory organs. It needs to be among the loudest and brightest of information presented to the individual. This creates what we know as a "Red Queen" effect whereby each seller needs not only to be able to place and present information corresponding to opportunities for exchange loudly and brightly in the environment, but *more* brightly and more loudly than other sellers. It is only in this way that the attention of the individual buyer will be focused to perceive that opportunity for exchange by the salience property of perception.

We can relate this effect to either the 4Ps (McCarthy 1960) or 7Ps (Booms and Bitner 1981) in order to understand the challenge, it presents. The effect of the ubiquitous internet interacting with cognitive constraints in global markets is to make it more difficult to sufficiently Place and Promote one's goods and services and provide Physical evidence of their quality. Information concerning a given product must be Placed and then Promoted within the internet in such a way as to make it readily available to search, but it must be so placed and promoted *relative* to other information within the internet concerning substitutes within *global* markets. Information must also provide Physical evidence of the quality of goods and services, and that information must make a sufficiently strong impression on the sensory organs as to be noticed *relative* to other information concerning substitutes within global markets. These three Ps of marketing, already necessary for sellers to satisfy, become more difficult to satisfy in the global markets made possible by the internet of the Fourth Industrial Revolution.

The internet thus offers profound opportunities for realising potential exchanges in truly global markets, but that very aspect also presents challenges for realising those potential exchanges through search and discovery. This challenge is, in fact, symmetric. Opportunities for realising exchange are constrained for the *buyer* as for the seller by the cognitive constraints of the buyer. The buyer is constrained in the degree to which their search presents opportunities for exchange which place and present themselves so as to make a sufficient impression on their sensory organs.

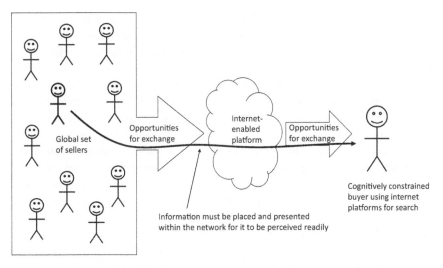

FIGURE 5.2 Cognitive constraints in internet-enabled markets.

The cognitive constraints of human beings mean that not all opportunities for exchange broadcast through the internet can be discovered, let alone perceived. Opportunities must be placed within the internet so that they are readily available to search, and presented so as to make a sufficiently strong impression on the sensory organs.

The seller is constrained in the degree to which the opportunities they broadcast for exchange can be discovered through internet-enabled search on the part of the buyer, and then presented and placed in the buyers' environment in such a way as to make a sufficient impression on their sensory organs as to be perceived.

In order to realise opportunities for exchange in global markets through internet-enabled search and discovery then, the seller must overcome some challenges posed by the nature of the technology and its interaction with the psychological process. They need to be able to place information broadcasting opportunities for exchange in such a position within the internet as for it to be readily discovered by search on the part of buyers before they cease that search. But that information discovered, it also must be placed and presented in the environment of the buyer in such a way as to make a sufficient impression on their sensory organs by being louder and brighter than other opportunities discovered by search. In the socioeconomic system transformed by the internet and the platforms it enables, the most valuable commodity in the world, so to speak, is attention. Without holding the attention of potential buyers, and therefore being successful in the struggle to hold it, no opportunities for exchange can be realised.

4 Disruption and re-coordination as global markets emerge: a hyper-charged economy

We have now established the micro-scale dynamics of the internet by relating the nature of the technology to the psychological process. We have discovered that the internet raises the possibility of behavioural change insofar as it enables *search* for opportunities for exchange on a truly global scale which has hitherto been almost impossible. Where such opportunities are discovered, there is the possibility for realising these opportunities for exchange on a global scale. In the first instance, there is a challenge presented by the nature of the internet to the ability for opportunities for exchange to be successfully broadcast to be discovered by internet-enabled search, and then for those opportunities to be actually perceived. Those opportunities need to be placed and presented in such a way as to have a sufficiently strong impression on the sensory organs. In the second instance, the internet creates further challenges for those who offer goods and services for which substitutes exist by introducing an element of hyper-competition into their business, while it creates opportunities for those who offer goods and services for which substitutes do *not* exist by introducing the possibility for hyper-growth in global markets if production capabilities allow. This is facilitated by the possibility for behavioural change from old, more localised modes of economic behaviour to new, more global modes of behaviour enabled by the internet. With this view of the micro-scale dynamics of behavioural change brought about by the emergence of the internet in hand, we may elevate our level of analysis to view the socioeconomic system as a whole and analyse the likely effects of the rise of the internet at this level.

The internet makes a new form of economic behaviour possible for buyers and sellers – a form in which the search which precedes decision-making is of a global nature. This manifests in a range of potential meso-rules across a range of markets which might be implemented over internet-based platforms. As the General Purpose Technology begins to diffuse, we would expect to observe, as we indeed have observed, a great deal of disruption as connections supported by pre-existing meso-rules which are not enabled by the internet are transferred to individuals who have adopted routines enabled by the internet. The hyper-competition introduced for sellers of goods and services for which a state of substitutability exists with respect to other goods and services will tend to disrupt existing business models and cause markets to deselect existing suppliers in favour of sellers who offer a cost/ benefit mix which is of globally competitive standards. As new meso-rules enabled by the internet spread, however, and come to have a hold on the behaviour of more and more individuals, we are likely to see, and are already starting to see, the re-coordination of socioeconomic systems around the new meso-rules and meso-populations associated with them.

Individuals and groups will become more successful and seize opportunities in this newly re-coordinated economy if they are able to inoculate themselves against the hyper-competition introduced by the internet and harness the opportunities it presents for hyper-growth. To seize the opportunities emerging in the economy re-coordinated around internet-enabled meso-rules requires particular smarts. This is not an economic system which is kind to people who try to compete. It will primarily reward those entrepreneurs who can spot gaps in the market which require the development of a good or service for which no state of substitutability exists with respect to other goods and services – at least for a time. It very much augurs strongly for Peter Thiel's exhortations (2014) to avoid competition and seek niches which do not require one to become a global best. As the diffusion of internet-enabled meso-rules continues, and the meso-populations which apply them become re-coordinated within the broader socioeconomic system, we will observe (as we already are) a socioeconomic system dominated by a diverse set of businesses each occupying a particular niche and servicing a global market alongside a few hyper-fit organisations which can survive hyper-competition.

However, seizing opportunities to be successful within this newly re-coordinated economy also requires smarts of a different kind. Opportunities for exchange need to be made readily available for discovery by search on the part of potential buyers, and when discovered they need to be placed and presented in the environment in such a way as to capture and hold potential buyers' attention. This is an economic system in which the struggle to hold the attention of prospective buyers is central. It will reward those entrepreneurs who can broadcast opportunities for exchange in a way that is strategically placed within the internet to make it more available for discovery by search, and also design that information so that it will be placed and presented in the environment of the potential buyer in a way that has sufficient impression on their sensory organs. As the diffusion of internet-enabled meso-rules continues, and the meso-populations which apply them become re-coordinated within the broader socioeconomic system, we will observe the emergence of a socioeconomic system dominated by a set of businesses which have a strong strategy for using internet-enabled platforms to successfully broadcast opportunities in global marketplaces to obtain hyper-growth by the discovery of these opportunities through search by prospective buyers. Those businesses which do not develop such a strategy will be unable to successfully discover opportunities for exchange as they will have not invested in succeeding in the most important competition of the internet age: the struggle for attention.

At the scale of the broader socioeconomic system, finally, we ought to recognise that the internet is likely to have an impact on the dynamics of socioeconomic systems which we wouldn't particularly observe from a micro-scale analysis. The internet enables rapid, near-instantaneous, effectively zero-cost communication with a virtually limitless audience spread anywhere across the globe who have access to the internet. This allows for candidate meso-rules, once they are originated, to spread far more rapidly than they would were they to have were the communication of the ideas that would become the knowledge that would become the rule to have to travel through communication networks not enabled by the internet. So in general, as we observe new meso-rules enabled by the internet spread, and the socioeconomic system becomes dominated by internet-enabled platforms for global marketplaces, we will observe a far more chaotic socioeconomic system. Traditionally, new meso-rules have been originated and then taken some half century to fully diffuse – disrupting the socioeconomic system initially and then causing it to re-coordinate. In the Fourth Industrial Revolution, we can expect this process to become radically shortened. We may expect diffusion to proceed over periods of decades, if not years, if not even months or even weeks, and thus for disruption and re-coordination to become a far more noticeable feature of life in socioeconomic systems.

5 Summary: global markets and the struggle for attention present opportunities to be seized and challenges to be mitigated

In this chapter we applied the Brisbane Club model to analysing the likely effects of the first mega-technology of the Fourth Industrial Revolution: the internet. We saw that in terms of the new connective structures that may be realised within socioeconomic systems, the global opportunities the internet creates and the challenges it poses are profound. It is a technology which poses the challenges and offers the opportunities of truly global markets, but also poses challenges insofar as a world in which it exists is a world in which the struggle to hold the attention of prospective buyers is central.

We saw that the internet is a vast network of computers storing data which might be transferred upon request by the execution of a transfer protocol. It allows vast amounts of data to be shared between people almost instantaneously at effectively zero marginal cost. It thus facilitates communication and social networks to arise which were hitherto unimaginable: any two persons with an internet connection can communicate almost instantaneously and effectively at zero cost. It provides the infrastructure for many of the technologies we have observed in the early twenty-first century: information communication technologies, social media, Big Data, apps, the Internet of Things, augmented reality, and, most importantly, platforms for market interaction.

By allowing for communication at effectively zero cost almost instantaneously between any two individuals, the internet significantly increases the capabilities of the individual to discover opportunities for exchange through *search* on a truly global scale. It thus presents the possibility for behavioural change from old, more localised modes of economic behaviour to new, more global modes of behaviour enabled by the internet. This presents good opportunities for buyers as they are more able to discover goods and services which are preferable for them in a more global market. It offers either challenges or opportunities, depending on whether a state of substitutability exists for their goods or services. If such a state does exist, the effect of the internet is to introduce a degree of hyper-competition from global markets, and a business must provide one of the *best worldwide* mixes of costs and benefits through prices and product attributes to be successful. If it does not, then the effect of the internet is to create opportunities for hyper-growth in global markets if production capabilities allow. These opportunities, however, can only be realised as long as the possibility for exchange is discovered through internet-enabled search, which requires a strategy be developed for making the relevant information easy to access within the internet, and for that to be placed and presented in such a way as to have sufficient impression on the sensory organs of potential buyers. Success in the struggle to hold the attention of potential buyers is all-important in the Fourth Industrial Revolution.

At the macro-scale of the socioeconomic system, the emergence of new meso-rules across markets which may be implemented on internet-enabled platforms is and will continue to create disruption as markets to deselect existing suppliers in favour of sellers who offer a cost/benefit mix which is of globally competitive standards. As the diffusion of these new internet-enabled meso-populations continues, however, we will observe the re-coordination of socioeconomic systems. These systems will be dominated by a diverse set of businesses each occupying a particular niche and servicing a global market alongside a few hyper-fit organisations which can survive hyper-competition. However, those businesses will also have a strong strategy for using internet-enabled platforms to successfully broadcast opportunities in global marketplaces to obtain hyper-growth by the discovery of these opportunities through search by prospective buyers. All the while, the increasing density of communications networks in the Fourth Industrial Revolution will mean that these diffusion processes will become much more rapid, and the disruption and re-coordination thereby brought a more regular aspect of socioeconomic systems. Life in the Fourth Industrial Revolution will become more chaotic because of the internet, and it will present challenges, but it will present profound opportunities to those prepared for it.

Technical appendix

The internet is a network of computers storing data which may be transferred upon request by the execution of a transfer protocol from one device to another. It is a technology which allows for the sharing of vast amounts of data between any two persons at effectively zero marginal cost. Now what this allows for which is particularly salient for socioeconomic systems is a new form of what economists (for instance, famously, Stigler, 1961) and psychologists (for instance, famously, Simon, 1956) call *search*. Search, in the sense which is salient in socioeconomic systems, is an action a_i^S which leads to information v' arising in the environment, which, perceived in the context of an environment v_{N_i}, contains the possibility of obtaining goods or services x_{ji} from j. That is, search is an action a_i^S for which

$$a_i^S \Rightarrow v' \subset v_{N_i} : \rho\left(v' \subset v_{N_i}\right) \supset x_{ji}$$

The effect of the internet, allowing for the sharing of vast amounts of data between any two persons at effectively zero marginal cost, means that new search actions have become feasible which were hitherto not feasible. These actions involve initiating data packet transfer protocols which would reveal new potential counterparties. That is, we have a range of search actions a_i^S which the internet makes possible, and so we have an extension of human capability such that

$$a_i^S \notin B \rightarrow a_i^S \in B$$

Now of course this not a *sufficient* condition for new behaviour arising, but none-theless it is a *necessary* condition which makes possible the formation of new economic connections in socioeconomic systems by individuals deciding to exchange goods and services. That is to say, the internet makes it possible that we observe changes of behaviour

$$a_i^* \mathrel{\mathpalette\D@\relax} x_{ji} \to a_i^* \supset x_{ji}$$

Obviously, the scale of this possibility brought about by the internet creates vast opportunities for i to obtain new goods and services x_{ji}.

Now it may be the case, of course, where i was previously not interacting with j, such that $a_i^* \mathrel{\mathpalette\D@\relax} x_{ji}$, because they were interacting with some other individual k previously, such that $a_i^* \supset x_{ki}$. If the effect of the internet is to allow i to discover new opportunities to obtain goods and services, then this creates the possibility that new feasible opportunities arise to obtain goods and services from j, $x_{ji} \subset a_i \in B$, and it may be possible that a state of substitutability exists for some cost or benefit δ in that environment. That is, we might have, for $a_i \mathrel{\mathpalette\D@\relax} x_{ji}$ and $a_i' \mathrel{\mathpalette\D@\relax} x_{ki}$ that

$$\exists \bar{\delta} : g_{a_i \supset x_{ki}} \sim g_{a_i' \supset x_{ji}}$$

So if this is the case, i's access to the internet and its search capabilities, which allows them to discover j and the potential to obtain goods and services x_{ji} from them, creates competition for k where hitherto there had been none. Provided that j could, in this case, obtain costs/benefits δ at some point which exceeds the state of substitutability, they could make the course of action which has i obtaining goods and services x_{ji} from them more preferable than obtaining goods and services x_{ki} from k. Thus the internet creates challenges for existing suppliers who now face a new set of competitors, unless of course they are inoculated by their product being non-substitutable for any new products discoverable with the internet.

But if we consider the internet from the perspective of j, we see that the internet also creates vast opportunities for profitable interactions. Profits for j accrue from connections $ji \in g(N)$ in which sales of goods and services x_{ji} are made at prices p_{ji}

$$\pi_j = \sum_{i \in N : ji \in g(N)} p_{ji} x_{ji} - c_j(x_{ji})$$

What the internet does for j is to vastly increase the range of potential connections $ji \in g(N)$ from which these profits may be derived. Of course, these opportunities for profits are exactly that – opportunities. There are challenges presented by the internet to realising such opportunities on the part of j which have to do with meeting the other necessary conditions for i to actually choose to buy their product – for $a_i^* \supset x_{ji}$. We already considered the technical problem of making their goods and services more preferable than existing goods and services, but the core of these problems goes deeper.

The core of these problems is that j relies on the knowledge $g_{a_i \supset x_{ji}}$ in the mind of i of how and why to act in a certain way being such that $x_{ji} \subset a_i^*$. Even if that knowledge is yet to be incorporated into the mind of individual i, this problem reduces to the perception of the objects and events connected by such knowledge $g_{a_i \supset x_{ji}}$ as would cause them to choose to obtain the product x_{ji}. The perception of the good or service x_{ji} as part of a potential exchange is, of course, central to this problem. Perception depends critically upon salience, and so the primary challenge for j is for the objects and events connected by such knowledge $g_{a_i \supset x_{ji}}$ as would cause i to choose to obtain the product x_{ji} being placed and present in such a manner as to make a sufficient impression on i's sensory organs. Recall that some percept h will be perceived if and only if the salience $\sigma(v')$ of the information $v' : \rho(v') = h$ corresponding to it is sufficiently large (a constant $\bar{\sigma}$) with respect to the salience of the overall environment $\sigma(v_N)$. That is,

$$h \in \rho(v' \subset v_N) \Leftrightarrow \sigma(v') - \sigma(v_N) \geq \bar{\sigma}$$

This is a difficult challenge to rise to in environments where the information $v' : \rho(v') = h$ for which the objects and events $h \in H_g : g(H_g) = g_{a_i \supset x_{ji}}$ which would make up those connected by the implications of obtaining goods and services x_{ji} are communicated by the internet. The internet contains vast amounts of information which can be revealed by search on the part of i, and j has to ensure that the information which would correspond to the knowledge which would cause i to obtain goods and service from them, $a_i^* \supset x_{ji}$, is easily accessible in that search, and presented and placed in the results thereof in such a way as to make a sufficient impression on the sensory organs.

References

Azuma, Ronald, (1997) "A survey of augmented reality", *Presence*, 6(4), pp. 355–385

Azuma, Ronald, Baillot, Yohan, Behringer, Reinhold, Feiner, Steven, Julier, Simon and MacIntyre, Blair, (2001) "Recent advances in augmented reality", *IEEE Computer Graphics and Applications*, 21(6), pp. 37–47

Barney, Darin, (2004) *The Network Society*, Polity, Cambridge

Bartlett, Jamie, (2014) *The Dark Net*, Random House, London

Belk, William, (2016) "Understanding the amazing Internet of Things (IoT) – innovation creates value", *Hackernoon.com*, available at URL: https://hackernoon.com/understanding-the-amazing-internet-of-things-iot-innovation-creates-value-6a9a93af33d5 (accessed 18/04/2018)

Berners-Lee, Tim, (2000) *Weaving the Web*, Harper Perennial, New York

Booms, Bernard H. and Bitner, Mary J., (1981) "Marketing strategies and organizational structures for service firms", in Donnelly, James H. and George, William R. (eds.), *Marketing of Services*, American Marketing Association, Chicago, pp. 47–51.

Boyd, Danah M. and Ellison, Nicole B., (2007) "Social network sites: Definition, history and scholarship", *Journal of Computer-Mediated Communication*, 13(1), pp. 210–230

Brown, Carl, (2014) *App Accomplished*, Addison Wesley, Boston

Brugger, Niels, (2010) *Web History*, Peter Lang, Bern

Brynjolfsson, Erik and McAfee, Andrew, (2017) *Machine, Platform, Crowd*, W.W. Norton & Co., New York

Cantoni, Lorenzo and Tardini, Stefano, (2006) *Internet*, Routledge, London

Castells, Manuel, (2009) *The Rise of the Network Society*, 2nd Edition, Wiley, Hoboken

Chang, Ha-Joon, (2010) *23 Things They Don't Tell You About Capitalism*, Penguin, London

Clegg, Brian, (2017) *Big Data*, Icon Books, London

Coleman, Gabriela, (2014) *Hacker, Hoaxer, Whistleblower, Spy: The Many Faces of Anonymous*, Verso, New York

Hafner, Katie, (1998) *Where Wizards Stay Up Late*, Simon & Schuster, New York

Heiner, Ronald, (1983) "The origin of predictable behavior", *American Economic Review*, 73(4), pp. 560–595

Heiner, Ronald, (1985) "Origin of predictable behavior: Further modelling and applications", *American Economic Review*, 75(2), pp. 391–396

Jordan, Tim, (2008) *Hacking*, Polity, Cambridge

Kirkpatrick, David, (2011) *The Facebook Effect*, Random House, London

Leiner, Barry M., Cerf, Vinton G., Clark, David D., Kahn, Robert E., Kleinrock, Leonard, Lynch, Daniel C., Postel, Jon, Roberts, Larry G. and Wolff, Stephen, (1999) "A brief history of the Internet", available at URL: arXiv:cs/099901011v1 (accessed 23/01/1999)

Lin, Jeffrey, (2017) "Creating the right products for VR, AR, or MR", *Hackernoon.com*, available at URL: https://hackernoon.com/creating-the-right-products-for-vr-ar-or-mr-3a093c5ba1a0 (accessed 18/04/2018)

McCarthy, Jerome E., (1960) *Basic Marketing: A Managerial Approach*, McGraw-Hill, New York

Obar, Jonathan A. and Wildman, Steve, (2015) "Social media definition and the governance challenge: An introduction to the special issue", *Telecommunications Policy*, 39(9), pp. 745–750

Parker, Geoffrey G., van Alstyne, Marshall W. and Choudary, Sangeet P., (2016) *Platform Revolution*, W. W. Norton & Co., New York

Peng, Vicki, (2016) "Mobile in 2016 – The next wave of mobile-first & augmented reality", *Medium.com*, available at URL: https://medium.com/swlh/mobile-enterprise-in-2016-the-next-wave-of-mobile-first-540d23f14b95 (accessed 18/04/2018)

Porter, Micahel E., (1979) "How competitive forces shape strategy", *Harvard Business Review*, 57(2), pp. 137–145

Porter, Michael E., (1980) *Competitive Strategy*, Free Press, New York

Schatz, Daniel, Bashroush, Rabih and Wall, Julie, (2017) "Towards a more representative definition of cyber security", *Journal of Digital Forensics, Security and Law*, 12(2), pp. 53–74

Schmidt, Eric, Rosenberg, Jonathan and Eagle, Alan, (2014) *How Google Works*, Hachette, New York

Sherman, Chris and Price, Gary (2001). *The Invisible Web*. Medford: Information Today

Shirky, Clay, (2008) *Here Comes Everybody*, Penguin, London

Simon, Herbert A., (1956) "Rational choice and the structure of the environment", *Psychological Review*, 63(2), pp. 129–138

Stigler, George, (1961) "The economics of information", *Journal of Political Economy*, 69(3), pp. 213–255

Sundstrom, Matt, (2015) "Designing humane augmented reality user experiences", *in*Blog, available at URL: www.invisionapp.com/blog/designing-humane-augmented-reality-user-experiences/ (accessed 18/04/2017)

Thiel, Peter, (2014) *Zero to One*, Crown Business, New York

Vedomske, Michael and Myers, Ted, (2016) "Everything you need to know about the internet of things", *Hackernoon.com*, available at URL: https://hackernoon.com/everything-you-need-to-know-about-the-internet-of-things-ce815339c9f9 (accessed 18/04/2018)

6

THE OCEAN IN YOUR POCKET

Case studies in global markets and the struggle for attention

The rise of ubiquitous mobile and wearable smart devices and the rise of networks of Internet-connected devices and appliances (Internet of Things or IoT) jointly represent the first of the three core technological cornerstones of the Fourth Industrial Revolution as it relates to impacts on the economy. The internet has been around since the middle of the Digital Revolution in the late 1980s, but the comparative ubiquity and accessibility of the internet today, the rise of social platforms, and the maturation of smartphone technology, operating systems, and application marketplaces, along with IoT-centred production efficiencies realised through data collection and communication, ensure that sustained economic growth derived from internet-centred technology continues throughout the Fourth Industrial Revolution (4IR).

This chapter proceeds to focus on mobile and wearable smart devices, rather than IoT applications, not because IoT applications are irrelevant, but because there is an arguably richer array of pertinent use cases to draw from. Several of these are examined in this chapter to motivate an understanding of how the economic value is created, in light of the previous discussions.

The first source of economic value in the personal smart device centres on new market creation and market access. The second source of economic value is derived from the convenience factor it adds to numerous regular life processes, reducing the amount of time, money and effort required to perform these tasks. The third source of economic value is derived from the efficient use of fragmented time, during which it is feasible to pull out your smartphone momentarily, but not particularly feasible to access the internet in any other way. In addition, there are many separate utility gains which affect quality of life, such as free entertainment, which are not directly represented in official GDP figures. We are not interested here in the technical details of the incredible technologies which make the internet possible. Those discussions are best left to other books where they have been well-covered. We are interested in these developments purely from the perspective of the utility gains to the end user and the aggregated effects this has for the economy and society at large.

1 The smartphone and wearable technology

Mobile computing devices have taken over the world in the last decade. Although people will argue that smartphones have been around since the Nokia Communicator in 1996, the debut of the iPhone in 2007 is almost universally seen as a pivotal point for the advent of the age of the smartphone. By the end of 2012, over one billion smartphones were in circulation around the world, and in 2019, this figure is nearing three billion (Statista 2019). The simultaneous rise in popularity of various wearable smart devices, most prominently smartphones and fitness trackers, provide a simple example of the Internet of Things in a commercial context. In most cases, however, these items of wearable technology depend upon a smartphone for access to a local network and the broader internet. Therefore, we just consider the role of a smartphone in the following case studies, as the economic benefits of wearable technology tend to be a subset of those accruing to the smartphone.

People derive value from the smartphone firstly because it enables them to realise all the benefits of access to the internet, but in a more flexible manner. No longer do people have to expend the time and energy to locate and sit down in front of a desktop computer or laptop to access the internet; people can conveniently access the internet wherever they are in a matter of seconds. The value of moving computing and internet access from desktop to mobile can be represented by the time saved each time a person intends to access the internet, in addition to the benefits derived from each situation in which access to the internet would have been infeasible given the resources on hand, if not for the availability of a smartphone. The ease of continual access to the internet has given rise to new behavioural characteristics, for example, diminished attention spans and cognitive capacity due to an outsourcing of working memory (Ward et al. 2017), and this has countless flow-on effects, one such being a reduced ability for students to concentrate in university lectures (Coleman 2014) and a distinct change in behaviour among pedestrians who are distracted by their smartphones, which may lead to an increased risk of traffic accidents (Jiang et al. 2018).

2 Education applications

Education as an economic good is valued because it generally supports the aspirational penultimate ends of status, security, and strength. Regarding status, people typically choose to allocate resources toward obtaining an education because eloquence or the mastery of skills and abstract knowledge sets tends to improve their status among their peers in their community. This is particularly the case if the education was obtained from a prestigious institution (Brewer and McEwan 2009). Regarding security, people will typically choose to obtain education because they may believe that it will subsequently improve their value as an employee in the labour marketplace, therefore increasing their chances of obtaining a stable, well-paying job. An investment into their self-education may also help them attain security, through a better understanding of risk mitigation and insurance strategies. Regarding strength, people typically choose to invest their time, money, and energy into obtaining an education if they believe that the connections they can forge with their lecturers and fellow students, in addition to those forged through extra-curricular activities, will improve their personal influence and their ability to generate opportunities which align with their own higher-order objectives. Higher education is unusual because it can be both a private good and a quasi-public good, in that it accrues private benefits to an individual, which subsequently have positive externalities for the rest of society (Fedeli and Forte 2013).

Smartphones have created economic value in education because of the new methods for learning which have become available. Many educational providers now offer a mobile application through which a person can engage in learning outside a classroom, for instance, while commuting on public transportation. Additional value is created because those commuter hours might otherwise be unproductive, but the smartphone provides a means for that value to be captured. The language-learning platform Duolingo is an excellent example of such an education provider which has risen to prominence in the last decade with its enjoyable mobile applications. People derive value from being able to learn languages without having to go to the effort of spending money and time on in-person language classes, and since the application is accessible via the smartphone, Duolingo can be used anywhere at any time. The app also allows users to create groups with their friends inside the platform, which allows users to support and compete with each other. By addressing the foundational end of social-belonging in addition to the usual aspirational ends, Duolingo is able to increase the utility derived by users.

3 Entertainment applications

There is some uncertainty as to the precise definition and scope of mobile entertainment (Hew et al. 2016). Nevertheless, smartphones can be used for entertainment purposes in many ways which may or may not contribute to GDP. For example, most modern smartphones include built-in cameras, and the use of the camera for photography or videography would be considered a form of entertainment, but this would not contribute towards GDP unless the media created by the user were subsequently sold.

Mobile entertainment, or M-Entertainment, maps to the foundational ends of somato-stability, where positive stimulation of the mind through fun and entertainment promotes good health, as well as social-belonging, if users consume the entertainment along with their friends or as part of a community. Games compose a major element of mobile entertainment. Most smartphones permit the user to play games through both built-in and third-party applications available in the relevant app store. People may also derive entertainment value from the use of their smartphones through the streaming of video content, for example, on YouTube, or feature films and shows, for example, from Netflix.

Wong and Hiew (2005) introduced a simple but useful model to understand the different forms of mobile entertainment as they relate to the internet and commerce, as shown in Figure 6.1. Area 1 in the diagram corresponds to the set of mobile entertainment services which involve a monetary exchange over the internet with the smartphone user. This would include services such as premium games which require purchases through the app store to use. Area 2 corresponds to free mobile entertainment services which do not require contact with third-party service providers, but which require a network connection to operate. This would include free games, for example, multiplayer sports games, which can be played with friends over a local Wi-Fi network. Area 3 in the figure corresponds to those mobile entertainment services which are free and which can be consumed offline, without access to the internet. For example, a chess application might have provisions for the user to play the engine running on the smartphone CPU, even while disconnected from the internet.

The key elements which determine whether consumers will engage in a particular form of mobile entertainment are generally categorised as perceived ease of use (PEOU) and perceived usefulness (PU), which are in turn influenced by the level of trust that the user has in the service, the perceived financial cost (PFC), and the quality of the services (QS) (Hew et al. 2016).

The entertainment applications of smartphones are still growing rapidly, especially in emergent economies. For example, Ma (2017, p. 160) observed that

> young internet users in China are more focused on entertainment services than the traditional forms of usage of the internet for information searches and email messages. For a large part of their time online, they play online games, watch videos of TV programs and movies, assume online personas in the virtual world and form online communities to have fun together. As smartphones have become the top channel for internet access in China, the young generation of users enjoy themselves whenever and wherever, increasingly consuming, sharing and arguing about the entertainment content on their hand-held devices during their "fragmented time" (for example, during a subway commute or while waiting in line) throughout the day (vis-a-vis the fixed time before a PC).

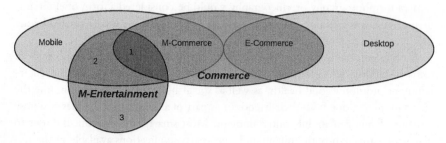

FIGURE 6.1 A simple mobile entertainment model.

Source: Adapted from Wong and Hiew (2005)

4 Text and voice: from reading and typing to listening and speaking

The gradual rise of voice-based natural-language user interfaces over the last decade is changing the way in which people interact with their personal smart devices and access the internet. Global technology companies now provide voice-enabled smart hubs which connect with other consumer devices in consumer IoT networks. Most smartphones are also equipped with voice assistants which are able to search the Internet and perform a variety of moderately complex tasks, controlled via voice command. The early forms of voice search were directory assistance (DA) systems in the 1990s (Tur and De Mori 2011). The biggest challenges, which were largely overcome in the early 2010s, involved accurate natural language recognition and the ability to convert this into a coherent set of tasks for the device to perform before responding (Park et al. 2011). Voice search systems and other commercial spoken dialogue systems (SDSs) more broadly have come a long way in the last fifteen years, and the advances in processing and memory capability within smartphones has provided the necessary computational power to run improved natural-language processing software.

The ability to perform voice search and other fundamental tasks using smartphones creates economic value for end users because speaking with your voice and listening for the response does not require the user to hold the device or focus their visual attention onto the device while typing. Therefore, compared to the older methods of typing commands and text search prompts into smart devices, or reading the responses provided by the device or the results of a search query, significant utility gains are realised, because the user's hands and eyes are freed up to perform other tasks simultaneously. For instance, a person might be preparing food in the kitchen or driving a car, and can now search the internet without pausing the first activity. This implies that time savings are realised, permitting people more time to allocate towards pursuing the higher-order ends. With voice-controlled smart devices it is also possible to be mobile rather than fixed, so long as the user remains within hearing range of the smart device.

The ability to control smart devices by voice also enables some of the benefits of smart devices to be realised by consumers who are either illiterate or otherwise disabled, who might struggle to navigate using a smartphone if they have to type commands or search queries by hand, and thus be required to spell or see the screen (Phillips, Nguyen, and Mischke 2010).

5 A tool for democratisation? Who controls the flows?

One of the most fundamental aspects of any economic marketplace is the transactions which occur within it. Every transaction represents an exchange of value between suppliers and demanders, that is, between producers and consumers. Further, every exchange of value that occurs in an economic marketplace implies a corresponding economic flow, whether of money and capital, or goods and services, or information and knowledge, or people. The question of who, if anyone, or what economic institution, controls these economic flows is of utmost importance to understanding where the power dynamics across all levels of the economy are really structured.

Trade flows of physical goods often involve the use of domestic or international trade routes. Land-based trade routes have evolved from the ancient roads designed for the use of animals hauling cargo to the modern array of highways, railroads, and tunnels designed for large road trains and freight trains hauling hundreds or thousands of tonnes of cargo today (Pepe 2018). Sea-based trade routes have largely remained the same, but travel distances have been shortened with canals, and the ships making the journeys are significantly larger. During the last hundred years, air trade routes have also become operational, usually used for lightweight, urgent, or premium cargo. In all cases, as the world economy has grown through the last three industrial revolutions, the trade routes have become much denser with traffic.

These routes are exceedingly important to the upkeep of the global economy, since the ability of businesses to sell their products and consumers to purchase them depends upon the ability of trade to flow within economic marketplaces (Koehn 1994). These represent both profits and livelihoods. Since ancient times, therefore, savvy rulers and merchants have understood the power that comes with the ability to extend influence over the trade routes and therefore over the flows of value in the economy (Gaile and Grant 1989). For example, if an independent party came to control the trade route itself, they may be able to impose a tax on merchants who wish to pass through the territory or make use of the highway. If the tax is priced appropriately, the merchants will stand to gain more from paying the tax and conducting their usual business than they would by not using the highway. Such an independent party may be able to exert its influence in other ways, for example, by setting other arbitrary rules which it has the capability to enforce, such as only permitting buyers and sellers of certain characteristics to transact. A typical example from countless examples over history since ancient times is the building of Petra by the Nabateans between the Gulf of Arabia and the Dead Sea (Benjamin 2001), which gave the Nabateans effective control of the incense trade route between Arabia and Damascus (Eckenstein 2005, p. 49).

In the modern age, nation-states still place immense value on both the physical control of trade routes and control over the rules by which trade must take place. Both of these factors play a significant role in transnational public policy (Bown and Reynolds 2015). For example, the United States tends to use its Navy in peacetime efforts to patrol international waters, and particularly high-traffic international trade routes, in an attempt to ensure that its strategic competitors do not gain too much power over these regions and that international trade shipments of goods and resources can move unhindered. The Malacca Straits in the Indian Ocean represent a high-traffic route for shipments between East Africa or Europe and East Asia, but for China this is likely to represent a strategic risk because the region is largely controlled by Indonesia and Singapore, who tend to have stronger relationships with the United States than with China. For this and many other reasons, China is investing heavily in its One Belt One Road initiative in a broader plan to secure a China-centred trading network. As another classic example of interference in trade, most countries around the world implement tariffs on specific categories of goods being supplied by merchants hailing from various countries.

This same variety of analysis applies to flows of money and capital, flows of breaking news, and flows of information and data. Whether commerce, media, or communications, the economic institutions which manage the physical exchange between sender and recipient, and the institutions which set the conditions under which the exchange may take place, are afforded great influence and power. The institutional shift to the internet during the Digital Revolution, and in particular through the use of smartphones during the Fourth Industrial Revolution, has completely changed the nature of economic flows, by digitizing and commoditising the economic marketplaces through which deals are agreed upon and the metaphorical trade routes through which the precious cargo is delivered. People derive value from this shift because, according to the previously mentioned seven penultimate ends of human action, people value having more time to allocate to higher-order ends, which is realised when transactions are faster. These digital communications are also generally cheaper, leaving people with the same outcome but with fewer financial resources spent to procure it. People also recognize that information loses value with age. Therefore, people are willing to even pay a premium to obtain data which is closer to real-time.

Ethical issues arise, however, when third-party institutions and organisations choose to interfere in the digital flows of information. For example, a government may believe it has the right to control trade flows, but can the same reasoning be applied to information flows? Another grey area arises when private, unelected companies are the third-party institutions which manage a private platform through which users become de facto producers and consumers of information and news updates. These platform companies derive enormous market power from their ability to determine how producers and consumers coordinate to find each other and negotiate deals (Grewall 2008), what terms and conditions of entry to the platform marketplace are imposed, and whether there is a participation fee.

6 Competing platforms, fragmentation, and the market for marketplaces

Before the advent of the internet, the number of physical marketplaces where people and businesses could come together to conduct commerce in any one industry was fairly limited. There are obviously upper limits on the number of suitable spaces available within a reasonable commute of both parties to the transaction (Toftgaard 2016). More precisely, the participation costs, which include the travel time and associated expenses in additional to any entry fees, dictated the number of people and businesses who would come to transact in the marketplace.

In the last century, many large companies, such as the Westfield Group and the Brookfield Properties Retail Group, earned substantial profits by establishing and managing physical shopping malls for many retailers and consumers to come together and do business. These shopping malls were highly successful as economic marketplaces, and by measure of regular traffic and sales volume within their walls, they tended to dominate other local marketplaces nearby. Only a few such physical marketplaces, judiciously located, were required to satisfy most of the buyers and sellers in a given city or town. Physical shopping malls were large and expensive architectural structures, requiring large amounts of capital to construct and maintain. There were large barriers to entry for prospective new marketplace entrepreneurs. As a physical platform and an economic marketplace, the shopping mall itself had only a handful of competitors (such as community markets or a rival shopping mall) vying for the attention of the same local buyers and sellers.

Fast-forward to the present day, and the internet of the Digital Revolution has drastically reduced the barriers to entry for entrepreneurs wishing to establish an economic marketplace, enabling them to create online platforms and storefronts (Sutherland and Jarrahi 2018). Further, the ubiquitous smartphone of the Fourth Industrial Revolution has drastically reduced the participation costs for buyers and sellers to participate in these online marketplaces built on top of the internet (Kazan et al. 2018), while increasing the absolute number of buyers and sellers potentially willing to participate through their mobile internet access. The only marginal costs now involve the effort to take the phone from their pockets, navigate to the relevant mobile application or website in the browser, and either create a listing to sell a product on the platform or search for and purchase items which have been listed by sellers.

As alluded to in the previous chapter, the lower barriers to entry and the global nature of the internet have transformed the market for economic marketplaces from the relatively protected industry that once was the network of local twentieth-century shopping malls to the hyper-competitive global industry of E-Commerce and M-Commerce. From one perspective, this high level of competition among internet platforms and marketplaces presents a welcome diversity of offerings with which buyers and sellers can develop a strategy to engage (Miller and Niu 2012). On the other hand, there are lost efficiencies through fragmentation because the value of the platform marketplace itself is proportional to how many people are using it, in line with the network effect (Ruutu, Casey, and Kotovirta 2017; but see Fletcher and Nielsen 2017). Many buyers and sellers may end up operating on different platforms, partially negating the benefits of global commerce through internet-enabled technology (Nelson-Field and Riebe 2011). Instead of being primarily grouped together by locality, buyers and sellers may find themselves in numerous fragmented groups according to their preferred platform or online marketplace. This may not present a problem, however, if the different platforms "serve distinct institutional interests" (Taneja 2013).

The ability for global buyers to purchase items from global sellers on the other side of the world has enabled economic value to be created through more choice and the associated higher probability that the buyers will find a seller with a product that better fits their needs. The ability of global sellers to access such a large marketplace of potential buyers through online platforms has also enabled many businesses to experience hyper-growth. Another result is that the increased number of options for buyers to sort through before making a purchase increases the likelihood of not making an optimal purchase decision. These search frictions permit sellers to maintain their profit-creating mark-ups in what might otherwise be assumed to be a highly competitive global marketplace (Dinerstein et al. 2018). Internet search providers such as Google derive their market power by capitalising on buyers' desire to optimise their purchasing decision given their resource constraints, by lowering search frictions. In turn, businesses go to great lengths to fight for the attention of their potential buyers, with the hope to be more easily noticed. Businesses also have to judge whether participation in an online marketplace is worth it at all (Ryan, Sun, and Zhao 2012; Mantin, Krishnan, and Dhar 2014).

This short discussion has been framed in terms of buyers and sellers of physical products, but this discussion equally applies to seekers and disseminators of information and media, such as updates from your friends and social networks, and information about current events around the world. Social media platforms and messaging platforms such as Facebook, Instagram, and Snapchat are fundamentally marketplaces for social information, gossip, and communication (Cao et al. 2013). These economic goods are "purchased" with the time and attention that users allocate to the platform in accordance with the perceived value of this information (Goolsbee and Klenow 2006). Due to network effects, these platforms offer a more convincing value proposition to users simply by having the friends of potential users on the platform (Srinivasan and Venkatraman 2018). The market for messaging platforms, however, is oversaturated and suffers the archetypical fragmentation problem. When confronted with the choice of sending a simple message via Whatsapp, Signal, WeChat, LINE, KakaoTalk, Facebook Messenger, email, a simple SMS, or any one of the many other messaging tools, it is easy for consumers to feel frustrated due to the complexity and the fragmented conversations which may spread across many diverse platforms. Strong social connections are a major factor in the consumer decision to prefer one social platform over another (Riles, Pilny, and Tewksbury 2018). Many challenges remain, particularly in relation to whether and how it would be appropriate to regulate various digital platforms, and whether any of these platforms may eventually capture the regulators (Nechushtai 2018; Nooren et al. 2018).

References

Benjamin, Jesse. 2001. "Of Nubians and Nabateans: Implications of Research on Neglected Dimension of Ancient World History." *Journal of Asian and African Studies* 36(4): 361–382.

Bown, Chad P., and Kara M. Reynolds. 2015. "Trade Flows and Trade Disputes." *Review of International Organizations* 10(2): 145–177.

Brewer, Dominic J., and Patrick J. McEwan, eds. 2009. *Economics of Education*. Amsterdam, Netherlands: Elsevier.

Cao, Huanhuan et al. 2013. "A Maslow's Hierarchy of Needs Analysis of Social Networking Services Continuance." *Journal of Service Management* 24(2): 170–190.

Coleman, Raymond. 2014. "Demise of the Academic Student Lecture: An Inevitable Trend in the Digital Age." *Acta Histochemica* 116(7): 1117–1118.

Dinerstein, Michael, Liran Einav, Jonathan Levin, and Neel Sundaresan. 2018. "Consumer Price Search and Platform Design in Internet Commerce." *American Economic Review* 108(7): 1820–1859.

Eckenstein, Lina. 2005. *A History of Sinai*. Boston, MA: Adamant Media Corporation.

Fedeli, S., and F. Forte. 2013. "Higher Education as Private Good and as Quasi Public Good: The Case of Italy." Pp. 197–224 in *Constitutional Economics and Public Institutions*. Edward Elgar Publishing Ltd.

Fletcher, Richard, and Rasmus Kleis Nielsen. 2017. "Are News Audiences Increasingly Fragmented? A Cross-National Comparative Analysis of Cross-Platform News Audience Fragmentation and Duplication." *Journal of Communication* 67(4): 476–498.

Gaile, Gary L., and Richard Grant. 1989. "Trade, Power, and Location: The Spatial Dynamics of the Relationship between Exchange." *Economic Geography* 65(4): 329–337.

Goolsbee, Austan, and Peter J. Klenow. 2006. "Valuing Consumer Products by the Time Spent Using Them: An Application to the Internet." *The American Economic Review* 96(2): 108–113.

Grewall, David Singh. 2008. *Network Power: The Social Dynamics of Globalization*. New Haven and London: Yale University Press.

Hew, Teck Soon, Lai Ying Leong, Keng Boon Ooi, and Alain Yee Loong Chong. 2016. "Predicting Drivers of Mobile Entertainment Adoption: A Two-Stage Sem-Artificial-Neural-Network Analysis." *Journal of Computer Information Systems* 56(4): 352–370.

Jiang, Kang et al. 2018. "Effects of Mobile Phone Distraction on Pedestrians' Crossing Behavior and Visual Attention Allocation at a Signalized Intersection: An Outdoor Experimental Study." *Accident Analysis and Prevention* 115: 170–177.

Kazan, Erol, Chee Wee Tan, Eric T. K. Lim, Carsten Sørensen, and Jan Damsgaard. 2018. "Disentangling Digital Platform Competition: The Case of UK Mobile Payment Platforms." *Journal of Management Information Systems* 35(1): 180–219.

Koehn, Nancy F. 1994. *The Power of Commerce: Economy and Governance in the First British Empire*. New York: Cornell University Press.

Ma, Winston. 2017. *China's Mobile Economy: Opportunities in the Largest and Fastest Information Consumption Boom*. West Sussex, UK: John Wiley & Sons Ltd.

Mantin, Benny, Harish Krishnan, and Tirtha Dhar. 2014. "The Strategic Role of Third-Party Marketplaces in Retailing." *Production and Operations Management* 23(11): 1937–1949.

Miller, T., and J. Niu. 2012. "An Assessment of Strategies for Choosing between Competitive Marketplaces." *Electronic Commerce Research and Applications* 11(1): 14–23.

Nechushtai, Efrat. 2018. "Could Digital Platforms Capture the Media through Infrastructure?" *Journalism* 19(8): 1043–1058.

Nelson-Field, Karen, and Erica Riebe. 2011. "The Impact of Media Fragmentation on Audience Targeting: An Empirical Generalisation Approach." *Journal of Marketing Communications* 17(1): 51–67.

Nooren, Pieter, Nicolai van Gorp, Nico van Eijk, and Ronan Fathaigh. 2018. "Should We Regulate Digital Platforms? A New Framework for Evaluating Policy Options." *Policy and Internet* 10(3): 264–301.

Park, So-Young, Jeunghyun Byun, Hae-Chang Rim, Do-Gil Lee, and Heuiseok Lim. 2011. "Natural Language-Based User Interface for Mobile Devices with Limited Resources." *IEEE Transactions on Consumer Electronics* 56(4): 2086–2092.

Pepe, Jacopo Maria. 2018. "Eurasia before Europe: Trade, Transport and Power Dynamics in the Early World System (1st Century BC – 14th Century AD)." Pp. 77–115 in *Beyond Energy*. New York: Springer.

Phillips, Mike, John Nguyen, and Ali Mischke. 2010. "'Why Tap When You Can Talk?': Designing Multimodal Interfaces for Mobile Devices That Are Effective, Adaptive and Satisfying to the User." Pp. 31–60 in *Advances in Speech Recognition: Mobile Environments, Call Centers and Clinics*, edited by A. Neustein. New York: Springer.

Riles, Julius Matthew, Andrew Pilny, and David Tewksbury. 2018. "Media Fragmentation in the Context of Bounded Social Networks: How Far Can It Go?" *New Media and Society* 20(4): 1415–1432.

Ruutu, Sampsa, Thomas Casey, and Ville Kotovirta. 2017. "Development and Competition of Digital Service Platforms: A System Dynamics Approach." *Technological Forecasting and Social Change* 117: 119–130.

Ryan, Jennifer K., Daewon Sun, and Xuying Zhao. 2012. "Competition and Coordination in Online Marketplaces." *Production and Operations Management* 21(6): 997–1014.

Srinivasan, Arati, and N. Venkatraman. 2018. "Entrepreneurship in Digital Platforms: A Network-Centric View." *Strategic Entrepreneurship Journal* 12(1): 54–71.

Statista. 2019. "Number of Smartphone Users Worldwide from 2014 to 2020 (in Billions)." www.statista.com/statistics/330695/number-of-smartphone-users-worldwide/.

Sutherland, Will, and Mohammad Hossein Jarrahi. 2018. "The Sharing Economy and Digital Platforms: A Review and Research Agenda." *International Journal of Information Management* 43: 328–341.

Taneja, Harsh. 2013. "Audience Measurement and Media Fragmentation: Revisiting the Monopoly Question." *Journal of Media Economics* 26(4): 203–219.

Toftgaard, Jens. 2016. "Marketplaces and Central Spaces: Markets and the Rise of Competing Spatial Ideals in Danish City Centres, c. 1850–1900." *Urban History* 43(3): 372–390.

Tur, Gokhan, and Renato De Mori, eds. 2011. *Spoken Language Understanding: Systems for Extracting Semantic Information from Speech*. West Sussex, UK: John Wiley & Sons Ltd.

Ward, Adrian F., Kristen Duke, Ayelet Gneezy, and Maarten W. Bos. 2017. "Brain Drain: The Mere Presence of One's Own Smartphone Reduces Available Cognitive Capacity." *Journal of the Association for Consumer Research* 2(2): 140–154.

Wong, Chin Chin, and Pang Leang Hiew. 2005. "Mobile Entertainment: Review and Redefine." Pp. 187–192 in *4th Annual International Conference on Mobile Business, ICMB 2005*.

PART III

Artificial intelligence

Radical automation and expansion of human capability

7

THE *I, ROBOT* FUTURE

Human work in an age of artificial intelligence

Artificial intelligence is technically the oldest of the three mega-technologies of the Fourth Industrial Revolution. It has existed since the 1950s, and earlier in theoretical form. But recent advances made in computing power and energy efficiency, as well as machine learning, have made it a far more potent technology with respect to socioeconomic systems and given it vigour in the early twenty-first century. Despite this relatively long diffusion period, the surge in applications of artificial intelligence will have by far the most profound effects on everyday life in the Fourth Industrial Revolution.

In this chapter we will apply the Brisbane Club model to analysing the likely effects of the mega-technology of artificial intelligence and the production technology it offers. There has been a great deal of research already done within economics using standard models of economic growth and labour markets segmented by task allocation to model the economics of artificial intelligence (Nordhaus, 2015; Acemoglu and Restrepo, 2016, 2017, 2018). The Brisbane Club model encourages us to take a different approach to the economics of artificial intelligence by examining in depth the dynamics by which artificial intelligence causes behavioural change, where standard models tend to leave this to assumption. The Brisbane Club model, in essence, encourages us to take a rigorous approach to the data presented by various studies of the technology itself (Brynjolfsson and McAfee, 2011, 2014; Ford, 2015; Frey and Osborne, 2013; Citi Global Perspectives & Solutions, 2016; Agrawal, Gans and Goldfarb, 2018; Zuvatern and Sullivan, 2017) to establish a relationship between the technology and the psychological process to project the likely impact it will have on behaviour. We will see as a result of this that artificial intelligence has profound implications as a technology which creates a substitute for the human labourer, both challenges and opportunities. But we will also see that there is a future for human work in an age of artificial intelligence. While the future we have identified is not dissimilar to the future identified, in particular, by Brynjolfssson and McAfee (2011, 2014, 2017), insofar as we argue that there is a future for work in production which requires judgment, creativity, and tacit knowledge, we give that future a very specific definition and meaning in the context of the Brisbane Club model.

We will begin, again, by considering what exactly artificial intelligence *is* and what capabilities for human action it creates. We will then use this to establish the relationship between the technology and the psychological process to assess how it is likely to drive a change of behaviour from old modes of behaviour to the new modes of behaviour it enables. We will then consider some limits to the extent of this behavioural change presented by non-substitutabilities between artificial intelligence and human labour. In establishing the nature of artificial intelligence, the relationship it has with the psychological process and behavioural change, and the limits of this relationship, we will draw heavily on research published elsewhere by Markey-Towler (2018). This understanding arrived at of the micro-scale dynamics generated by artificial intelligence, we will then use it to analyse how the technology is likely to continue to cause disruption of the broader socioeconomic system, and project what an economy re-coordinated around meso-rules enabled by it looks like.

1 The machine with a mind: what artificial intelligence is

The nature of artificial intelligence is suggested by its very name – a uniquely informative name. It is a technology which seeks to replicate (or mimic the outputs of, for the tech-heads reading along) the operation of a human intelligence. It is actually not a new technology, as it emerged with computer science in the 1950s and coevolved therewith afterward. We can see from two early and utterly seminal contributions to computer science and artificial intelligence how computer science was, from the outset, considered to be an exercise in building an artificial intelligence.

In a famous 1950 paper in *Mind*, Alan Turing, having just secretly invented a new, vastly improved computer machinery for breaking Nazi encryptions, explored how the workings of the machinery he had developed related to the workings of the human mind. He introduced the idea here that the mind, much like the computer, could be understood as a system for processing, transforming, and storing information, and then repeating. He introduced the idea that the process of thought might be likened to the passage of "tape" through a (archaic) computer. A contribution by the mathematical genius John von Neumann explored the other "direction" of this relationship between mind and machine. In his *The Computer and the Brain (1958)* he explored how computing machines might be developed by reference to the workings of the human mind to better improve their functioning. Their function, after all, was to automate and replicate (or mimic, again for the tech-heads reading along) the process of human computation. The mechanical structure of the machine would manifest sets of logical operations that the human mind might apply while transforming information to solve a particular problem,

placed in sequence or in parallel, and then use these "organs" to process information. Thus the computer would come to resemble something like an artificial
brain, automating the functioning of a process that would otherwise be applied by
a human mind. The mind could be understood to be akin to the computer, and
the computer could be understood to be akin to the mind. The computer became
an artificial intelligence.

Both of these contributions to computer science were, interestingly, seminal
contributions also to the development of cognitive psychology when applied to
studying the functioning of the human mind by Herbert Simon (1968) and his
long-time collaborator Alan Newell (1990). Together with their collaborator John
Shaw (Newell, Shaw and Simon, 1958) they would famously make use of computers to show how even the greatest feats of the human mind might be obtained by
placing simple logical operations in sequence to create a program for transforming
information. They used their programs to show how cognitive processing might,
for instance, derive the first two chapters of Russell and Whitehead's *Principia Math-
ematica*, or (as in Simon, 1998) derive Newton's laws by fitting equations to astro-
nomical data. Steven Pinker (1999) has noted how cognitive psychology gradually
came to the realisation that the human mind doesn't just work *like* a computer, it *is* a
computer. Artificial intelligence will often therefore draw on cognitive psychology
to design the programs manifesting in the mechanical structures of computers so
that their functioning mimics the functioning of a cognitive process. Ray Kurzweil
for instance (2012), developing insights made by Friedrich Hayek (1952), among
others, has characterised artificial intelligence as a pattern recogniser, mimicking
the manner in which the mind uses a system of classification to categorise objects
and events in the environment at higher and higher levels of abstraction. Alternatively, Agrawal, Gans and Goldfarb (2018), developing insights made by George
Kelly (1963), among others, have characterised artificial intelligence as "prediction
machines," mimicking the manner in which the mind construes the likely future
course of events based on objects and events in the environment.

This is important because such processes of classification and prediction are the
basis for human *action*, from which human *work* arises. Indeed the model of the
psychological process at the core of the Brisbane Club model reveals this to us. It
is by classifying and categorising objects and events in our environment, and forming a judgment of their relationship to predict the future course of events, that
we arise at an understanding of our environment which might orient our action
within it (Markey-Towler, 2018). So by automating the processes which give rise
to human *thought*, artificial intelligence automates the processes which give rise to
human *action*. If the mechanical structure which manifests the artificial intelligence
can be integrated within a mechanical structure which executes work, we can use
machines to automate not only human action, but also human action *as guided by
thought*.

An artificial intelligence as we have discussed it so far has a "fixed" programmatic structure, while we know that the structure of the human mind can *evolve*
through the creation of new connections and the fading of old ones (Hayek, 1952;

Edelman, 1978). As a way to eliminate this difference between mind and machine, Arthur Samuel showed that, since computers transform information into operations (Samuel, 1953), it was possible to have those operations modify the programmatic structure of the machine's organs (Samuel, 1959). These "meta" programs for updating programs would be called "machine learning" algorithms. They could be written so as to update the programmatic structure of the machine based on whether its functioning led to a better or worse outcome relative to some criterion, and thus improve the functioning of the machine relative to that criterion as it "learned." Samuel himself used the example of a machine playing a game of checkers to show how machine learning algorithms could cause the programs embedded within it to become better and better at achieving the criterion of making "good" moves in the game. The effect of Samuel's innovation, therefore, was to allow for artificial intelligences to not merely automate the functioning of a human mind, but also to show how that mind would evolve and develop based on feedback from the environment. Samuel, in effect, helped to realise how the development process about which Piaget (1923) wrote, whereby mental schema grow and evolve based on feedback from the environment, could be automated and replicated in a machine.

As advances were made in the late twentieth century in computing power and energy efficiency, academic and industrial research into the algorithms which might manifest an artificial intelligence surged. There are now many accessible primers and entry points into this literature on artificial intelligence and machine learning (for instance: Kelnar, 2016; McClelland, 2017; Jeffries, 2017) which reduce to a fundamental commonality as regards the nature of artificial intelligence technology. Artificial intelligence, especially when endowed with machine learning algorithms, is a technology which seeks to mimic the functioning of the human mind, and which can therefore mimic human action guided by a process that mimics human thought.

Artificial intelligence, broadly construed, is at the heart of many of the technologies of the Fourth Industrial Revolution. Most obviously, of course, it underlies the vigorous automation of routine production processes we are beginning to observe worldwide (Brynjolfsson and McAfee, 2011; Frey and Osborne, 2013; Citi Global Perspectives & Solutions, 2016). This, obviously enough, underlies the emerging "drone" economy, where automated drones endowed with some level of artificial intelligence take the place of human operators of machines. But what is perhaps a little disturbing for some is how this automation is being extended to areas that are traditionally considered inoculated from automation. Where "knowledge" work dedicated to transforming information in routine ways was traditionally thought to be somewhat inoculated, as opposed to more physical routine work, the sheer power of modern artificial intelligence, especially endowed with machine learning, is challenging that presumption (Ford, 2015; Zuvatern and Sullivan, 2017). Artificial intelligence, especially when endowed with machine learning, is also incredibly powerful when combined with Big Data as a way of identifying trends and relationships which would otherwise take a human being vast amounts of time to discover (Clegg, 2017; Zuvatern and Sullivan, 2017). Closely related to this technology, insofar as artificial intelligence endowed with machine learning is what Agrawal, Gans and Goldfarb (2018) have called a "prediction machine" which is designed to form more and more accurate assessments of data based on "experience," it is underlying many advancements in biological and medical science which allow for better diagnoses based on symptoms input into an artificial intelligence and better treatment based on genetic sequencing by artificial intelligence drawing on data analysed by artificial intelligence. Wherever an algorithm can be written to automate a process of transforming information into action, artificial intelligence is powering the Fourth Industrial Revolution ahead.

2 The economics of a machine with a mind: building a substitute for *us*

Artificial intelligence is a profound technology in its own right. It is, to put it somewhat dramatically, a technology we have made in our own image. It is a technology which is also profound in its likely impact on socioeconomic systems. This technology does not only expand the capabilities for human action as prior technologies have tended to (Lawson, 2010). It does this, but its core characteristic is that, insofar as it mimics human action guided by a process that mimics human thought, it provides a *substitute* for human action. It not only complements human action by automating certain tasks human action might perform, but also is a substitute for human labourers.

To put this in the language of the Brisbane Club model, artificial intelligence creates (in principle) a state of substitutability between a production plan which involves human labourers, and a production plan which involves machines endowed with artificial intelligence. The technology means that there exists (in principle) a state in which a production plan which relies on human labour can be substituted for a production plan which relies on artificial intelligence without a significant change in the preferability of outcomes following from those plans. Therefore, we know that there exists (in principle) an incentive structure for which the individual deciding between those production plans can be induced to choose that associated with using artificial intelligence rather than human labour. The most obvious candidate for causing such a substitution is of course the ongoing price of maintaining artificial intelligences, which is likely to plummet relative to wages to such a point as makes a change of behaviour from labour-based production plans to artificial intelligence–based production plans desirable. But the product attributes of artificial intelligence are also a candidate cause for such behavioural change induced by a state of substitutability – the processing power of an artificial intelligence in general vastly outstrips that of a human being, it lacks the biological limitations of a human labourer, and it is entirely programmable and absent of cognitive processes contrary to the desires of the producer. So in the first instance, as artificial intelligence technology improves and becomes more affordable, we are very likely to observe it inducing a behavioural change from old modes of production which involve human labour to new modes which involve artificial intelligence.

It is very tempting to, as Martin Ford (2015) in particular has, along with an array of celebrities, see this as not merely a challenge but as a threat. But it is important to recognise that this possibility for behavioural change made possible by artificial intelligence technology which substitutes away from human labour also offers profound *opportunities*. Wherever a set of tasks are being done through costly labour that might be better employed elsewhere and for which an algorithm may be written and embedded within a machine, artificial intelligence allows for the substitution of that labour by an automated machine. This of course offers the opportunity to realise astounding production possibilities through production plans implemented using artificial intelligence. As the capabilities of artificial intelligence are improved and their cost declines, we are likely to see ever greater dominance of machines over labour in production, and we are likely to see the capabilities of such production expand dramatically. This dramatically expands the scope for forming value-generating connections in socioeconomic systems through the exchange of goods and services by exploiting these production capabilities. Keynes (1930) and definitely Marx and Engels (1848) were probably premature in their prophesying of a utopian future in which human labour is all but unnecessary and we live off the output of our machines, freed of the slavery of necessity and devoting ourselves to our particular interests, but they may very well be merely premature rather than wrong.

There are, however, of course definite and undeniable challenges presented by artificial intelligence technology and the behavioural change it supports. In principle, it creates a state of substitutability for human labour which makes behavioural change from production plans involving human labour to plans involving artificial intelligence increasingly likely as the technology evolves. What *is* immediately apparent is that such labour as will be substituted for by artificial intelligence will be subject to the loss of income obtained from providing that labour. It is *not* immediately apparent that such human labour will be allocated to employment of roughly similar remuneration. This is largely an empirical question which can only be answered as the data emerge. So we do face the prospect, as artificial intelligence emerges and becomes increasingly substitutable for human labour, of behavioural changes manifesting in production plans which realise an increasing tendency for human labour to be substituted for artificial intelligence, and for that human labour to not be allocated to new jobs. The scope of artificial intelligence technology for creating a state of substitutability with human labour means this prospect is not especially localised to a particular sector of the economy – it is likely to be a general phenomenon. Martin Ford's (2015) terrifying vision of a plutocratic neo-feudal *I, Robot* dystopian future is therefore not without reason. We do, in short, face the spectre of mass unemployment: many workers across socioeconomic systems *do* face the real prospect of being without work and income.

Obviously the Brisbane Club model reveals artificial intelligence to be a profound technology in this manner. As a substitute for human action which can mimic the process of human thought and action, it offers incredible opportunities but also sobering challenges. It offers incredible opportunities as a production technology for expanding production capabilities and expanding the scope for forming value-creating connections in economic systems through the exchange of goods and services produced by production plans which employ artificial intelligence. But it also, in principle, presents us with the challenge that is the spectre of mass unemployment as production plans substitute human labour for artificial intelligence broadly across the economy.

However, with respect to these challenges presented by artificial intelligence technology, we have assumed that *in principle* the technology creates a state of substitutability between human labour and the machine endowed with artificial intelligence. It is by no means necessarily apparent immediately that this principle is general, and it is entirely possible that exceptions exist. Where these exceptions exist, we cannot say that artificial intelligence creates a state of substitutability where an incentive structure can be found such that the outcomes expected to attend upon a production plan involving human labour and one involving artificial intelligence are roughly equivalently preferable. So where such exceptions exist, human labour is relatively inoculated against the challenges presented by artificial intelligence, and instead is actually positioned to be exposed more to the opportunities it presents.

3 The economic limits of artificial intelligence: where machines are non-substitutable for human labour

Drawing on research published elsewhere by Markey-Towler (2018), we can readily establish three kinds of capability for human action in which a state of substitutability between production plans involving human labour and production plans involving artificial intelligence *cannot* be said to exist. This can be done fairly readily by comparing the natures of human labour and artificial intelligence. By doing this we can readily establish differences between the two. Non-substitutabilities between production plans using human labour and artificial intelligence arise from these differences.

The differences between human labour and artificial intelligence arise from the fact that an artificial intelligence is a mechanical system for processing information, transforming it by higher-order categorisation and classification into some sort of function through algorithms embedded within its mechanical structure. The base code of that structure has been programmed by a human being. A human being on the other hand is a system with *consciousness* which processes information by transforming it by higher-order categorisations and classifications into some sort of function based on schema reflected in its biological structure which have been shaped by *evolution* and a *development* process. A human being is thus differentiated from an artificial intelligence insofar as it has consciousness, the innate structure of its schema have been shaped by aeons of evolutionary pressures, and that innate structure has been extended and built upon by decades of interaction with the social and physical worlds.

We cannot say, given this, that we might substitute a production plan involving human labour for a production plan involving artificial intelligence and obtain roughly equivalent outcomes in terms of preferability. There are economic limits to the existence of a state of substitutability which arise from the consciousness, evolutionary history, and developmental process of a human being. Those workers which engage in work which requires the capabilities created by these differences between human labour and artificial intelligence are therefore likely to be somewhat inoculated from the effects of artificial intelligence. Indeed, they are likely positioned to be able to exploit the opportunities it offers.

3.1 Mistakes and emotions as mothers of invention

A conscious, biological system such as a human being is able to make *mistakes* in a way that a more purely mechanical structure does not. It is well known, of course, that many of the great inventions in history have been discovered quite by accident. It is unclear whether it would be even desirable to program an artificial intelligence to malfunction. But it is also unclear whether the outputs of such malfunction could be recognised to be of value without the intervention of a conscious human being. So in this particular, it seems that production plans involving artificial intelligence would not be able to be substituted for production plans involving human labour without a significant change in the preferability of the outcomes obtained. It would be difficult to imagine a production plan without human labour uncovering valuable new techniques by mistake.

Further, a conscious biological system has *emotions*, which, at present, a purely mechanical system does not have. Two emotions are particularly salient in this regard for their motivating power: fear and boredom. Nederkoon et al. (2016) showed that boredom can be so awful that people are willing to inflict physical *pain* on themselves to relieve it. Similarly, Joseph Le Doux (1996) showed that fear is so potent a feeling that its neural bases are actually *prior* to the sensory cortex. These two emotions provide powerful motivators to develop new techniques which, in the first instance, save the worker from monotony, and in the second, preserve the worker from the object of fear. As yet, the lack of such emotions in machines endowed with artificial intelligence means it is difficult to imagine a state of substitutability between production plans involving human labour and production plans involving artificial intelligence. It would be difficult to imagine a production plan without human labour uncovering valuable new techniques motivated by boredom or fear.

So in this regard, we can establish that there is a limit to the existence of a state of substitutability between production plans which rely on human labour and production plans which rely on artificial intelligence. The latter are unlikely to be able to generate creative inventions from mistakes or the motivations provided by fear or boredom. So where creative invention is required to realise a production plan, we are unlikely to observe the substitution of artificial intelligence for human labour as the Fourth Industrial Revolution progresses. Indeed quite the contrary, artificial intelligence is likely to *complement* such human labour and present the worker with profound opportunities by expanding their production capabilities.

3.2 Deep creativity, judgment, consciousness, and Gödel's theorem

Roger Penrose (1989) in particular argued that Gödel's famous incompleteness theorems show that there is some ability endowed by the consciousness alone to discern *truth* where logic nonetheless fails. This argument is subject to some debate, but it is an interesting one which as yet seems to hold. What Gödel proved was that there were certain true statements within given logical systems which could not be verified by operations within those systems. To put it differently, we could program a machine to process information in a particular way, but there would be true statements according to the logical rules embedded in the program which couldn't be verified by it.

What this means, if Penrose's argument holds, is that human consciousness is capable of exercising *judgment* in a way that is not (presently) possible with a machine, even one endowed with artificial intelligence. This limits the extent to which a production plan which requires the exercise of judgment, especially in "fuzzy" situations with conflicting data, can substitute between human labour and artificial intelligence and obtain outcomes of roughly equivalent preferability. In such environments, the arguments made by Zuvatern and Sullivan, (2017) and Agrawal, Gans and Goldfarb (2018) hold – machine intelligence will *complement* and *aid* the exercise of human judgment by providing informational inputs for decision-making which vastly outstrip the human capability for data processing. It would be difficult to imagine a production plan which requires the exercise of judgment to be implemented using artificial intelligence alone.

Now further, we established above that there is a role for human labour in the Fourth Industrial Revolution where it has the capability to generate creative inventions. The argument for this is deepened substantially by Gödel's theorem, again if Penrose's argument holds. If, following the Brisbane Club model, we understand the mind to be a network structure, the exercise of judgment, which is the unique capability of human consciousness, might be understood to be the construction of connections between ideas and their "truth-values." If this is true, it would suggest that human consciousness has the ability to create connections *ex nihilio*. Such connections are the "bisociations" about which Arthur Koestler (1964) wrote and which he showed to be the basis for human creativity in art, science, and technology. Where great advances have been made in art, science, and technology, it has been, Koestler showed, by genius recognising a connection between objects and events in the world which had hitherto not been recognised and creating a connection *ex nihilio*. Dopfer, Potts and Pyka (2016) could be said to be arguing, further, that this capability of the human consciousness also underlies our *organisational* creativity – recognising new ways to combine people and assets to extend our production capabilities. This again limits the extent to which a production plan which requires a form of creativity in technology or strategy can substitute between human labour and artificial intelligence and obtain outcomes of roughly equivalent preferability. It would be difficult to imagine a production plan which requires a form of creativity in technology or strategy to be implemented using artificial intelligence alone.

So we can establish then that there is a further limit to the existence of a state of substitutability between production plans which rely on human labour and production plans which rely on artificial intelligence. The latter are unlikely, with the present state of the technology, to be able to exercise judgment or manifest what we might call "deep" creativity in technology or strategy. So in these particulars, where judgment or "deep" creativity in technology or strategy is required to realise a particular production plan, we are unlikely to see the substitution of artificial intelligence for human labour as the Fourth Industrial Revolution progresses. Indeed, again, quite the contrary is true, artificial intelligence is likely to *complement* such human labour and present the worker with profound opportunities by expanding their production capabilities.

3.3 Tacit knowledge, development, and evolution

A quite practical problem reveals the last of the major theoretical challenges posed by the difference between human labour and artificial intelligence to the existence of a state of substitutability between production plans which rely on human labour and those which rely on artificial intelligence. It is the nature of human beings as biological systems with an *evolutionary* and *developmental* history. We know that that human mind has certain innate structures which have been shaped by hundreds of millions of years of evolution (Plomin, 2018; Pinker, 2002). They are intricate, complex, and not particularly well known to us because they are so deeply embedded within the non-conscious brain and entangled with developed structures. We know also that the human mind *develops* structures as it matures by the presentation of new connections through play and experimentation and their incorporation into mental schema for categorisation and classification (Piaget, 1923; Dewey 1910). Both of these processes have served to shape schema in the mind for orienting the human being to the environment in such a manner as is (sometimes, by no means always) functional for behaving in the appropriate manner in the vastly complex and individuated array of environments that might exist in the world. And substantial portions of the mental schema thus developed exist in the mind in such a way as is extremely difficult to express in any existing linguistic system even if they are conscious, a region of the mind Michael Polanyi (1966) famously called the "tacit dimension." We become aware of such tacit knowledge whenever we get a "feeling" about a particular situation based on certain "cues" in the environment which we know to indicate something about it, but we find it extremely difficult to explain why.

This poses challenges to the existence of a state of substitutability between production plans which rely on artificial intelligence and production plans which rely on human labour which is both fundamental and one of feasibility. In terms of fundamental engineering problems, it is difficult to imagine an artificial intelligence being able to replicate the sophistication and subtlety of a human mind when a good deal of that sophistication and subtlety comes from knowledge which we find difficult to express. It would be very difficult to engineer something which mimics the innate "base" code of the human mind to the fullest extent possible for this reason. It would be very difficult as well to engineer something that mimics the developed structures of the human mind for this reason. Now it is, in principle, possible for machine learning to be able to mimic the *developmental* process and potentially mimic the building of developed structures to compensate for this, but here we run into a problem of economic feasibility. Even if we were to be able to develop a mechanical structure which mimics the development process well enough, it takes *at least* two decades for the human mind to achieve anything like maturity in its structure such that it is sufficiently sophisticated and subtle to orient the human being properly to the physical and social environment. This might be expedited somewhat by the mechanical attributes of an artificial intelligence insofar as it does not require sleep, has extraordinary processing speeds relative to the human mind, and can be distributed across a network of interconnected machines. However, we can still very readily imagine this will be a process of some years, and is unlikely to become economically viable as a substitute for human labour for some time yet.

So we can establish that in this regard there is a limit to the existence of a state of substitutability between production plans which rely on human labour and production plans which rely on artificial intelligence in realms of human action which demand a sufficiently subtle and sophisticated knowledge of the social and physical worlds which is difficult to express in any linguistic system. For such production plans as require sophisticated and subtle tacit knowledge of how to orient oneself in the social or physical world, we are unlikely to observe an artificial intelligence being able to be substituted for human labour and for the same outcomes to obtain. Human labour is endowed with an entanglement of innate mental schema developed over hundreds of millions of years and developed mental schema developed over decades which it is difficult to imagine being cost effective (as yet) to mimic. So we are unlikely to see the full substitution of artificial intelligence for human labour in such realms as the Fourth Industrial Revolution progresses. Indeed, we are likely to see artificial intelligence *complementing* such human labour and presenting the worker with profound opportunities by expanding their capabilities for production.

4 Disruption and re-coordination as *I, Robot* rises: part utopia, part plutocracy

We have now established the dynamics brought about by artificial intelligence at the micro-scale of socioeconomic systems by relating the nature of the technology to the psychological process. We have discovered that artificial intelligence in principle creates a state of substitutability between production plans which rely on

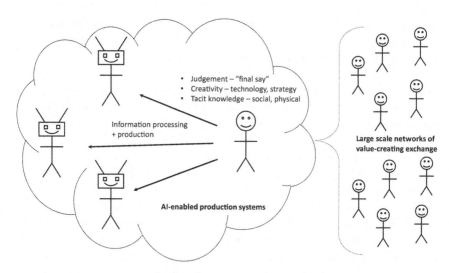

Information processing + production

- Judgement – "final say"
- Creativity – technology, strategy
- Tacit knowledge – social, physical

AI-enabled production systems

Large scale networks of value-creating exchange

FIGURE 7.1 AI-enabled production systems.

Future AI-enabled production systems radically expand production capabilities for any given input of human labour, and allow the saving of labour for the exercising of judgment, the cultivation of creativity, and the application of tacit knowledge.

human labour and production plans which rely on artificial intelligence. We have established that this *in principle* means that as the technology progresses, we face some significant challenges in terms of potential mass unemployment as behaviour changes. However, we have also discovered that this principle is not general, and that artificial intelligence technology presents some profound opportunities for expanding the range of production capabilities to almost a utopian extent. As yet, it is difficult to imagine artificial intelligence being substituted for human labour in realms which require the exercising of *judgment*, deep *creativity* in technology and strategy development, and subtle and sophisticated *tacit knowledge* of how to orient oneself in the social and physical worlds. In these arenas, artificial intelligence is likely to *complement* and offer profound *opportunities* for human workers engaged in such production plans to expand their capabilities. With this micro-scale view of the behavioural change brought about by artificial intelligence, we may elevate our analysis to project the likely effect of artificial intelligence on the scale of the socioeconomic system as a whole.

Artificial intelligence makes a new form of production plan possible – one in which artificial intelligence plays a key role. As meso-rules enabled by artificial intelligence begin to emerge and as existing connections between human workers and their employers are transferred to the suppliers of artificial intelligence software and hardware, we can expect to observe a significant degree of disruption. We cannot discount the possibility that we will observe mass unemployment emerging as artificial intelligence is substituted for human labour wherever it creates a state of substitutability and can provide a cost/benefit mix which exceeds it. As these meso-rules spread and come to have a hold on the production plans of more and more sectors of the economy, we will observe the re-coordination of socioeconomic systems around the meso-populations which have adopted meso-rules enabled by artificial intelligence. Eventually we will observe these meso-populations fully integrated within the connective structure of socioeconomic systems.

Individuals and groups who are inoculated from the effects of artificial intelligence as a substitute for human labour and who are instead poised to seize opportunities it presents in terms of production capabilities will become more successful and will seize the opportunities presented by this re-coordinating economy. Such individuals and groups are not those for whose labour a state of substitutability can be created by artificial intelligence technology – they are not individuals and groups for whose activities an algorithm, even a machine learning algorithm, can be written. Those individuals and groups who will become integrated within the connective structure of socioeconomic systems are those who can supply work for production plans which require the exercising of *judgment*, deep *creativity* in technology and strategy development, and subtle and sophisticated *tacit knowledge* of how to orient oneself in the social and physical worlds. For such individuals and groups, the newly re-coordinated economic system will be one where their production capabilities within its connective structure are stupendously extended by the complementarities offered by artificial intelligence to their work.

The newly re-coordinated economy which is likely to emerge from the process of diffusion of new meso-rules enabled by artificial intelligence is a strange one. It is part utopia, with a chance of dystopia. It is an economic system which produces vastly more than the labour which it requires in its production systems would suggest. It is a production system in which relatively few human beings will be able to operate production systems on a scale which is hitherto unimaginable, with their capabilities extended by artificial intelligence technology. This is a somewhat utopian world, one redolent of Keynes's and Marx's visions of the world in which we have solved the problem of scarcity. But it is a production system which requires comparatively little by way of human behaviour to operate relative to its scale. It is not immediately apparent that the labour necessary for such an economic system is commensurate with the size of the population at all, and it is therefore not immediately apparent that much of the population will be able to obtain remunerative work in production plans for which human labour is necessary. So while the economic system which re-coordinates around meso-populations applying meso-rules enabled by artificial intelligence is seductively utopian, it also suggests hints of potential plutocracy (as Martin Ford in particular has prophesied) of a select few whose labour is necessary for production plans of stupendous scale and value, and a many whose labour is unnecessary as artificial intelligence can be substituted for it.

5 Summary: human work in an age of artificial intelligence presents challenges, but also profound opportunities

In this chapter we applied the Brisbane Club model to analysing the likely effects of the oldest of the mega-technologies of the Fourth Industrial Revolution, but one which is really only now beginning to make itself noticeable in socioeconomic systems: artificial intelligence. We saw that artificial intelligence is a technology which provides profound opportunities in terms of the scale of connective structures of value-creating exchange that might be realised by its expansion of the range of human capabilities. But we also saw that it offers a (qualified) challenge in terms of the potential for mass unemployment it raises as socioeconomic systems are disrupted by its emergence and re-coordinate.

We saw that artificial intelligence is a technology which mimics the process of human thought and human action as guided by human thought. It thus facilitates automation on a grand scale not only of physical motor tasks, but also of any information processing task which can be reduced to an algorithm, even (with the advent of machine learning) one which needs to be constantly updated relative to the gap between outcome and objective. It is the technology behind the "drone economy," the technology which allows us to better make predictions using Big Data which could not be arrived at by human computation alone, and the technology which is transforming biomedical science and practice by offering new automated systems for data processing and diagnoses.

By allowing for the large-scale automation of tasks using machines which surpass human capabilities for processing and work, artificial intelligence offers profound opportunities for expanding the range of production, and the range of value-creating exchange connections which can be formed in socioeconomic systems. It offers challenges insofar as it creates an in-principle state of substitutability between production plans which rely on human labour and those which rely on artificial intelligence, which will likely increasingly cause the latter to be substituted for the former, with it not being immediately apparent that such human labour can be re-employed elsewhere. But these challenges are mitigated by the limits to the existence of a state of substitutability for human labour and artificial intelligence in production plans which require the exercising of *judgment*, deep *creativity* in technology and strategy development, and subtle and sophisticated *tacit knowledge* of how to orient oneself in the social and physical worlds. In such production plans, artificial intelligence will *complement* human labour rather than replace it. These conclusions are not dissimilar to those offered by Brynjolfsson and McAfee (2011, 2014, 2017), in particular, but we have given these concepts a very specific definition in the context of the Brisbane Club model of socioeconomic systems.

At the macro-scale of the socioeconomic system, the emergence of new meso-rules enabled by artificial intelligence will cause disruption as existing connective structures between human labour and its employment are eliminated. But as these meso-rules diffuse, the meso-populations which apply them will increasingly become re-integrated within a re-coordinated socioeconomic system. This will present opportunities for workers who can provide labour for production plans which require judgment, creativity, and tacit knowledge as they will be able to seize opportunities to become integrated within production plans with stupendous capabilities for creating valuable exchanges. Life in the Fourth Industrial Revolution will become somewhat more difficult insofar as the spectre of a plutocracy hangs over it between the potentially many who aren't required in an age of artificial intelligence and the few who are. But it will also become seductively utopian insofar as the production capabilities of an economy which has integrated artificial intelligence are such as Keynes and Marx dreamed of in their wildest visions of a future where the frontier of scarcity has been effectively abolished.

Technical appendix

Artificial intelligence, especially when endowed with machine learning algorithms, is a technology which seeks to mimic the functioning of the human mind, and which can therefore mimic human action guided by a process that mimics human thought. Advances in computing power and energy efficiency have made it such that this technology is now feasible to obtain. That is to say, we have an extension of human capabilities such that, for the obtention by j of an artificial intelligence we might call m_j

$$m_j \notin B \rightarrow m_j \in B$$

The effect of artificial intelligence is, in principle, to create a state of substitutability between a production plan a_j which involves human labour l_{kj} supplied by k to j but not artificial intelligence ($a_j \supset l_{kj}$ but $a_j \not\supset m_j$) and a production plan which involves artificial intelligence but not human labour ($a'_j \supset m_j$ but $a'_j \not\supset l_{ij}$). That is to say, the effect of artificial intelligence is that there is a mix of costs/benefits δ attached to various production plans at which point the substitution of the one plan for the other has little effect on the preferability of the outcomes to obtain from them

$$\exists \bar{\delta} : g_{a_j \supset l_{kj}} \sim g_{a'_j \supset m_j}$$

Provided that j could, in this case, obtain costs/benefits δ at some point which exceed the state of substitutability, it would be more preferable for them to implement a production plan which employs artificial intelligence rather than human labour. Provided certain technical conditions hold, we would therefore observe a change of behaviour

$$a_j \supset l_{ij} \rightarrow a'_j \supset m_j$$

As the ongoing prices for maintaining artificial intelligence decline and their attributes improve, we are likely to observe the substitution of production plans involving artificial intelligence for production plans involving human labour.

Notice that from the perspective of j, the capabilities offered by artificial intelligence offer extraordinary opportunities for realising value from production plans. Profits for j accrue from connections $jk \in g(N)$ in which sales of goods and services x_{jk} are made at prices p_{jk}

$$\pi_j = \sum_{k \in N: jk \in g(N)} p_{jk} x_{jk} - c_j(x_{jk})$$

The effect of artificial intelligence on this is twofold. The production capabilities it offers greatly expands the set of connections $jk \in g(N)$ that can be made by the exchange of goods and services x_{jk} at price p_{jk}, but as the technology progresses, this will increasingly be achieved at lower and lower costs of production $c_j(x_{jk})$.

Obviously from the point of view of i, the human labourer, artificial intelligence presents a clear and obvious challenge. As the technology progresses, it becomes increasingly likely that the labour individuals supply l_{kj} will be substituted by an artificial intelligence m_j, and that they will lose the income $w_{kj}l_{kj}$ at wage w_{kj} that they would obtain from that labour. This is immediately apparent, but it is not immediately apparent that this will be compensated for by another position of equivalent wage. Whether this is possible is largely an empirical question which is unlikely to be resolved until we observe the data.

However, we can predict the conditions under which i will be able to maintain the income $w_{kj}l_{kj}$ at wage w_{kj} that they would obtain from labour despite the emergence of artificial intelligence technology. This, simply enough, will occur whenever there is not a state of substitutability between a production plan a_j which involves human labour l_{kj} supplied by k to j but not artificial intelligence ($a_j \supset l_{kj}$ but $a_j \not\supset m_j$) and a production plan which involves artificial intelligence but not human labour ($a'_j \supset m_j$ but $a'_j \not\supset l_{ij}$). That is, there is no mix of costs/benefits δ attached to various production plans at which point the one plan can be substituted for the other and roughly equivalently preferable outcomes will obtain

$$\nexists \bar{\delta} : g_{a_j \supset l_{kj}} \sim g_{a'_j \supset m_j}$$

or, to be more precise

$$g_{a_j \supset l_{kj}} \succ g_{a'_j \supset m_j} \ \forall \ \delta$$

To establish the forms/attributes of labour l_{kj} for which this is true requires a comparison of the attributes of artificial intelligence and human labour to discover the classes of labour for which artificial intelligence cannot be substituted. Those classes of labour for which artificial intelligence cannot establish a state of substitutability will be those for which substituting a production plan employing human labour with a production plan using artificial intelligence will lead to a significantly less desirable outcome. We have done this theoretically above, but it is desirable and possible to conduct empirical analyses of the tasks required in various classes of employment and assess the degree to which each class may be substituted for based on projections of the capabilities of artificial intelligence. The Oxford Martin studies (Citi Global Perspectives and Solutions, 2016; Frey and Osborne, 2013) have done just this and, at present, reveal roughly 70% of existing classes of labour (roughly speaking, jobs) are susceptible to being substituted for based on current projections of artificial intelligence capabilities.

References

Acemoglu, Daron and Restrepo, Pascual, (2016) "The race between machine and man: Implications of technology for growth, factor shares and employment", NBER Working Paper No.22252

Acemoglu, Daron and Restrepo, Pascual, (2017) "Robots and jobs: Evidence from US labor markets", NBER Working Paper No.23285

Acemoglu, Daron and Restrepo, Pascual, (2018) "Artificial intelligence, automation and work", NBER Working Paper No.24196

Agrawal, Ajay, Gans, Joshua S. and Goldfarb, Avi, (2018) *Prediction Machines*, Harvard Business Review, Cambridge, MA

Brynjolfsson, Erik and McAfee, Andrew, (2011) *Race against the Machine*, Digital Frontier Press, Lexington

Brynjolfsson, Erik and McAfee, Andrew, (2014) *The Second Machine Age*, W.W. Norton & Co., New York

Brynjolfsson, Erik and McAfee, Andrew, (2017) *Machine, Platform, Crowd*, W.W. Norton & Co., New York

Citi Global Perspectives & Solutions, (2016) "Technology at work v2.0: The future is not what it used to be", Technical report, Citi and Oxford Martin School, available at URL: www.oxfordmartin.ox.ac.uk/downloads/reports/Citi_iGPS_iTechnology_iWork_i2.pdf.

Clegg, Brian, (2017) *Big Data*, Icon Books, London

Dewey, John, (1910) *How We Think*, D.C. Heath and Co., Lexington

Dopfer, Kurt, Potts, Jason and Pyka, Andreas, (2016) "Upward and downward complementarity: the meso core of evolutionary growth theory", *Journal of Evolutionary Economics*, 26(4), pp. 753–763

Edelman, Gerald, (1978) *Neural Darwinism*, Basic Books, New York

Ford, Martin, (2015) *Rise of the Robots*, Oneworld Publications, London

Frey, Carl B. and Osborne, Michael, (2013) "The future of employment: How susceptible are jobs to computerisation?" Technical report, Oxford Martin School, Oxford, available at URL: www.oxfordmartin.ox.ac.uk/publications/view/1314.

Hayek, Friedrich, (1952) *The Sensory Order*, University of Chicago Press, Chicago

Jeffries, Daniel, (2017) "Learning AI if you suck at math", *Hackernoon.com*, available at URL: https://hackernoon.com/learning-ai-if-you-suck-at-math-8bdfb4b79037 (accessed 18/04/2018)

Kelly, George A., (1963) *A Theory of Personality*, W. W. Norton & Co., New York

Kelnar, David, (2016) "The fourth industrial revolution: A primer on artificial intelligence", *Medium.com*, available at URL: https://medium.com/mmc-writes/the-fourth-industrial-revolution-a-primer-on-artificial-intelligence-ai-ff5e7fffcae1 (accessed 18/04/2018)

Keynes, John Maynard, (1930) "Economic possibilites for our grandchildren", in *Essays in Persuasion*, Harcourt Brace, New York, pp. 358–373

Koestler, Arthur, (1964) *The Act of Creation*, Picador, London

Kurzweil, Ray, (2012) *How to Create a Mind*, Penguin, London

Lawson, Clive, (2010) "Technology and the extension of human capabilities", *Journal for the Theory of Social Behaviour*, 40(2), pp. 207–223

LeDoux, Joseph, (1996) *The Emotional Brain*, Simon and Schuster, New York

Markey-Towler, Brendan, (2018) "The economics of artificial intelligence", available at SSRN: https://ssrn.com/abstract=2907974

Marx, Karl and Engels, Friedrich, (1848) *The Communist Manifesto*, Penguin, London

McClelland, Calum, (2017) "The difference between artificial intelligence, machine learning, and deep learning", *Medium.com*, available at URL: https://medium.com/iotforall/

the-difference-between-artificial-intelligence-machine-learning-and-deep-learning-3aa67bff5991 (accessed 18/04/2018)

Nederkoon, Chantal, Vancleef, Linda, Wilkenhoner, Alexandra, Claes, Laurence and Havermans, Remco, (2016) "Self-inflicted pain out of boredom", *Psychiatry Research*, 237, pp. 127–132

Newell, Alan, (1990) *Unified Theories of Cognition*, Harvard University Press, Cambridge, MA

Newell, Alan, Shaw, John C. and Simon, Herbert A., (1958) "Elements of a theory of human problem solving", *Psychological Review*, 65(3), pp. 151–166

Nordhaus, William D., (2015) "Are we approaching an economic singularity?" NBER Working Paper No.21547

Penrose, Roger, (1989) *The Emperor's New Mind*, Oxford University Press, Oxford

Piaget, Jean, (1923) *The Language and Thought of the Child*, Routledge, London

Pinker, Steven, (1999) *How the Mind Works*, Penguin, London

Pinker, Steven, (2002) *The Blank Slate*, Penguin, London

Plomin, Robert, (2018) *Blueprint*, Penguin, London

Polanyi, Michael, (1966) *The Tacit Dimension*, University of Chicago Press, Chicago

Samuel, Arthur L., (1953) "Computing bit by bit, or, digital computers made easy", *Proceedings of the I.R.E.*, 41(10), pp. 1223–1230

Samuel. Arthur L., (1959) "Some studies in machine learning using the game of checkers", *IBM Journal of Research and Development*, 3(3) pp. 210–229

Simon, Herbert A., (1968) *Sciences of the Artificial*, MIT Press, Cambridge, MA

Simon, Herbert A., (1998) "Discovering explanations", *Minds and Machines*, 8, pp. 7–37

Turing, Alan, (1950) "Computing machinery and intelligence", *Mind*, 59(236), pp. 433–460

von Neumann, John, (1958) *The Computer and the Brain*, Yale University Press, New Haven

Zuvatern, Angela and Sullivan, Josh, (2017) *The Mathematical Corporation*, Hachette, Paris

8

THE GHOST *AND* THE MACHINE

Case studies in the *I, Robot* future

The rise of artificially intelligent software, systems, and robots has begun to revolutionize many industrial production processes in recent years, and this represents the second of the three core technological cornerstones of the Fourth Industrial Revolution as it relates to impacts on the economy. From a technical standpoint, this was made possible by the development of improved machine learning and prediction algorithms to forecast contingencies before they eventuate; the commercialisation of affordable, lightweight computing hardware with sufficient power for use in new micro-robotics applications; and the development of improved sensory systems to interact with complex operational environments.

The use of robots in industrial production processes is not particularly new or exclusive to the Fourth Industrial Revolution. Pre-programmed robots have been in commercial use for decades. The 4IR is about more than mere automation. As Park (2017) puts it, the 4IR moves the goalposts from automation to smartization, whereby intelligently programmed software and robots are able to collect new data during the regular course of their operation, share it with other approved devices on the network, analyse the data, and use the conclusions to update their course of action. The 4IR took "dumb" autonomous machine and made them "smart." This step was essential to the development of technological marvels such as self-driving cars and trucks and next-generation industrial robotics (Levy 2018).

Artificial intelligence and advanced robotics, viewed together as an engine for economic growth and prosperity, are possibly the most potent of the three technological cornerstones of the 4IR discussed in this book, in terms of the still-unrealised potential to disrupt industrial processes. This chapter proceeds to focus on illustrating the key points of the previous chapter using several judiciously selected examples of applied use cases, while also summarising a few of the related economic impacts and institutional shifts which influence the ongoing health of the economy. The chapter also examines how this technology and its applications are used to create economic value and move society forward towards higher-order ends.

Advanced robotics can connect with the cloud and process humanly impossible amounts of data using remote hardware. We are not interested here in the technical details of the incredible algorithms or hardware developments which make artificial intelligence or advanced robotics possible. Those discussions are best left to other books where they have been well-covered. In this chapter, we are interested in these developments purely from the perspective of the utility gains to the end user and the aggregated effects this has for the economy and society at large.

1 Automation, capital, and labour

The first and most obvious source of economic value derived from artificial intelligence and advanced robotics is the partial outsourcing of complex or mentally draining repetitive human tasks and decision-making processes. These decisions may be either critical or non-critical to core operations, depending upon the nature of the industry and the efficiency of the artificial intelligence system. This may include optimizing a plausible solution to a complex problem or game scenario against an arbitrary set of objectives. The second source of economic value creation is grounded in the ability of artificially intelligent systems to automate entire production processes in the supply chain. This is in line with the well-established trend of replacing of boring, repetitive human work with better machinery and technological applications, which featured so prominently in the first three industrial revolutions. Robotic Process Automation (RPA) has evolved substantially, making it easier for software to perform ever more complex structured digital tasks (Davenport 2019, p. 105).

Although the tendency towards automation is excellent for economic growth and productivity, there are also potentially challenging distributional effects across the economy, in particular, across the factors of production (Eden and Gaggl 2018). For example, as routine tasks become easily automated, the economy will eventually see a lowering in the demand for labour allocated to those particular job roles or occupations. Many businesses will prefer to invest in automation systems to make their workers more productive. Therefore, income will be reallocated within the labour factor of production to other jobs which are less automatable (Autor and Dorn 2013). Further, income will be generally reallocated across the economy from labour to capital, leading to a reduction in the labour income share (Karabarbounis and Neiman 2014). The returns to capital are becoming relatively larger than the returns to labour inputs. This is one of several factors influencing the increasing wealth gap in advanced economies (Allen 2017). Wealth inequality has recently been driven along capital and labour lines. Those who own capital structures are able to capture more value from their operation due to the automation of human labour. Those who derive their income from their labour, who in many cases still see their average per capita incomes rising, are therefore falling behind capital owners in relative terms.

There exists a substantial scholarly literature within labour economics on the relationship of labour with artificial intelligence, and perhaps with information and communication technologies more broadly (Acemoglu and Autor 2011). As mentioned in the previous chapter, there are for this purpose considered to be two varieties of labour. The first involves the following of significant routines, otherwise known as pre-specified decision trees (Eden and Gaggl 2018). This variety of labour is relatively easier to automate, as it lends itself naturally to programming and "learnable" skills. The second variety of labour demands higher amounts of informed judgment, creativity, interpersonal skills, or tacit knowledge as inputs, which happen to be harder to automate due to the need for human empathy, creativity, and a broader understanding about reality.

Although many doomsayers may suggest otherwise, centuries of economic history suggest that the automation of tasks previously performed by humans does not appear likely to leave insufficient meaningful jobs in the economy for people desiring to work (Gruen 2017). Most jobs require a depth of human perception and connection – humanness, shall we say – which an inanimate machine, even a highly functional one, will never be able to replicate. The shift is not in the number of jobs available, but in the distribution and nature of jobs (Autor and Salomons 2018). Automation frees up human labour to solve more complex problems, embark on new ambitious projects, and create more value, augmented with the support of intelligent machines and systems to help with the execution (Nica 2016). One of the key papers in the economics literature to demonstrate this idea of capital-skill complementarity is Lewis (2011), who found strong evidence in several decades of data from U.S. manufacturing plants to support the idea that automation in the production process complements middle-skilled workers relative to low-skilled workers.

A concept illustration of this reallocation in the labour market is depicted in Figure 8.1. The general trend is that jobs with limited flexibility and well-defined, narrow tasks are those which tend to be prone to automation. These are not necessarily low-skill jobs, as suggested by Park (2017), as these jobs may require a high amount of skill which may have taken great effort or education to acquire, for example, jobs in translation services. There is also a generally steady demand for human-centred basic service jobs which do not require high levels of informed judgment based on experience, for example, waiting staff in various hospitality services (Cortes, Jaimovich, and Siu 2017). These latter kinds of jobs are difficult to automate because of their flexible nature and their dependence upon basic humanness to deliver a quality value proposition to customers, which would be near impossible for an intelligent machine to emulate. These jobs, however, typically command lower wages, since genuine human empathy and a few basic skills are all that are required to perform the job effectively; therefore, the pool of potential candidates is quite large. The higher-paid jobs, for which demand is generally increasing, are those which require a deep contextual knowledge of problems and the broader objectives, along with sufficient creativity and flexibility to adapt and create new value, supported and executed by intelligent machine systems. Often

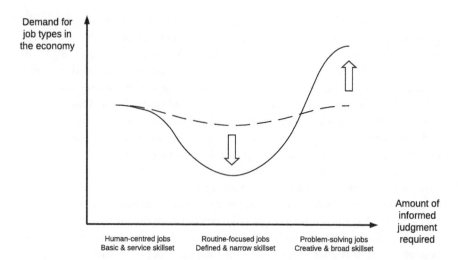

Demand for job types in the economy

Amount of informed judgment required

Human-centred jobs
Basic & service skillset

Routine-focused jobs
Defined & narrow skillset

Problem-solving jobs
Creative & broad skillset

FIGURE 8.1   Shifts in the distribution of jobs during the Fourth Industrial Revolution.

This is a generalised concept illustration. Actual data will vary across countries and industries.

only a small handful of candidates will have the requisite experience and capacity to help with the specific needs of the business, and the value created is often substantial, justifying the higher wages.

As workers are gradually displaced from routine-focused jobs, most tend to find new work in one of the other two categories of jobs shown in Figure 8.1. Since the average wages in each of these two categories tend to differ markedly, it has been suggested that this is why automation tends to increase wage inequality. The ability for workers to shift towards the higher-paying jobs is therefore dependent upon their ability to acquire the requisite skillsets. It comes as no surprise, then, that the World Economic Forum suggested in its 2016 Future of Jobs report (World Economic Forum 2016) that the top ten most employable skills in 2020 would include complex problem solving, critical thinking, creativity, people management, the ability to coordinate with others, emotional intelligence, good judgment and decision-making ability, a service orientation, negotiation skills, and cognitive flexibility.

It is important to emphasize that artificial intelligence has the ability to automate things which are predictable and routine, not things which are necessarily classed as "low-skill." For this reason, the oft-quoted proxy of skill is education, from which the argument has been frequently made that the antidote to automation is an investment in more education. This is a misleading conclusion which the evidence does not support. For example, many lawyers perform regular tasks which are presently being replaced with artificially intelligent software tools. These include such things as the preparation of simple legal documents, the extraction of data from title deeds for property disputes, and the use of predictive coding software in legal disclosure processes (Chelliah 2017).

In light of this, Acemoglu and Restrepo (2018) developed an economic frame-work in which capital can compete with high-skill labour on complex tasks, to account for the fact that traditionally "high-skill" jobs are also threatened by the disruptive forces of automation. Unlike earlier studies such as Acemoglu and Autor (2011), which used a simple comparative advantage ranking, Acemoglu and Restrepo's novel framework identifies two distinct impacts of automation, specifi-cally a displacement effect and a productivity effect. To quote the authors: "The displacement effect, by taking away tasks from the directly affected factor, harms the labor market fortunes of that factor, while the productivity effect tends to increase the wages of all factors" (Acemoglu and Restrepo 2018, pp. 206–207).

Another important aspect of the economic shifts in capital and labour due to automation is the rise of entrepreneurship. As workers are displaced from their former jobs and the returns to capital rise, a natural third option which many are already choosing presents itself. This involves establishing themselves as owners of certain intellectual property and niche capital items, then entering into licensing or service agreements with other businesses to generate income for themselves. Increasingly, these individuals will also earn an income from the gig economy, for example, by driving for Uber, Lyft, or Grab, or by offering freelance services over the internet. There is strong evidence to suggest that the number of these solo self-employed business owners is rising (Sorgner 2017).

While not discussed as often, there are also revenue implications of automation for governments, at least in the majority of advanced economies which have a significant proportion of tax revenues based on labour. If a business replaces some of its employees with artificially intelligent systems and robots, the government incurs a loss because robot "labour" is not generally taxed. In most countries, capital investment is taxed at lower rates than human labour. Tax policy, therefore, can be an effective policy instrument through which governments can attempt to influence the rate of automation in the economy (Abbott and Bogenschneider 2018). One proposal to correct the current absence of tax neutrality is to introduce an "automation tax," which proponents argue would encourage businesses to find primarily non-tax reasons for the automation of human labour.

2 Prediction and contingency planning

One natural application of artificial intelligence and advanced robotics involves the processing of large amounts of information and data to obtain useful predictions and inform subsequent preparation for future contingencies. The sheer amount of relevant data which is available in many industrial contexts and the urgency of the final output precludes any human from undertaking a comprehensive analysis within a sufficient time frame to be useful. In addition to analysing future con-tingencies, prediction can also apply to the present tense. For example, artificially intelligent prediction can be used to judge whether a condition is met in various contexts such as quality management, cancer detection, identity verification, credit card fraud and money laundering detection, and others. It can be used to overcome human biases, which have been well-studied in the psychological and behavioural economic literatures. Artificial intelligence also finds natural applications in sales and marketing, where algorithms can be used to, for example, identify customers who have a high likelihood of cancelling subscriptions.

Artificially intelligent machines have notably been used to predict game theoretic best responses and optimal strategies in applications such as chess and Go, games used for decades in artificial intelligence research. A significant cause for the rapid improvement in artificially intelligent machines in the last decade is the advances that have been made in computing power and in deep learning methodologies. For example, the AlphaZero engine developed by the Alphabet-owned company DeepMind made headlines in 2018 for its impressive feats in defeating several of the world's best human and computer chess players (Silver et al. 2018). The engine relied on parallel neural networks running on tensor operating units managed by Google. Compared to the chess engine Stockfish, which tends to examine tens of millions of potential board positions before making a prediction on the best move to make, AlphaZero tended to only examine several tens of thousands in the same timeframe, but still outperformed on average, illustrating the potential of deep learning to more efficiently help with decision-making in complex scenarios across a much broader array of use cases.

With this capability, there is good reason to suspect that in the not-too-distant future, artificially intelligent engines may take a more integral role in feeding information to company board meetings and strategic planning, to help them understand their complex, ever-shifting marketplace more clearly and take action to strengthen their business.

3 Comparative advantages of human and machine prediction

Human prediction is often biased, whether due to an inability to collect enough relevant information to make an informed judgment, or due to pre-conceived notions of reality, or even due to a misunderstanding of the rules of statistics. The predictions of smart machines, however, are usually optimal given the veracity of the information presented to them.

In their landmark chapter "The New Division of Labor," Agrawal, Gans, and Goldfarb (2018, p. 54) identify the comparative advantages which humans and artificially intelligent machines possess when it comes to the formulation of useful insights and predictions from complex data. They state: "Humans and machines both have failings. Without knowing what they are, we cannot assess how machines and humans should work together to generate predictions." The chapter proceeds to examine four possibilities in which one can understand the value which artificial intelligence–enabled tools bring to the table, based on the presence and reliability of available data. These are illustrated in Figure 8.2.

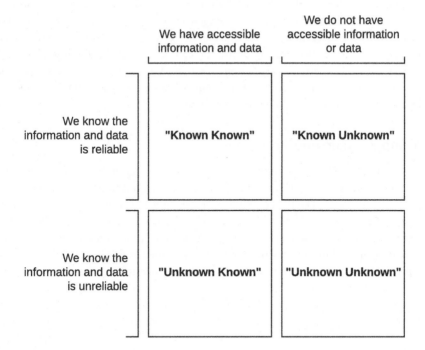

FIGURE 8.2   The four data scenarios.

Understanding the occasions when artificial intelligence prediction tools will be either valuable or useless.

The ideal scenario involves a "Known Known," in which data is accessible and known to be reliable. In this situation, machine prediction engines perform at their best. As more high-quality data is fed to them, their predictive ability increases. In cases with complex problems, machines tend to outperform humans and have the advantage. The second scenario involves a "Known Unknown," in which the data is reliable but barely any data is available. This is often the case for extremely rare events such as natural disasters and freak accidents, where the data is well known and heavily analysed, but the relative lack of comparable events makes it difficult for machine prediction tools to deliver useful inputs directly from the data without the support of some extra framework or theory. In these, situations, human intuition and judgment are often a better predictor than the machines.

For the "Unknown Unknown" situations, in which the data is available but known to be unreliable, both humans and machines struggle. This might occur when a completely new category of event arises which bears only some similarity to previous scenarios for which data exists. It also might occur when something entirely unexpected takes place which would not have been foreseen by any plausible machine learning prediction, due to no basis existing in the data for the expectation of its occurrence. The fourth data scenario is the "Unknown Known," in which the problems within the data are fortunately known to humans, but unable to be ascertained by the artificial intelligence machine. In this case, the results provided by the machine are almost guaranteed to be biased. There is some hope, however, that if the exact nature of the bias can be understood, then human steps may be taken to interfere and attempt to correct for the bias. The danger occurs here if artificial intelligence is followed unquestioningly because a human failed to consider the reliability of the information inputs.

4 Supply chain optimization

Several large companies have been recently realising great logistical efficiencies through the deployment of artificial intelligence systems and advanced robotics in the supply chain. Let us take the clothing and apparel industry as an example. Manufacturers often struggle with the decision of what location would be most suitable for the establishment of their manufacturing plants. Emerging economies have seen sustained growth in apparel manufacturing as an industry in the last few decades, making this aspect of supply chain optimization a crucial challenge for the business owners to overcome. Many environmental factors influence the decision, including country risk factors, choice of local community, the availability of transport and key facilities, and political stability. Unsurprisingly, many businesses make suboptimal decisions while attempting to choose the best plant locations based on their subjective assessment of all available options. Various rubrics and formal chart-based methods exist which provide some guidance for this human decision process. Nevertheless, artificial intelligence methods have been developed in the last couple of decades which perform better (Liang and Wang 1991; Kuo, Chi, and Kao 2002). There is evidence to suggest that supervised artificial neural networks represent a viable alternative to rubrics in determining the optimal plant location problem (Leung, Guo, and Wong 2013).

Effective production scheduling is a perennial challenge for manufacturers. For simpler cases involving a single shop location or perhaps an assembly line problem, various techniques and models exist, such as job shop scheduling (Adam et al. 1993), flow shop scheduling (Nagar, Heragu, and Haddock 1996), machine scheduling (Dimopoulos and Zalzala 2001), and assembly line scheduling (Zhang et al. 2000). Cut order planning, usually known as COP, is another essential strategy for apparel manufacturers because it enables them to seek cost savings given a set of criteria that pertain to the nature of the inputs to production. COP is also typically the first activity in the workflow of the fabric cutting team in apparel manufacturing. Depending on the apparel company, an estimate for the optimal COP is derived by some combination of human judgment and industrial software. Recent developments, however, have yielded promising algorithms which lend themselves nicely to artificial intelligence solutions. Many of these new methods, often taking the form of genetic algorithms, can be implemented using computers to help optimise the scheduling process according to the maximisation of the order satisfaction level and the minimization of the time taken.

References

Abbott, Ryan, and Bret Bogenschneider. 2018. "Should Robots Pay Taxes? Tax Policy in the Age of Automation." *Harvard Law & Policy Review* 12(1): 145–175.

Acemoglu, Daron, and David H. Autor. 2011. "Skills, Tasks and Technologies: Implications for Employment and Earnings." Pp. 1043–1171 in *Handbook of Labor Economics*. Amsterdam, Netherlands: Elsevier.

Acemoglu, Daron, and Pascual Restrepo. 2018. "Low-Skill and High-Skill Automation." *Journal of Human Capital* 12(2): 204–232.

Adam, N., W. Bertrand, D. Morehead, and J. Surkis. 1993. "Due-Date Assignment Procedures with Dynamically Updated Coefficients for Multilevel Assembly Job Shops." *European Journal of Operational Research* 68(2): 212–227.

Agrawal, Ajay, Joshua Gans, and Avi Goldfarb. 2018. *Prediction Machines*. Boston, MA: Harvard Business Review Press.

Allen, Robert C. 2017. "Lessons from History for the Future of Work." *Nature* 550(7676): 321–324.

Autor, David H., and David Dorn. 2013. "The Growth of Low-Skill Service Jobs and the Polarization of the US Labor Market." *American Economic Review* 103(5): 1553–1597.

Autor, David, and Anna Salomons. 2018. "Is Automation Labor Share-Displacing? Productivity Growth, Employment, and the Labor Share." *Brookings Papers on Economic Activity* 2018 (Spring): 1–87.

Chelliah, John. 2017. "Will Artificial Intelligence Usurp White Collar Jobs?" *Human Resource Management International Digest* 25(3): 1–3.

Cortes, Guido Matias, Nir Jaimovich, and Henry E. Siu. 2017. "Disappearing Routine Jobs: Who, How, and Why?" *Journal of Monetary Economics* 91: 69–87.

Davenport, Thomas H. 2019. *The AI Advantage: How to Put the Artificial Intelligence Revolution to Work*. Cambridge, MA: MIT Press.

Dimopoulos, C., and A. Zalzala. 2001. "Investigating the Use of Genetic Programming for a Classic One-Machine Scheduling Problem." *Advances in Engineering Software* 32(6): 489–498.

Eden, Maya, and Paul Gaggl. 2018. "On the Welfare Implications of Automation." *Review of Economic Dynamics* 29: 15–43.

Gruen, David. 2017. "The Future of Work." *Policy* 33(3): 3–8.

Karabarbounis, Loukas, and Brent Neiman. 2014. "The Global Decline of the Labor Share★." *Quarterly Journal of Economics* 129(1): 61–103.

Kuo, R. J., S. C. Chi, and S. S. Kao. 2002. "A Decision Support System for Selecting Convenience Store Location through Integration of Fuzzy AHP and Artificial Neural Network." *Computers in Industry* 47: 199–214.

Leung, S., Z. X. Guo, and W. K. Wong. 2013. *Optimizing Decision Making in the Apparel Supply Chain Using Artificial Intelligence (AI)*. Cambridge, UK: Woodhead Publishing.

Levy, Frank. 2018. "Computers and Populism: Artificial Intelligence, Jobs, and Politics in the Near Term." *Oxford Review of Economic Policy* 34(3): 393–417.

Lewis, Ethan. 2011. "Immigration, Skill Mix, and Capital Skill Complementarity." *Quarterly Journal of Economics* 126(2): 1029–1069.

Liang, G. S., and M. J. Wang. 1991. "A Fuzzy Multi-Criteria Decision-Making Method for Facility Site Selection." *International Journal of Production Research* 29(11): 2313–2330.

Nagar, A., S. Heragu, and J. Haddock. 1996. "A Combined Branch-and-Bound and Genetic Algorithm Based Approach for a Flowshop Scheduling Problem." *Annals of Operations Research* 63(1–4): 397–414.

Nica, Elvira. 2016. "Will Technological Unemployment and Workplace Automation Generate Greater Capital-Labor Income Imbalances?" *Economics, Management and Financial Markets* 11(4): 68–74.

Park, Hang Sik. 2017. "Technology Convergence, Open Innovation, and Dynamic Economy." *Journal of Open Innovation: Technology, Market, and Complexity* 3(1): 24.

Silver, David et al. 2018. "A General Reinforcement Learning Algorithm That Masters Chess, Shogi, and Go through Self-Play." *Science* 362(6419): 1140–1144.

Sorgner, Alina. 2017. "The Automation of Jobs: A Threat for Employment or a Source of New Entrepreneurial Opportunities?" *Foresight and STI Governance* 11(3): 37–48.

World Economic Forum. 2016. *The Future of Jobs: Employment, Skills and Workforce Strategy for the Fourth Industrial Revolution.* Geneva, Switzerland: Forum Publishing.

Zhang, Y., P. Luh, K. Yoneda, T. Kano, and Y. Kyoya. 2000. "Mixed-Model Assembly Line Scheduling Using the Lagrangian Relaxation Technique." *IIE Transactions* 32(2): 125–134.

PART IV

Blockchain

Decentralising power, authority, and the design of systems of governance

9

THE ENTREPRENEURSHIP OF RULES

Institutions in an age of blockchain

Blockchain is the "youngest" of the mega-technologies of the Fourth Industrial Revolution, and operates on the infrastructure provided by the internet. It was invented, dramatically, by the pseudonymous Satoshi Nakamoto in a 2009 whitepaper in order to solve the problem of preventing the double-spending of "coins" in a ledger of cryptocurrency holdings and payments. But, perhaps unwittingly, Nakamoto discovered more than a way to keep a ledger of cryptocurrency. The discovery of blockchain constituted the discovery of a new *institutional* technology (Davidson, De Filippi and Potts, 2018). It provided a technology by new which platforms for interaction might be developed by anyone with access to a laptop with institutional governance emergent from the protocols embedded within their infrastructure.

In this chapter we will draw on the Brisbane Club model to analyse the likely impacts of the mega-technology that is blockchain and the possibilities for institutional discovery it offers. We will do so by drawing on the emerging "institutional cryptoeconomics" literature (Davidson, De Filippi and Potts, 2018; Berg, Davidson and Potts, 2018) to establish what we mean when we say that blockchain is an institutional technology. We will see, in doing so, that blockchain is an extremely exciting technology which offers profound opportunities for what Berg, Davidson and Potts (2018) call "institutional discovery," by allowing for private individuals to develop decentralised institutional governance solutions to various problems confronting them. We will also develop research published elsewhere by Markey-Towler (2018) to establish how such institutional systems are adopted by an evolutionary process and the factors governing the exertion of selection pressures therein, and see that the developers of blockchain-based platforms with institutional governance face significant challenges for coordinating expectations across a population of potential adopters. Despite these challenges, we will see that blockchain offers new possibilities for the emergence of community-based solutions to various socioeconomic problems.

We will proceed, first, by drawing on the emerging institutional cryptoeconomics literature to consider the nature of blockchain technology and the capabilities for human action it creates. We will here establish the capabilities for new modes of behaviour it makes feasible relative to existing modes. We will then draw on and develop research published elsewhere by Markey-Towler (2018) to establish the relationship between these capabilities and the psychological process to understand how these new modes of behaviour might be realised, and thus the selection pressures exerted on various blockchain-based platforms with institutional governance. We will then take this understanding of the micro-scale dynamics facilitated by blockchain as an institutional technology and place it within the context of a macro-scale analysis of the disruption it will create within the broader socioeconomic system, and project the likely form of a socioeconomic system re-coordinated around meso-rules enabled by blockchain.

1 The ledger of facts: the blockchain as a foundation for privatised institutional governance of platforms

Blockchain is not a typical technology with which we are familiar. It does not merely enhance productivity by offering business a new technology for keeping ledgers of data (as Swan, 2015, Tapscott and Tapscott, 2016; Mougayar, 2016 argue). While it operates on platforms enabled by the internet, it is also not merely a platform technology which facilitates exchange (Catalini and Gans, 2017; Parker, van Altsyne and Choudary, 2016). Rather, the institutional cryptoeconomics literature shows that it presents the next step in the evolution of the internet as a platform technology as an *institutional* technology which provides for the formulation of privatised governance of those platforms (Davidson, De Filippi and Potts, 2018). It is, if you like, a technology which allows us to establish governance structures for determining what behaviours are appropriate and necessary within a particular system of interaction, much as markets, firms, governments, clubs, and commons have traditionally done (Williamson, 1975, 1985; Ostrom, 1990).

That blockchain is an institutional technology might not be immediately apparent to the reader, so we will briefly demonstrate the argument of the institutional cryptoeconomics literature. Blockchain is a distributed ledger technology which makes use of decentralised consensus algorithms to keep a record of socioeconomic facts. The ledger is "distributed" because each node in a network within the internet keeps a copy of the ledger, and it is "decentralised" because it is updated only once consensus is achieved *across* that network on the next "block" of facts to be incorporated into the "chain" of such blocks which constitutes the ledger. A multitude of algorithms for achieving consensus have been proposed and are still being developed, with the common aim of decentralising consensus on the ledger of socioeconomic facts (Ometoruwa, 2018), reflecting the origins of the technology in the cryptoanarchist movement (see May's 1992 manifesto). For instance, the famous "proof of work" algorithm proposed by Satoshi Nakamoto (2009) requires *every node* in the network to verify the work done by a single node to compile the "true" block to be added to the ledger of economic facts, which is proved by expending computational power. Next-generation algorithms such as "proof of stake" seek to mitigate the energy-intensity of verifying the "true" block to be added to the ledger by having nodes which stake crypto-assets elect a particular node to compile it.

So blockchain allows a decentralised network to come to a consensus on a ledger of socioeconomic facts which is distributed among them. That is, block-chain allows a decentralised network to come to a consensus on a ledger which maintains a verified record of who interacted with whom, when they interacted, and the result of that interaction in terms of the effect it had on the state of the system as a whole. Now, any interaction, before it can be entered into the verified record of socioeconomic facts, must meet certain requirements established by rules embedded in the protocols of the blockchain infrastructure on which that ledger is kept. These protocols establish what interactions are legitimate and valid for entry into the ledger of socioeconomic facts. Thus, the technology creates *rules* about what are legitimate and valid interactions within a platform which will be verified by the network as a whole which supports that platform. It is these rules, which we call *institutions* in economics (North, 1990; Hodgson, 2010; Lawson, 2016), which establish the right and proper modes of interaction in society which can be verified and legitimated. Once verified and legitimated, interactions can then be *enforced* within the system of institutional governance thereby established. Hence block-chain, like markets, firms, governments, clubs, and commons (Williamson, 1975, 1985; Ostrom, 1990), is an *institutional* technology by which systems of governance can emerge to determine what behaviour is appropriate and/or necessary in any given situation. It establishes the domain of legitimate and valid interactions which can take place within a given platform implemented on the internet.

What is different about blockchain as an institutional technology is its hybrid nature. It enables institutional systems of governance which are of an intermediate form between firms and markets. The institutional systems of governance which emerge from the protocols embedded in blockchain infrastructure are subject to a significant degree of *design*, which they share in common with, typically, firms, governments, and clubs (Coase, 1937; Williamson, 1975, 1985). However, the institutional systems of governance which emerge from the protocols embedded in blockchain infrastructure are typically systems for the governance of interactions which are *voluntarily* entered into, which they share in common with markets and commons (Hayek, 1945; Williamson, 1975, 1985; Ostrom, 1990). Like firms and governments, therefore, particular institutional systems enabled by blockchains can emerge relatively rapidly, but they facilitate voluntary exchange and coordination of interaction on the large scale of markets.

This means that blockchain significantly accelerates a process Berg, Davidson and Potts (2018) have called "institutional discovery." Institutional systems and institutional technologies, like any other systems enabled by other technologies, are subject to a process of discovery wherein entrepreneurial experimentation leads to various systems which iterate variations on the underlying capabilities of the technology. Traditionally we have only seen large-scale experimentation with institutional technologies take place on a time scale of decades if not centuries as firms emerged slowly from localised experiments in organisation, governments emerged from wars and constitutional conventions, and commons emerged from repeated interactions within communities. With blockchain, large-scale experimentation with institutional technologies to develop institutional systems of governance for platforms on the scale of markets occurs *within* time scales of decades if not years or even months. Anyone with access to a laptop can design an institutional system of governance for a new platform of voluntary socioeconomic interaction and then release it into the internet, inviting others to participate in its development.

Blockchain therefore expands the capability, on a scale hitherto unheard of, for human interaction to take place in the context of a variety of different institutional systems. Where traditionally individuals were relatively constrained to interact within institutional systems for particular markets, firms, governments, commons, and clubs, individuals are now more able to interact within a variety of different institutional systems enabled by blockchain technology. Blockchain expands the range of *possibilities* for systems of institutional governance within which one may decide to conduct one's affairs. It makes far more possible what Trent MacDonald (2015) has called "crypto-secession" from entire systems of institutional governance such as governments in particular by offering a range of new platforms for interaction governed by institutional systems which emerge from the protocols embedded within a blockchain infrastructure. It makes far more possible what Hirschman (1970) called "Exit" at the level not only of particular interactions, but at the level of the institutional systems within which those interactions take place, not only through crypto-secession, but also through "forking," whereby a subset of a particular blockchain network decides to implement a new, different system of institutional governance to the network at large (Berg and Berg, 2017).

We have already observed such experimentation on a large scale which challenges existing institutional systems in such diverse arenas of socioeconomic life as the monetary system, the system of contracts, voting, and the establishment of identity. The first experiment in blockchain-based institutional systems of governance was, of course, in the realm of cryptocurrencies, with Satoshi Nakamoto's famous Bitcoin protocol, which enabled a decentralised, peer-to-peer monetary system with a stable money supply. This of course was followed by a flurry of experiments with variations on the blockchain protocols for cryptocurrencies which drove, and are still driving, a process of institutional discovery in monetary systems. Very soon after the development of cryptocurrency, Nick Szabo's (1994) vision of the algorithmically executed "smart contract" was implemented within the Ethereum protocol, which made use of blockchain infrastructure to develop a "smart ledger" containing such algorithmically executed smart contracts (Buterin, 2013; Wood, 2014). This again was followed by a flurry of experiments with variations on the blockchain protocols for smart contracts such as the EOS network (Grigg, 2017), which drove and is still driving a process of institutional discovery in the governance of contracts. Allen, Berg and Lane's (forthcoming) explorations of the possibilities for blockchain to support new institutional systems for voting are already being realised with the emergence of such platforms as Horizon State (2018). At present, the possibilities for blockchain to support even new institutional systems for the establishment of *identity* (traditionally such a sole province of government-based institutional systems) are being explored (Berg et al., 2017). Wherever the governance of a particular aspect of socioeconomic life has existed, blockchain-based institutional systems are beginning to experiment with offering possibilities for realising governance through decentralised, distributed means.

What we can see here then is that blockchain expands the capabilities for entrepreneurial action into the design of institutional systems of governance for platforms of socioeconomic interaction in a way hitherto unimagined. It offers significant opportunities to discover new systems for establishing the right and proper mode of interaction in socioeconomic systems using blockchain as an infrastructure for achieving decentralised consensus on a distributed ledger of socioeconomic facts. It is entirely possible for such systems to be *privatised* and emerge from communities committed to their ongoing development entirely outside of the authority of government. It therefore creates new opportunities for entrepreneurial action to design and for communities to develop new decentralised institutional systems for the governance of socioeconomic interaction to solve problems in *any* realm of socioeconomic life which require institutional governance.

However, while blockchain offers such profound opportunities for the emergence of new institutional systems of governance from the community level to solve problems which require governance, it is no forgone conclusion that such opportunities will be realised. Entrepreneurial action may design a blockchain-based platform governed by an institutional system emerging from the protocols embedded within its infrastructure, but the ongoing development of that platform by its adoption as a platform for interaction within an institutional system is not guaranteed. For this to occur, individuals need to adopt such blockchain-based platforms for interaction and the institutional systems they manifest.

2 Adopting a privatised platform with institutional governance: substitution between rule systems

The decision on the part of an individual to adopt a blockchain-based platform for interaction and the institution systems to which they are subject is a holistic one about the system in which to pursue entire courses of action. To understand the adoption of such systems for interaction, and the preconditions for their successful selection by evolutionary pressures, we need to approach the behavioural changes of individuals which exert that pressure in a holistic way. We need to understand what is required of an institutional system of governance for a platform for socioeconomic interaction before individuals will adopt it as such by conducting their affairs within it and deciding to participate in its development. In doing so, we will draw on and develop research published elsewhere by Markey-Towler (2018), which provided a sketch of such an analysis.

In the first instance, the Brisbane Club model suggests that a change from conducting one's affairs within a particular institutional system and on the platform subject to it to another can be implemented if a state of substitutability exists between conducting one's affairs in the one and the other. So as long as there exists a state, for instance a particular incentive structure, in which one might conduct one's affairs within an existing institutional system and the platform subject to it and expect to achieve roughly equivalently preferable outcomes from conducting one's affairs in a blockchain-based system, a change from conducting one's affairs in the former to the latter can be implemented. Once the blockchain-based system offers a better incentive structure than that for which a state of substitutability exists, a behavioural change will occur and an individual will begin conducting their affairs within it.

In order for a state of substitutability to exist, there must be no breaks in the chain of substitution between conducting one's affairs within an existing institutional system and a blockchain-based one. There are two potential causes for such breaks, which need to be addressed before any blockchain-based institutional system and platform subject to it can support a state of substitutability and thus be adopted. The first potential barrier to a state of substitutability is the existence of *requirements* for any institutional system, and the second is the opportunities for realising *complementarities* that it offers. In order for any blockchain-based institutional system of governance to be adopted then, it must support expectations which indicate that it meets the institutional *requirements* for any such system, and offers sufficient opportunities for realising *complementarities* within it.

Such institutional requirements as are necessary to support expectations which would cause an individual to adopt a blockchain-based institutional system to conduct their affairs within are fairly straightforward to identify. The institutional system implemented on a blockchain-based platform must support expectations that contracts struck within the system will be honoured and executed and that records of property rights within it will have security and integrity. It must support expectations that disputes over contracts and property rights will be reconciled equitably. In general, it must support expectations that there will be *governance* which will make all the typical expectations of reciprocity and exchange which one requires to conduct one's affairs feasible. Without such expectations that institutional requirements will be met, the individual cannot possibly expect that they will obtain outcomes of *any* preferability by conducting their affairs within the blockchain-based system in question.

An institutional system for a particular platform must also offer sufficient opportunities to realise *complementarities* in the conducting of one's affairs, by facilitating *many* forms of interaction with others. Adopting a platform subject to a blockchain-based institutional system becomes more preferable the more of one's affairs may be conducted within it, and the more interactions one may form in the course of those affairs. In order to be adopted by an individual, a blockchain-based platform subject to an institutional system must support expectations that such complementarities may be realised. This requires, therefore, that individuals expect that many *others* will also adopt the system with whom they may interact in the course of their affairs and realise complementarities with. Without such expectations that complementarities may be realised by interactions with others on a blockchain-based platform subject to institutional governance, it is very difficult for individuals to expect that they will obtain outcomes of *any* preferability by conducting their affairs within it.

A blockchain-based institutional system must support such expectations of requirements being met and the feasibility of realising complementarities, but we have to go further than the sketch provided by Markey-Towler (2018) in order to understand exactly how those expectations are formed and applied so as to guide individuals to adopt such systems by conducting their affairs within them. That is, *behavioural* requirements must also be met before the necessary expectations can be formed and applied that would guide individuals to adopt an institutional system of governance for a blockchain-based platform and participate in its development. By applying the behavioural model at the heart of the Brisbane Club perspective, we can obtain insight into how this can be achieved.

In the first instance, ideas which would become expectations if incorporated into mental networks concerning a given blockchain-based platform subject to institutional governance and the opportunities it offers as a system for conducting one's affairs within have to be communicated to a population of potential adopters. We know from the behavioural model at the heart of the Brisbane Club perspective that the likelihood that these ideas will be so incorporated into the mind of the population of potential adopters is subject to a number of factors. The form of the ideas which maximise the likelihood of expectations forming about the extent to which institutional requirements are met and opportunities for realising complementarities are available is shaped by those factors. They are *simple*; they connect objects and events in the environment with a powerful hold on the individual's *attention*, build on *existing* ideas in the mind, do not *contradict* ideas that are applied when they are presented, and make changes at the *periphery* of mental networks rather than their core. *Narratives*, we have seen, are an important way to convey such ideas so as to maximise the likelihood that they will be incorporated into mental networks and become expectations that a particular system meets institutional requirements and provides for sufficient complementarities to be realised as to be desirable to conduct one's affairs within.

These expectations formed in the mental networks of various potential adopters of blockchain-based platforms with institutional governance do not guide behaviour until they are *applied* to forming judgments about the environment in which that population exists. This requires that information in the environment be placed and presented relative to perception so as to call those ideas to mind when necessary. The manner in which that information must be so placed and presented is determined by the salience and chains properties of perception. Objects and events which form the elements of expectations that institutional requirements will be met, and sufficient opportunities for realising complementarities provided within a blockchain-based system, need to be placed and presented in the environment so as to have a sufficiently strong impression on the sensory organs as to satisfy the salience property. Otherwise, objects and events which are strongly connected *to* such objects and events need to be placed and presented so as to have a sufficiently strong impression on the sensory organs that their perception via the salience property causes the latter to be perceived via the chains property. If all such information which corresponds to the elements of expectations that institutional requirements will be met and sufficient opportunities for realising complementarities offered by a blockchain-based system can be so placed and presented, we will observe that those expectations are applied, and that they guide behaviour so as for individuals to adopt the blockchain-based system.

The challenge presented by these necessities for individuals to adopt a blockchain-based platform go further than this however. For it is not enough to have them satisfied for any given individual. The application of expectations formed that a blockchain-based system meets institutional requirements and provides scope for realising sufficient complementarities as for it to be preferable to conduct one's affairs within must be *coordinated* across the population of potential adopters. That is to say, there must be coordination of environments across the population of potential adopters such that expectations formed about the expected outcomes of conducting affairs within a blockchain-based system are applied and guide behaviour in a correlated manner. If this coordination does not occur, expectations for realising complementarities will go unfulfilled for lack of counterparties with whom to interact. Obviously, this is a very difficult thing to achieve, and so significant challenges must be overcome in order to seize the opportunities that are presented for community-based development of institutional governance for the solution of problems faced by those communities.

So, we can see that in order for a blockchain-based platform subject to institutional governance to be adopted by individuals who decide to participate in building it by conducting their affairs within it then, certain preconditions need to be met. A state of substitutability must exist between the rule structures for existing platforms and the rule structures for new blockchain-based platforms. In order for this to be the case, expectations of the outcomes which would follow the adoption of such a platform must reflect a belief that institutional requirements for the security of contracts and property rights will be met, and sufficient opportunities for realising complementarities with other adopters of that platform will be available. For these expectations to guide behaviour however, they need first to be formed, and then applied in forming judgments of the environment faced by members of the population of potential adopters. This requires that ideas which would become such expectations be communicated in such a form as makes them likely to be incorporated into mental networks, and then information placed and presented in the environment so as for those ideas to be applied to guide behaviour toward adopting a blockchain-based platform. This must be *coordinated* across the population of potential adopters, which presents significant challenges to be overcome in order for blockchain-based platforms subject to institutional governance to be adopted and developed as such.

3 Disruption and re-coordination as privatised institutional governance emerges: a new era for community-based solutions

We have now established the dynamics which are likely to be brought about at the micro-scale of socioeconomic systems by the emergence of blockchain by studying its interaction with the psychological process from which socioeconomic systems form. We have discovered that blockchain is an institutional technology which facilitates the privatised development of new decentralised systems of institutional governance for platforms in which socioeconomic interaction takes place. It thus facilitates behavioural change whereby individuals substitute from existing platforms with institutional rule structures to new blockchain-based platforms with privatised, decentralised institutional governance. Blockchain thus presents wonderful opportunities for the emergence of community-based solutions to problems which require institutional governance. However, entrepreneurial action in this space faces significant challenges in order to seize these opportunities in terms of forming and coordinating expectations that the institutional requirements of such blockchain-based systems will be met and that sufficient opportunities for realising complementarities are available in order for there to be coordinated adoption of these technologies across a population of potential adopters. With this micro-scale view of the behavioural change brought about by blockchain technology, we may elevate our analysis to project the likely effect of this new institutional technology on the scale of the socioeconomic system as a whole.

Blockchain makes a new form of platform subject to institutional governance possible – one in which socioeconomic interaction takes place on a platform subject to privatised, decentralised institutional governance which may be designed bespoke to solve the problems facing particular communities. As meso-rules enabled by blockchain technology begin to emerge, we can expect to see significant disruption not so much in terms of the connective structure of socioeconomic systems as in terms of the systems of institutional governance in which those connective structures are built. Where blockchain offers better possibilities for institutional governance of socioeconomic interaction, we can expect systems built on it to be substituted for existing systems of institutional governance. Of course, these possibilities offered by the new institutional technologies will allow for new connections to emerge which were not possible within existing institutional systems as well, so we might very well expect the disruption to institutional systems to actually cause structure in socioeconomic systems to *grow*. As meso-rules enabled by blockchain continue to diffuse then, re-coordination will occur not so much in terms of the connective structure within which the meso-populations using such rules are embedded, but instead in terms of the alignment of institutional systems of governance within which that connective structure forms. Eventually, we will observe an economy re-coordinated around meso-populations applying meso-rules which support interaction within a new mixture of platforms enabled by institutional technologies, which will include those which are subject to privatised, decentralised systems of governance enabled by blockchain.

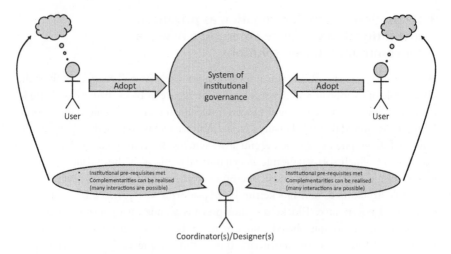

FIGURE 9.1 Coordination problems in blockchain adoption.

Blockchain allows for the privatised design and development of systems of institutional governance, but designers need to form and coordinate expectations that institutional pre-requisites will be met, and complementarities can be obtained.

Individuals, groups, and communities who will become successful and seize opportunities presented by this re-coordinating economy are those which can effectively design platforms enabled by blockchain to solve various problems with institutional governance which make new value-creating connections possible. Such individuals, groups, and communities will design institutional systems of governance which define appropriate and necessary forms of behaviour in socioeconomic systems which encourage the formation of value-creating connections where they are currently felt to be in deficit. But they will also be able to design them so as to support the formation and application of expectations which will guide behaviour on the part of a population of potential adopters to decide to conduct their affairs within the platforms enabled by blockchain and thereby participate in their development. Those individuals, groups, and communities will therefore be able to communicate ideas about the platforms and institutional governance they have developed that would become such expectations which are simple, build on existing ideas at the periphery of mental networks without greatly contradicting them, and connect objects and events with a powerful hold on the attention of a population of potential adopters. But they will also be able to *coordinate* those expectations by so placing and presenting information in the environment of the population of potential adopters as to cause the expectations to be applied to guiding behaviour to adopt their blockchain-based platform subject to institutional governance as a system in which to conduct their affairs.

The newly re-coordinated economy which will likely emerge from the diffusion of new meso-rules enabled by blockchain will not, in terms of its value-creating connective structure, likely look that particularly different to what it would otherwise have looked like. However, the institutional context in which that connective structure exists will likely look very strange to our present sensibilities. It is quite likely that a far more diverse set of institutional systems will support the formation of that connective structure which are bespoke to the institutional needs of those who form that structure. That set of institutional systems will include privatised, decentralised systems of institutional governance implemented on blockchains. It is quite likely that in spite of the main change being on the level of institutions, the development of such more bespoke institutional governance structures will facilitate the formation of new value-creating structures which address deficits the individuals, groups, and communities who develop those structures wish to have addressed. While there are significant challenges to effectively implementing blockchain-based platforms with institutional governance in terms of obtaining their adoption as systems in which to conduct socioeconomic interaction, the opportunities presented by blockchain are significant. This technology promises to enable a new era for community-based solutions to problems which require institutional governance by providing the capability for those communities to develop privatised, decentralised institutional systems.

4 Summary: the entrepreneurship of rules faces significant challenges, but also presents extraordinary opportunities

In this chapter we applied the Brisbane Club model to analysing the likely effects of the youngest of the mega-technologies of the Fourth Industrial Revolution: blockchain. We saw that blockchain is a technology which offers significant opportunities for community-based solutions to socioeconomic problems through the development of privatised, decentralised institutional systems of governance for platforms in which value-creating connections are formed. But we saw that realising these opportunities requires addressing significant challenges in terms of implementing the adoption of a blockchain-based platform subject to such privatised, decentralised institutional governance.

We drew on the emerging institutional cryptoeconomics literature to see that blockchain is an institutional technology which facilitates the development of privatised, decentralised institutional systems for platforms on which socioeconomic interaction takes place. By enabling the development of privatised, decentralised institutional systems to emerge in this manner, blockchain makes possible a new process of "institutional discovery" in which new systems of institutional governance based on blockchain can be substituted for existing rule structures. It is a technology which is disrupting existing institutional systems, from those for money and contracts to those for establishing identity.

We then saw, drawing on and developing research published elsewhere by Markey-Towler (2018), that the realisation of such behavioural change faces significant challenges. In order for a population of potential adopters to decide to conduct their affairs within an institutional system of governance on a particular platform enabled by blockchain requires the coordination of expectations such that a state of substitutability exists between existing and new rule structures. This requires that the institutional system implemented on blockchain meet institutional requirements concerning the security and integrity of property rights and the honouring and execution of contracts, as well as providing sufficient opportunities to realise complementarities through interaction in the system. The expectations which this supports must then be actually formed by being incorporated into the mind through the communication of ideas which are simple, extend existing ideas at the periphery of mental networks without contradicting them greatly, and connect objects and events with a powerful hold over the attention of the population of potential adopters. These expectations must then be coordinated to guide behaviour toward adopting and participating in the development of a blockchain-based system of interaction by the placing and presenting of information in the environment so as for them to be applied.

At the macro-scale of the socioeconomic system, the emergence of new meso-rules enabled by blockchain will likely not create so much disruption of existing value-creating structures as it will create disruption for existing institutional systems. As the socioeconomic system re-coordinates around meso-populations applying meso-rules enabled by blockchain which support interaction on blockchain-based platforms subject to privatised, decentralised institutional governance, we are likely to observe the connective structures within which they are embedded occur in the context of a more diverse set of institutions. That set of institutions will include more bespoke platforms subject to institutional systems which are the result of entrepreneurial action, and probably support the formation of new value-creating connective structures which the individuals, groups, and communities responsible for developing those institutional systems believed were in deficit. The platforms and systems of institutional governance which make up that set will be those for which the significant challenges have been risen to of forming and coordinating expectations of sufficiently preferable outcomes following the conducting of affairs within them. Life in the Fourth Industrial Revolution therefore offers the hope of a new era for community-based solutions to emerge through privatised, decentralised institutional governance of platforms of socioeconomic interaction. But it is nonetheless a life not without significant challenges in securing those opportunities, and requires significant effort on the part of entrepreneurs at the level of the individual, group, and community to develop the applications of blockchain technology which make them possible.

Technical appendix

A sketch of a model of the evolution of institutional systems implemented using institutional technologies drawing on the insights of the Brisbane Club has been offered elsewhere by Markey-Towler (2018) in the inaugural issue of the *Journal of the British Blockchain Association*. We will take this model and develop it further here.

Blockchain is an institutional technology which enables the development of an institutional system. We will call such an institutional system l, and the set of actions – transactions, contracts, registrations, etc. – which are validated and legitimated within them $S(I)$. For simplicity, we say that some course of action a_i^* selected by an individual i– such as the striking of a contract or registering property – takes place within an institutional system l if it is contained within the set of actions which are validated and legitimated within them, that is

$$a_i^* \in S(I)$$

We can use this to characterise at any given point the platform $P(I)$ for interactions for which I forms the system of institutional governance. We say that the platform $P(I)$ is characterised at any given point by the interactions which take place within it, that is

$$P(I) = \left\{ a_i^* \in \left\{ a_j^* \right\}_{j \in N} : a_i \in S(I) \right\}$$

We could (crudely) characterise the evolution of this platform, and thus the institutional technology which enables its governance, by the evolution of its size (it's cardinality, $|P(I)|$) over time

$$\frac{\partial}{\partial t} |P(I)| = \frac{\partial}{\partial t} \left| \left\{ a_i^* \in : a_i \in S(I) \right\} \right|$$

Now traditionally this has been relatively trivial due to the lack of large-scale experimentation with institutional technologies, and models of firm growth have been more or less sufficient to capture the evolution of particular institutional systems manifest in firms. The effect of blockchain technology is to accelerate this process significantly by greatly expanding the capacity for human action to take place in a *variety* of different institutional systems, by providing them with an infrastructure to be developed on. That is, with blockchain technology, it is more possible to have a behavioural change from some course of action taking place within an existing institutional system I to some course of action taking place within a new blockchain-based system I'

$$a_i \in S(I) \to a_i' \in S(I')$$

Where behavioural change takes place such that interaction increasingly takes place on a platform for which a blockchain-based institutional system provides governance, we can say that the process of evolution is selecting that system. This behavioural change is a holistic one, so we need to approach it holistically with the Brisbane Club model in order to understand the conditions under which it will occur, and thus a blockchain-based institutional system will be selected by the process of institutional evolution and discovery.

In the first instance, if for a particular incentive structure δ a state of substitutability was to exist between two courses of action $a_i \in S(I)$ and $a'_i \in S(I')$ which would take place in different institutional systems, that is

$$\exists \overline{\delta} : g_{a_i \in S(I)} \sim g_{a'_i \in S(I')}$$

then as long as the individual can expect sufficiently preferable outcomes to follow from acting within the latter institutional system as exceeds this point of substitutability, a behavioural change will obtain between interacting within existing institutional systems and new institutional systems. In order for this to be the case, the institutional system I' must support expectations $g_{a'_i \in S(I')}$ which indicate that there are no breaks in the chain of substitution between interactions within existing institutional systems and new institutional systems. In order for this to be the case, the institutional system I' must meet institutional *requirements* which support expectations that contracts struck within the system will be honoured and executed and that ensure the security and integrity of records of property rights within it, but it must also support expectations of realising sufficient *complementarities* within the platform which that institutional system governs. For some $a'_i \in S(I')$, complementarities exist if

$$g_{a'_i \supset a, \alpha'} \succ g_{a'_i \setminus \alpha'}$$

and are capable of being satisfied if $\alpha' \in B$. In the context of a platform with an institutional system of governance implemented using blockchain, these complementarities are realised by being able to conduct more interactions rather than less within them – for instance $\alpha' = x_{ij}$, in the context of some contract between i and j. The model sketched out by Markey-Towler (2018) ends here, but we ought to go further, for this model does not inform us of when such expectations will be called to mind and coordinated so as to guide behaviour toward adopting this or that institutional technology.

Supposing that a blockchain-based institutional system I' can support such expectations $g_{a'_i \in S(I')}$, these must be, further, incorporated into the mind and then applied in order to guide behaviour so as to take place in the system I'. The conditions which maximise the likelihood of the former being the case are sufficiently formally complex as to be unnecessary for us to state here. But informally, the likelihood that these expectations are incorporated into the mind of the individual i, $g_{a'_i \in S(I')} \subset g_i(H_i)$, is increasing the *fewer* connections are contained within them, the more they connect objects and events with a strong hold on the individual's *attention*, the more they build on *existing* mental networks, and the less they *contradict* connections in $g_i(H'_i)$ or would change mental networks at their *core*. Narratives, we have seen, are a potent way to convey such ideas (Shiller, 2017).

The conditions which make the latter the case – that expectations will actually be applied so as to guide behaviour $g_{a'_i \in S(I')} \subset g_i(H'_i)$ – derive from the manner in which perception interacts with the environment through the salience and chains properties. Recall that some percept h will be perceived if and only if the salience $\sigma(v')$ of the information $v' : \rho(v') = h$ corresponding to it is sufficiently large (a constant $\bar{\sigma}$) with respect to the salience of the overall environment $\sigma(v_N)$. That is,

$$h \in \rho(v' \subset v_N) \Leftrightarrow \sigma(v') - \sigma(v_N) \geq \bar{\sigma}$$

Recall further that chains exist wherever some percept h is connected to another h' by a sufficiently strong connection $R_{hh'} \in g(H)$ in mental networks. If the "strength" of some connection $R_{hh'}$ can be represented by a metric $s(R_{hh'})$, which is commensurate with the salience metric $\sigma(\cdot)$, then $s(R_{hh'})$ being sufficiently large (a constant $\bar{s}$) relative to the salience of the environment $\sigma(v_N)$ means that the perception of h may cause the perception of h'. That is, (and this may be generalised to pertain to groups $\{h\}$ of anterior percepts)

$$h \in H' \ \& \ \exists R_{hh'} \in g(H) : s(R_{hh'}) - \sigma(v_N) \geq \bar{s} \Rightarrow h' \in H'$$

So the environment must be framed so as for the objects and events connected by expectations $g_{a'_i \in S(I')}$ or their perceptual antecedents to be placed and presented in such a way as to make a sufficiently large impression on the sensory organs.

If the such expectations can be supported by the design of an institutional system, incorporated into the mind, and then applied to guide behaviour in a coordinated manner, then in principle we will observe the differential adoption of the institutional technology on which that system is implemented.

References

Allen, Darcy W. E., Berg, Chris and Lane, Aaron M. (forthcoming), *Cryptodemocracy*, World Scientific

Berg, Alastair and Berg, Chris, (2017) "Exit, voice, and forking", available at SSRN: https://ssrn.com/abstract=3081291

Berg, Alastair, Berg, Chris, Davidson, Sinclair and Potts, Jason, (2017) "The institutional economics of identity", available at SSRN: https://ssrn.com/abstract=3072823

Berg, Chris, Davidson, Sinclair and Potts, Jason, (2018) "Institutional discovery and competition in the evolution of blockchain technology", available at SSRN: https://ssrn.com/abstract=3220072

Buterin, Vitalk, (2013) "Ethereum: A next-generation smart contract and decentralized application platform", available at URL: http://ethereum.org/ethereum.html (17/09/2018)

Catalini, Christian and Gans, Joshua S., (2017) "Some simple economics of the blockchain", Rotman School of Management Working Paper No.2874598; MIT Sloan Research Paper No. 5191–16, available at SSRN: https://ssrn.com/abstract=2874598 or http://dx.doi.org/10.2139/ssrn.2874598

Coase, Ronald, (1937) "The nature of the firm", *Economica*, 4(16), pp. 386–405

Davidson, Sinclair, De Filippi, Primavera and Potts, Jason, (2018) "Blockchains and the economic institutions of capitalism", *Journal of Institutional Economics*, 14(4), pp. 639–658

Grigg, Ian, (2017) "EOS – an introduction", available at URL: https://eos.io/documents/EOS_An_Introduction.pdf (accessed 17/09/2018)

Hayek, Friedrich, (1945) "The use of knowledge in society", *American Economic Review*, 25(4), pp. 519–530

Hirschman, Albert, (1970) *Exit, Voice and Loyalty*, Harvard University Press, Cambridge, MA

Hodgson, Geoffrey and Knudsen, Thorbjorn, (2010) *Darwin's Conjecture*, University of Chicago Press, Chicago

Horizon State, (2018) "Horizon state: Ensuring every voice counts", available at URL: https://horizonstate.com/Horizon-State-Whitepaper.pdf (accessed 28/12/2018)

Lawson, Tony, (2016) "Comparing conceptions of social ontology: Emergent social entities and/or institutional facts?", *Journal for the Theory of Social Behaviour*, 46(4), pp. 359–399

MacDonald, Trent J., (2015) *Theory of Unbundled and Non-territorial Governance*, RMIT University, doctoral thesis.

Markey-Towler, Brendan, (2018) "Anarchy, blockchain and Utopia: A theory of political-socioeconomic systems organised using blockchain", *Journal of the British Blockchain Association*, 1(1), pp. 1–16

May, Tim, (1992) "The crypto anarchist manifesto", available at URL: www.activism.net/cypherpunk/crypto-anarchy.html (accessed 3/11/2018)

Mougayar, William, (2016) *The Business Blockchain*, Wiley, Hoboken

Nakamoto, Satoshi, (2009), "Bitcoin: A peer-to-peer electronic cash system", available at URL: https://bitcoin.org/bitcoin.pdf (accessed 14/09/2018)

North, Douglass, (1990) *Institutions, Institutional Change and Economic Performance*, Cambridge University Press, Cambridge

Ometoruwa, Toju, (2018) "Solving the blockchain trilemma: Decentralization, security & scalability", *CoinBureau.com*, available at URL: www.coinbureau.com/analysis/solving-blockchain-trilemma/ (accessed 17/09/2018)

Ostrom, Elinor, (1990) *Governing the Commons*, Cambridge University Press, Cambridge

Parker, Geoffrey, van Altsyne, Marshall and Choudary, Paul, (2016) *Platform Revolution*, W.W. Norton & Co., New York

Shiller, Robert, (2017) "Narrative economics", *American Economic Review*, 107(4), pp. 967–1004

Swan, Melanie, (2015) *Blockchain: Blueprint for a New Economy*. O'Reilly, Sebastpol, CA.

Szabo, Nick, (1994) "Smart contracts", available at URL: www.fon.hum.uva.nl/rob/Courses/InformationInSpeech/CDROM/Literature/LOTwinterschool2006/szabo.best.vwh.net/smart.contracts.html (accessed 17/08/2018)

Tapscott, Don and Tapscott, Alex, (2016) *Blockchain Revolution: How the Technology Behind Bitcoin is Changing Money, Business and the World,* Portfolio/Penguin, London, UK.

Williamson, Oliver, (1975) *Markets and Hierarchies*, Free Press, New York

Williamson, Oliver, (1985) *The Economic Institutions of Capitalism*, Free Press, New York

Wood, Gavin, (2014) "Ethereum: A secure decentralised generalised transaction ledger EIP-150 revision", available at URL: http://yellowpaper.io (accessed 17/09/2018)

10

LEADERLESS REVOLUTIONS

Case studies in the entrepreneurship of rules

The rise of blockchain technology in the last decade has helped make significant progress towards achieving viable decentralisation of governance in economic institutions, while maintaining the integrity of complex systems. This represents the third of the three core technological cornerstones of the Fourth Industrial Revolution as it relates to impacts on the economy. As described in the previous chapter, blockchain technology is by far the newest of the three mega-technologies considered in this book, with the concept having only been around for the last decade. Blockchain technology is also the most nascent of the three, with most of its full potential and many transformative applications as yet unrealised or at least not widely adopted (Wang, Chen, and Xu 2016).

1 Coordination, rules, governance, law, and order

The most prominent use case for blockchain in recent years has been cryptocurrency, and this has served to rapidly bring blockchain to the top of the agenda within technology conferences and financial circles around the world (Herian 2018). The global cryptocurrency market cap peaked at many hundreds of billions of U.S. dollars and is still an immense twelve-figure sector representing a significant amount of global wealth. Despite high levels of volatility and an uncertain future, this use case is unlikely to disappear anytime soon. Nevertheless, there are many other use cases for blockchain technology which will have arguably more substantial economic effects in the long run, not only in a monetary sense, but in a structural and institutional sense as well. These use cases have been receiving an increasing amount of attention and interest from researchers and from industry (Risius and Spohrer 2017).

How is this possible? For starters, our society and institutions, our businesses and government, our clubs and associations, and all other systematic forms of interaction between sufficiently large groups of human beings – these all have this in common: a *coordination problem*. Let us elaborate on this point. In the most basic sense, each human being can be characterised as an independent actor with agency to choose their own actions; in other words, a free economic agent. As discussed in an earlier chapter of this book, each human being will tend to act in a way which they perceive will help them achieve their foundational, aspirational, and transcendental ends, as a means to achieving the ultimate end which they are striving for, consciously or otherwise.

Participation of the individual in a functional institution, however, implies the existence of some set of rules or norms which define the proper, rational, or accepted set of actions, as a subset of the set of all possible actions. This set of rules or norms may be large and complex, for example lengthy tomes of legal statutes and industry regulations, or it may be minimalistic, for example, the well-known "non-aggression principle." These rules or norms may be grounded in a higher moral code of virtue, based on an understanding of rights and responsibilities, or they may simply represent consequentialist expediency. Regardless of the normative ethical theory a human being subscribes to, one thing is clear: rules and norms foster predictability through their adherence.

Small deviations from these rules or norms occurs regularly for a variety of reasons, but these deviations, while they represent an economic cost to the society, are bearable and are small and infrequent enough to not threaten the viability of the institution. Unintentional deviations can often be attributed to imperfect information and unfamiliarity. Intentional deviations from the rules which are performed in a public manner for purported public gain is often a form of activism, while intentional deviations performed in a private manner for private gain are often a form of corruption.

The substantial deviation from these rules or norms by a sufficiently large number of people, however, leads to chaos. Sufficient chaos introduces unpredictability, and unpredictability diminishes the ability of people to realise the aspirational end of security. Unpredictability also leads to economic losses as decisions which are based on a set of expectations about the future prove to be suboptimal when those expectations are not realised. As the amount of chaos rises, eventually the society or institution reaches a critical point at which it is no longer able to usefully function.

One of the landmark papers on the economics of governance is Dixit (2009), which put forward the argument that market economies cannot properly function without the following prerequisites: (1) the security of property rights; (2) the enforcement of contracts; and (3) collective action. Well-defended property rights create the optimal conditions for people to be incentivised to save and invest, and worry less about allocating excessive time and energy to protecting their possessions. The enforcement of contracts ensures that each party can realise its mutual gains from conducting economic transactions, without fear of being cheated. Appropriate collective action permits the internalisation of externalities, as well as the proper management of public goods and public bads.

Trust is perhaps the only thing on which all of economics relies, because trust is essential to economic transactions and commerce. However, trust and the verification of authenticity are different concepts. Werbach (2018) relates the story of a typical incident which happened in mid-2016, where about 11,000 individuals committed about $150 million worth of the Ether cryptocurrency towards a distributed autonomous organisation (DAO), only for the blockchain to undergo a hard fork (split) into two groups after a bad actor stole $50 million from the DAO. Due to the immutability of the blockchain, one of the resulting groups accepted that the hack occurred and carried on with the thief having stolen funds, while the other group broke away and decided to reverse the event. Werbach uses this anecdote as an example to support the idea that an overarching legal system is complementary to blockchain in engendering trust, arguing that "the blockchain is an ingenious solution for verification but to promote trust requires something more."

Nevertheless, as Stringham (2017) points out, for the vast majority of everyday transactions in society, the economic cost of relying on the legal system to enforce contractual obligations often greatly surpasses the marginal benefits to be gained from the value of the transaction. Further, the opportunity cost of the lengthy amount of time that would often be invested in pursuing legal enforcement is usually high. Stringham also cogently argues that the location of the economic marketplaces also plays a large role, because it can be harder to enforce contracts which take place in remote locations or in certain online contexts, or across jurisdictional boundaries. There is a large body of observed evidence to suggest that economic markets tend to emerge and function largely independent of government enforcement. Private governance arrangements built on technology such as the blockchain have the potential to reduce average transaction costs caused by a lack of enforcement.

In a legal sense, blockchain is remarkable because it permits two or more parties to enter into some form of contractual agreement in cases where (1) the parties wish to preserve their anonymity, and (2) the parties are unable to rely upon an understood legal or social context to ensure the enforcement of the contract. The ability of blockchain to offer a means of creating trust in so-called no-trust environments is one of the most promising properties of the technology, and is the focus of much current attention by specialists in contract governance (Eenmaa-Dimitrieva and Schmidt-Kessen 2019). Unfortunately, the legal academic literature has not properly addressed the substantial differences that are a result of the variations in node selection, network size, the consensus mechanism, and the readability and writability of the blocks.

Drescher (2017) neatly summarises the technical conflicts which arise when finding the right balance between the security of a blockchain system and the speed of its operation, or when finding the right balance between the privacy of the users and data on the blockchain on the one hand and trust-enhancing transparency on the other hand. This leads to a simple categorisation of four types of blockchain systems, which are depicted in Figure 10.1.

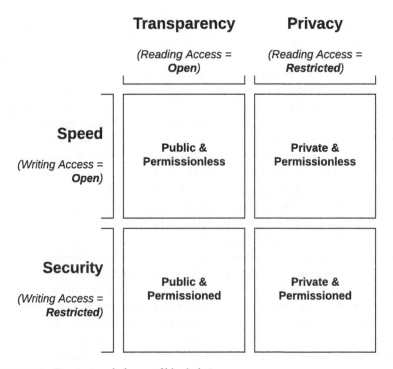

FIGURE 10.1 Four general classes of blockchain.

There are two general conflicts, the resolution of which describes four categories of blockchain. The first conflict pertains to writing access, and the second conflict pertains to reading access (Drescher 2017).

It is therefore important to recognise that all blockchains are not equal in terms of their performance and suitability as a technology for underpinning transactions in an economic marketplace. When the term "public blockchains" is used, typically this represents public and permissionless systems. On the other hand, the term "consortium blockchain" typically refers to private and permissioned blockchains (Zhu et al. 2018). Another, more specific term which has been used is "fully-private blockchain." These are typically private and permissioned blockchains, but are entirely managed and used by one organisation, group, or individual, distinguishing them from the more general class of consortium blockchains. For fully-private blockchains, their ability to maintain the integrity of stored data is deemed more interesting than their ability to support a decentralised system of trust (Feng et al. 2018).

While the smart contracts inherent to blockchain technology have many applications, they have several fundamental differences to legal contracts. Savelyev (2017) nicely summarised these differences; for instance: (1) smart contracts create no future legal obligations, (2) smart contracts generally cannot be breached, (3) vitiated consent does not affect the smart contract's validity, (4) smart contracts are perfectly egalitarian, (5) smart contracts may not *a priori* distinguish legal and illegal content, and (6) smart contracts are executed autonomously. The programming language in which the smart contracts are coded also has a bearing on their legal suitability, as pointed out by Governatori et al. (2018), who argue that although most smart contracts today are written in imperative language, there are distinct benefits to adopting a declarative approach which clearly states the legal items agreed to, abstracted from the computational operations required to execute the contract. Even more recently, Rory Unsworth (2019) penned an excellent chapter on the emerging role of blockchain in the world of legal contracts, which was published in a book edited by Corrales, Fenwick, and Haapio (2019). Unsworth notes that several challenges inevitably arise in any transition process, from legal clauses in current contracts to programmatic clauses in smart contracts. For example, despite some similarities, many traditional legal clauses follow a complex structure, often with characteristics unique to the particular context of the contract, which makes an attempted translation to computational logic tedious. Unsworth suggests that Digital Contract Optimization (DCO) may help with this transition, and suggests that the processes of a DCO journey might include (1) clause extraction, (2) clause clustering, (3) importance assessment and expert allocation, (4) quality and scope assessment, (5) book investigation and benchmark creation, and (6) automated contract review. Blockchain technology is unlikely to replace traditional contracts in the foreseeable future, but may augment them in selected use cases (Jamison and Tariq 2018).

Apart from contract law, blockchain has the potential to disrupt the legal field more broadly, for example, in cases involving the definitions of private property and digital rights management (Käll 2018). This has potential legal and economic benefits for the creators of digital content, who may soon have easier methods of facilitating proper attribution and enforcing proper licensing and royalty payments in situations where online anonymity may presently offer loopholes. This in turn is likely to facilitate the development of new online business models which offer content creators more of the economic value which is currently controlled by platform intermediaries (O'Dair 2019). Blockchain may also find a natural future place in improving compliance processes. For example, the outdated know-your-customer (KYC) due diligence and verification process costs individual financial institutions hundreds of millions of dollars annually and is a regular frustration for customers (Moyano and Ross 2017). These economic costs are amplified by the fines imposed on banks under existing anti-money-laundering (AML) and KYC regulations. The use of an interbank distributed ledger may eventually reduce costs across the financial sector by precluding duplicate KYC verifications by different banks on the same customer.

One of the biggest challenges facing the broader adoption of blockchain technology into applied industry settings was always the establishment of the requisite supporting infrastructure. In the last couple of years, however, major technology companies have pioneered the provision of blockchain infrastructure in the Cloud, thus reducing the cost barriers for innovating companies to enter the marketplace with new blockchain applications. Microsoft is one example of a major technology company which now offers various formats of blockchain as a service (BaaS) through its Azure platform, freeing up new companies to focus on development instead of chasing the capital needed to setup expensive infrastructure. This industry shift mirrors the emergence of Cloud infrastructure as a service (IaaS) in the 2000s, and the market opportunity which that created for innovators (Pathak and Bhandari 2018). Ethereum in particular has grown in the last couple of years to become a dominant blockchain platform, powered by Ether tokens, and it has been highly popular among developers, who write custom smart contracts for their blockchain-powered applications using the language Solidity (Dhillon, Metcalf, and Hooper 2017). The Hyperledger project established by the Linux Foundation also encompasses a wide variety of blockchain tools and frameworks which have seen extensive use in enterprise applications (Lu 2018). Another looming challenge involves higher-level meta-centralisation, or "emergent centralisation" (De Domenico and Baronchelli 2019). As a technological ecosystem evolves around a certain variety of blockchain, the core decentralised system can itself grow to assume a centralised role in the integration of other systems. Organisations must not become too dependent on the correct functioning of blockchain-based systems, because even these fail from time to time. Forward-thinking organisations that wish to deploy blockchain-based systems need to be aware that broader systemic risks still need to be mitigated.

2 Alternative governance structures for institutions

One of the most fundamental opportunities for blockchain to create new economic value resides in the realm of governance. The distributed nature of blockchain systems is a powerful technological enabler for the emergence of decentralised governance structures for core economic institutions such as community organisations, companies, governments, and voting systems (Bheemaiah 2017). In turn, blockchain opens new opportunities in anticorruption efforts, and offers economic welfare gains through product and process innovation at the governance level.

2.1 The DAO

The concept of a Decentralized Autonomous Organization (DAO) is one of the simplest decentralised governance structures which is plausible to create with the help of blockchain technology. As an organisational structure, it must execute specific actions which have been decided upon via some mechanism for reaching consensus amongst the participating entities with a stake in the organisation. This consensus mechanism much be such that the participating entities (which constitute a network of "nodes") can be fully anonymous while being able to trust that compliance will be observed, or even enforced, across the network. It must also entail that a true record of all important information regarding the activities of the organisation is stored and protected from corruption or various attacks. While not representing an organisational hierarchy, the DAO is not exactly structured as a marketplace either. Hsieh et al. (2018) define DAOs as "non-hierarchical organizations that perform and record routine tasks on a peer-to-peer, cryptographically secure, public network, and rely on the voluntary contributions of their internal stakeholders to operate, manage, and evolve the organization through a democratic consultation process."

The DAO relies heavily upon the proper functioning of a peer-to-peer (P2P) network which can manage information and data in an organized and secure fashion. As institutions for economic production, P2P networks have existed in other forms for some time. Many of these P2P networks also double as institutions for economic consumption, leading some authors to dub the members of these networks "prosumers," as they are not only consumers of the economic goods and services (often information-based or digital products) but often producers simultaneously (Bauwens and Pantazis 2018, p. 65). With reference to the model of economic production, Bauwens and Pantazis distinguish between extractive P2P networks and generative P2P networks. The former class, in their view, includes many for-profit platforms such as Uber, Airbnb, and Facebook, which have a traditional company structure overseeing a large network of users which both create value for and derive value from other users by virtue of engaging in the network. The overarching company behind the network then extracts by various means a portion of this economic value, in a process referred to as surplus value extraction. The latter class of P2P networks typically includes more open source and not-for-profit networks such as Wikipedia and Linux. These generative models are typified by users being not only prosumers, but also the managers in a more real sense of the shared economic resource or common property which they collaboratively create and develop.

Organizations, as economic institutions, can take various forms. Takagi (2017, p. 28) offers a nice summary of the theory. Traditionally the distinction was made between markets (voluntary bargaining) and hierarchies (strict lines of authority), with hierarchies being the structure of choice when the transaction costs from operating in the marketplace become too high (Coase 1937). These costs encompass those associated with finding suitable customers or suppliers and subsequently enforcing contracts. Williamson (1975) argued that the sources of these transaction costs can be reduced to (1) bounded rationality with environmental uncertainty, and (2) opportunism with "small-numbers exchange relations" due to information asymmetries and hold-up issues, where customers become effectively "locked in" to their original supplier relationships. Hierarchies, whether explicit or implicit, within the context of a traditional organization, are understood to become the preferred mechanism when environmental uncertainty becomes sufficient to demand the regular and reliable communication associated with hierarchies, or when information asymmetry and opportunism need to be controlled by internal audits and strict information flows. Figure 10.2 provides a graphical illustration of the traditional understanding of markets versus hierarchies as economic organizations.

From an economic perspective, economic organizations are "created entities within and through which people interact to reach individual and collective

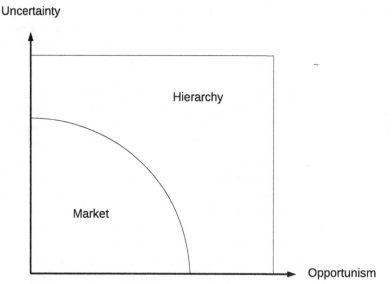

FIGURE 10.2   Markets vs. hierarchies.

The Coasean perspective on the boundaries of firms according to transaction costs, as formulated by Williamson (Takagi 2017).

economic goals" (Milgrom and Roberts 1992, p. 20). This is a broad definition which encompasses all hierarchies and markets. But from a legal perspective, organizations take on a distinct legal identity of their own so that they can enter binding contracts. Only some hierarchies and some markets are legal organizations. Takagi (2017) argues that DAOs, while not always legal organizations, should aim to represent a viable third option between the two extremes of markets and hierarchies in terms of transaction costs. Indeed, it is the costs at scale – both monetary costs and complexity costs – which will ultimately determine the long-term viability of blockchain use in business process execution. While investigating this question, Rimba et al. (2018) suggest that blockchain will ultimately assume two roles in business process execution: (1) that of a "choreography monitor" which processes messages and checks for conformity, and (2) that of an "active mediator" which coordinates collaboration among the participants. Even in more traditional organisations, permissioned blockchains provide opportunities to improve important functionality such as shareholder engagement systems (Van Der Elst and Lafarre 2019).

2.2 Open source economics and CBPP communities

Blockchain-based governance structures are likely to find a natural future home among various open source online projects and commons-based peer production (CBPP) communities. This is primarily because the distributed and decentralised structure of these projects and communities align with the aforementioned benefits of these governance structures.

The economic incentives associated with open source projects are unique, because individuals who allocate time to work on these projects typically forgo immediate monetary compensation, of the sort which is typically derived from proprietary projects. If these individuals work on these projects as part of their employment, there is also an opportunity cost which accrues to the employer, namely the effort which could have otherwise been put toward the main productive activity associated with the employment relationship, such as completing client work or an academic research project. On the other hand, Lerner and Tirole (2002) suggest that the delayed benefits of working on open source projects are driven largely by a strong signalling incentive to gain the respect and attention of their peers (the ego gratification incentive) and future employers (the career concern incentive). According to this framework, open source projects are more likely to be worked upon if they are highly visible to a large relevant audience, directly showcase the participant's talent, and do not require an inordinate amount of time and effort to complete.

This signalling incentive is deemed to be stronger in open source projects than in closed source projects because of (1) the greater transparency involved, (2) the ability for individual workers to take the initiative without interference from a supervisor, and (3) the development of firm-agnostic workplace skills. It also follows that the signalling incentive is strongest when the intended audience is highly sophisticated and therefore in a position to accurately judge the relevant value of the contributions put forward by the participant in the open source project. Participants in open source projects tend, therefore, to focus on specific issues and tasks which appeal to a niche group of other users. Often, a community will form around each project, which may create further social benefits and satisfaction from participation. Reciprocal altruism is a key factor in the growth of open source communities, as individuals who have freely benefited from the contributions of others to the project feel an obligation to "pay it forward" (Athey and Ellison 2014).

Such open source projects have been categorised as a form of private-collective innovation, in which public goods innovations are privately resourced without any promise of a private return (Gächter, von Krogh, and Haefliger 2010). There is a well-established tradition of private companies wishing to impose some governance structure onto an open source project in order to better reap the benefits of the private-collective innovation process; for example, technology companies regularly release portions of proprietary code to the public as part of a code release strategy (Lerner and Tirole 2005). The use of blockchain-based governance structures for open source projects, due to their natural suitability, will underpin many of the blockchain-based innovations that emerge in coming years.

In reality, open source online projects represent a common type of CBPP community. Peer production is characterised firstly by a decentralised authority to act and secondly by the presence of primarily social (rather than immediately financial) incentive structures (Benkler and Nissenbaum 2006). Benkler and Nissenbaum further point out that CBPP processes typically reflect three structural characteristics. Firstly, the product or the output produced must be highly modular to accommodate the pooled labour of various individual workers, whose efforts are neither homogenous nor centrally organised. As a result, the production process is often highly "incremental and asynchronous" (p. 401). Secondly, they argue that the modules must have heterogenous granularity, in order for both small and large contributions alike to noticeably move the project towards its goal. Thirdly, both quality control and the integration of these individual modules into the final product must be inexpensive.

Effective CBPP projects, therefore, are reliant on the existence of appropriate technology to facilitate the interaction of workers and the completion of individual chunks of work in a decentralised and secure manner. The internet was the first of these enabling technologies, and many CBPP communities work via specialised forums and wiki sites. The transparency and decentralisation inherent in blockchain technology provides the technological capability to move CBPP projects to a higher level of productivity by introducing trust and coordination, non-hierarchical governance, and more sophisticated incentive structures. This in turn may enable existing CBPP communities to scale without introducing a centralised bureaucratic system (Bollier 2015). Further, it may enhance the potential long-term economic impact of highly energetic grassroots movements or projects, which are known to typically suffer from disorganisation, poor information management, and unreliable recordkeeping (Findlay 2017). Blockchain is subsequently set to expand the possibilities of modes of production to more "generative" peer-to-peer networked models, instead of traditional "extractive" and hierarchical models, as explored by Bauwens and Pantazis (2018).

3 Some promising applications for blockchains

Innovative global businesses, start-up companies, governments, and international organisations have been deploying blockchain technology over the last few years across a wide variety of use cases, including digital identity and humanitarian assistance, the energy sector, medicine and healthcare, supply chain management, digital currency, mobile payments, and banking, among other applications.

3.1 Digital identity

The ability to possess a legitimate identity lies at the centre of modern economic systems and is essential to their efficient functioning. An individual's identity provides a means to identify themselves and all their personal assets and possessions. In terms of most economic marketplaces, people need to be reasonably satisfied that the other parties involved in any transaction, firstly, are indeed who they represent themselves to be, and secondly, possess the right to offer the money or goods being offered in exchange, either as the principal owner or as valid agent acting on behalf of the owner.

Typically, the identity of an individual can be represented by a list of details, including full name, date of birth, place of birth, nationality, and perhaps residential address and the details of immediate family. This identity can be further authenticated by the correct verification of unique data, which is generally achieved via one of three methods, as described by Kim and Jeong (2018). These three authentication methods are (1) knowledge-based authentication, for example, a password or a sequence of security questions with unique answers only known to the individual with the correct identity; (2) possession-based authentication, for example, hardware or software authentication devices which provide a unique multicharacter passcode every thirty seconds to the owner of the device; and (3) biometric-based authentication, for example, facial recognition, voice recognition, or fingerprint scanners (Huh and Seo 2018). Most countries keep track of the identities of their citizens, residents, and visa holders via a centralised national identification system which links all these details to a key numerical identifier which is managed by the government, such as a passport number or driver's license. Similar methods are used to identify companies and organisations. All these identifiers and their linked personal details are then stored in centralised government-controlled databases.

This works well enough if the centralised system is reliable. In many parts of the world, however, circumstances such as warfare, corruption, community distrust, and poor management render centralised identity systems unreliable. Recent estimates from the World Bank Identification for Development (ID4D) project conclude that over one billion people around the world remain unable to assert ownership and control over their identity (World Bank 2019). While identification is important across most industries, for some such as the banking sector, know-your-customer (KYC) and anti-money-laundering (AML) regulations impose quite stringent identification requirements, which may in some cases include letters of recommendation, proof of employment, birth certificates, and items such as utility bills. The implications for people who cannot reliably verify their identity are obvious and dire, in many cases rendering them unable to open bank accounts, purchase property, or even vote (Kshetri 2017a). Even individuals who live in relatively more advanced and stable economies experience fragmentation of online identification systems and a duplication of identity verification efforts. For example, a customer must typically undergo a new KYC verification process at each bank at which they wish to open an account. The storage of this data in a centralised database also makes it an attractive target for hackers and corrupt government employees who might gain access to the data and exploit it for their own private benefit.

There are growing efforts to explore the potential of blockchain technology to provide digital identity solutions in economic regions without stable centralised government identification systems. Since many of these regions also suffer from the effects of warfare or other crises, identification systems prove challenging for organisations working to provide aid and funding for rebuilding efforts. For example, the World Food Programme (WFP) has been recently trialling their Building Blocks program, which uses Ethereum blockchain technology to facilitate cash transfers and humanitarian assistance (World Food Programme 2019). Beginning in Pakistan in 2017, the WFP has moved to roll out the technology in refugee camps in Jordan. Many thousands of refugees living in these camps can now purchase groceries by using iris scanners at point-of-sale, which incorporates UNHCR's biometric authentication technology to link their groceries transaction to a record of cash value assigned to them by the WFP and stored in the blockchain. This setup eliminates the financial transaction fees that would occur were the transfers made through traditional banks and reduces the administration costs for the WFP in processing the transactions.

Zwitter and Boisse-Despiaux (2018) suggest that the following four criteria must be met if blockchain technology is to ultimately prove useful in new applications within the context of humanitarian aid.

1 The benefits must outweigh the development and scaling costs of the new technology.
2 Decentralization through distribution, and built-in trust through transparency, must be a necessary feature of the new technology.
3 The digital ledger, as a core of the new technology, needs to be immutable.
4 The features of the new technology must comply with legal norms, humanitarian principles, and professional codes of conduct.

The concept of "qualified money" has been discussed as a natural extension to blockchain-based digital identity solutions, whereby aid funding can be provided which can only be allocated toward specific purposes or used by specific communities. Further, records of all transactions stored on the blockchain provide greater accountability and transparency for donors and may help to restore trust in those operational segments of the not-for-profit sector which have come under fire for corrupt behaviour. This qualified money concept would also help to prevent illicit funding sources from entering the monetary supply chain. Blockchain is likely to become a powerful tool to fight corruption in contexts of systemic poor governance.

Another proven application of the digital identity blockchain use case lies with land registry. Conventionally, records of land ownership are managed by governments, but during crisis events or political unrest these registries can be tampered with or destroyed, leaving scarce records to establish proof of ownership. Kshetri (2017b) notes that the majority of land in rural Africa is unregistered; along with a lack of access to the formal financial system due to difficulties in establishing proof of identity, landlessness is arguably one of the most significant barriers to economic growth. In the case of both land registries and qualified money, however, caution will need to be exercised to ensure that sufficient flexibility is provided to deal with unusual or unforeseen scenarios using a proper degree of good human judgment and discretion. The danger is that overly inflexible processes programmed using automatically executed smart contracts may prove a hindrance in volatile crisis events.

Many other applications of blockchain-based identity systems are being proposed and developed; for example, identification-as-as-service systems (Lee 2017) and digital rights management (DRM) (Ma et al. 2018; Nizamuddin et al. 2019). For digital creators who suffer from copyright violation and a lack of attribution, blockchain could present an economically and technologically viable solution in the near future (Zeilinger 2018). Further challenges remain for blockchain-based identity systems, especially in terms of integrating with existing complex organisational structures and access controls. Solutions such as Uport rely on permissionless blockchains, while solutions such as Sovrin rely on permissioned blockchains. Traditional centralised systems rely on models such as Access Control Lists (ACLs) and Role-based Access Control (RAC) (Zhu and Badr 2018), but these are not as suitable for blockchain-based systems.

3.2 Energy sector

Beyond digital identity applications, the energy sector is also increasingly at the centre stage of applied blockchain technology. Renewable energy sources have substantially increased in recent times as a proportion of total inputs into energy supply, but the incorporation of renewable energy sources has proven a challenge for wholesale markets due to their relative volatility and the inability of the wholesale markets to reflect appropriate price signals in real-time. One proposed methodology to mitigate this issue is the establishment of smart microgrids which form local energy markets (LEMs) for local energy consumers, producers, and prosumers to trade energy at a smaller scale. The advocated advantages include the ability of this marketplace to provide an appropriate near real-time pricing mechanism for the energy supply and demand requirements in a certain geographical locality, and the attainment of energy cost reductions for participants. These LEMs can in theory be designed on a private blockchain, with the flexibility of coping with large numbers of participating agents, managing a one-side or two-sided marketplace, and either centrally set prices or a decentralised auction pricing mechanism (Mengelkamp, Notheisen, et al. 2018).

Blockchain-based LEM microgrid projects have already been established, for example the Brooklyn Microgrid (Mengelkamp, Gärttner, et al. 2018) and the Landau Microgrid Project (LAMP). For the case in which the network is built on the Ethereum blockchain, smart meters which share energy demand and supply information of each prosumer can be treated as light nodes and the provider of the blockchain platform is treated as a full node (Myung and Lee 2018). Specific progress has also been made on blockchain-based P2P electricity trading networks, such as Power Ledger, and there is potential for managing the battery charging networks for electric vehicles in a similar manner (Knirsch, Unterweger, and Engel 2018; Schlund 2018). Indeed, Liu et al. (2019) have developed a proof-of-benefit (PoB) consensus mechanism which is designed specifically for the unique characteristics of P2P electricity trading on a blockchain network. Multi-carrier energy systems, which facilitate the exchange of not only electricity but also heating and cooling, have also been assessed as theoretically feasible to operate fully on an Ethereum blockchain, with appropriate incentive mechanisms for the optimal allocation of local renewable energy generation (Yu, Meeuw, and Wortmann 2018). Other research has focussed on the viability of using blockchain networks to permit more efficient switching of energy suppliers, which would reduce barriers to entry and promote better competition (Hinterstocker et al. 2018).

3.3 Healthcare

The field of medicine and the healthcare sector in general are beginning to discover the potential applications for blockchain. The most promising use case appears to be the technical challenge of developing fully secure, patient-centred electronic health records (EHR) and electronic medical records (EMR) which preserve patient privacy and personal control over their medical data and clinical notes, permit read and write access to authorised medical professionals, and are cross-compatible with a variety of health systems without increasing the human administrative workload (Roman-Belmonte, De la Corte-Rodriguez, and Rodriguez-Merchan 2018). The scalability of the technology may prove a challenge (Zheng et al. 2018). Further, the emergence of geospatial blockchains permits the integration of location data into ledger entries, assisting with the mapping and authentication of events via proof-of-location (Boulos, Wilson, and Clauson 2018). A thorough literature review of blockchain applications in electronic health systems was conducted by Alonso et al. (2019). This review demonstrates that much of the early technological groundwork has been prepared. Once the technology reaches maturity, the sturdiest roadblocks to implementation will involve convincing key stakeholders that there is a need for change and training time-poor staff on how to use the new system.

A second promising medical use case involves the management of large quantities of anonymised public health data for the purpose of sharing knowledge between different medical institutions efficiently and securely with fewer manual processes (Nagasubramanian et al. 2018), providing inputs into health policy in the broader community and the government, and developing new treatments in partnership with third-party commercial and tertiary-sector research institutions. Zhang and Lin (2018) illustrate how this outcome can become feasible using their proposed sharing protocol and a system of two blockchains: one private and one consortium. The technology behind the wider sharing of medical data will also permit secure automation of remote patient monitoring (Griggs et al. 2018). Doubtless, the potential for greater patient involvement and data sharing, if realised, would herald a new era for the healthcare sector (Radanovic and Likic 2018).

3.4 Supply chains

Once upon a time, supply chains were of economic interest to the business community primarily for reducing the costs and the administrative burden associated with the international transportation of intermediate goods. The term "supply chain management" (SCM) was first introduced in the early 1980s, reflecting the increasing challenges associated with managing the scale and complexity of supply chains in modern companies, and resulting in the birth of a new discipline within business management. In today's world, SCM encompasses many business activities, such as forecasting, procurement, logistics, sales, and marketing. To service this need, businesses around the world spend billions of dollars annually on SCM software. Cutting-edge SCM software products now incorporate Industrial Internet of Things features such as cloud computing and various smart sensors featuring technologies based on GPS and RFID (Heiskanen 2017). Two substantial limitations face the current mainstream SCM software products, according to Gao et al. (2018). Firstly, supply chains by nature involve multiple companies which may be reluctant to be fully transparent and share their own commercially sensitive information, and each of which is likely to be running their own SCM software. Secondly, SCM software tends to be a target for hackers who aim to undermine system integrity and gain access to (or delete) information for fraudulent purposes. The manual entry of data also creates a higher risk of losses from human error and corruption. Traditional SCM systems which operate centralised databases are therefore particularly at risk of single-point failure.

The essentially distributed nature of supply chains has lent itself well to the progress of several highly promising business ventures and projects which are developing SCM systems that incorporate blockchain technology. Essentially, these ledgers feature a register of timestamps and tracking information along with product identification, which vastly improves the traceability of the goods and services along the supply chain. This data typically encompasses a minimum of five facts (Saberi et al. 2018): (1) a description of the product's nature, (2) a description of the product's quality, (3) the quantity of the product, (4) the current location of the product, and (5) the current ownership of the product. Naturally, the most pressing economic use case for blockchain-based SCM systems resides with high-value assets, such as diamonds, art, wine, and pharmaceutical products. Emerging companies such as Everledger are capitalising on this specific opportunity by helping track the provenance of high-value assets.

Some of the earlier efforts at developing blockchain-based SCM systems have struggled due to the technical limitations of the earlier-generation blockchains that were based on the proof-of-work protocol. For example, the transaction times and energy needs associated with adding new blocks proved a challenge for high-volume application scenarios. There are also stability challenges associated with using the proof-of-stake protocol in SCM systems, due to the unpredictable demands of blocks (Gao et al. 2018). The potential of blockchain technology in supply chain finance has also been investigated in much detail, with impacts across the various layers of order processing, shipping, invoicing, and payment (Hofmann, Strewe, and Bosia 2017). Innovation is continuing at a rapid pace in blockchain-based supply chains, and the state-of-the-art can be observed by attending relevant industry conferences. The broader adoption of blockchain-based SCM systems across the industry will take time, as further work needs to be done on the technology and regulatory standards (Wang et al. 2019).

3.5 Digital currency

The establishment of cryptocurrencies, decentralised virtual currencies which are not legal tender and rely upon distributed ledger technology, are what made blockchain technology famous, and they still to this day represent the most widely recognised application of blockchains. Since the first cryptocurrency, Bitcoin, emerged in 2009, the number of widely traded cryptocurrencies has grown to several thousand, with a total market capitalisation of several hundred billion dollars. These cryptocurrencies comprise both coins and tokens. The difference is that coins (e.g., Bitcoin, XRP, Litecoin) possess their own unique blockchains, while tokens (e.g., Tether, Chainlink) are built upon pre-existing blockchain infrastructure. For the latter, the most popular in recent times have been based on the ERC-20 tokens, which utilise the Ethereum blockchain (Dannen 2017).

For most cryptocurrencies, their market value is determined by normal interactions of demand and supply. The demand for crypto assets has grown enormously over the last decade in step with the increased awareness of their existence and varied purposes. The characteristics of the supply vary by the crypto asset. For example, outside of their availability on crypto exchanges, some cryptocurrencies can be electronically mined and some have pre-programmed limitations on total supply, such as hard upper limits or time-based releases of new tokens via an air-drop mechanism. In line with what would be expected according to the economic theory for competitive markets with a sole homogeneous good, data suggest that the profitability of mining crypto assets (e.g., Bitcoin) tends towards zero over time (Derks, Gordijn, and Siegmann 2018). One of the recurring practical issues with cryptocurrencies is their relatively high price volatility (Ciaian, Rajcaniova, and Kancs 2016), which led to the introduction of a few "stablecoins" which have their value theoretically pinned to a fiat currency in an effort to provide a more reliable reference value for users. Another issue is the prevalence of hard forks, a governance failure which effectively splits the cryptocurrency into two opposing factions, which ultimately undermine market value and trust (Trump et al. 2018).

There is ongoing debate on whether the treatment of cryptocurrencies by end consumers better supports their primary empirical categorisation as a currency (that is, a financial medium of exchange) or as a security (that is, a tradable financial asset) (Campbell-Verduyn 2018b). The evolving reality appears to support the argument that cryptocurrencies fulfil both purposes. Cryptocurrencies are presently used as currencies in contexts such as online payments for e-commerce products and online casinos. Certain individuals have also been known to use them as a means of anonymous wealth extraction from countries (such as China) which heavily restrict outward capital flows. Cryptocurrencies have been treated as securities by speculators who simply buy them and hold them in the hope that their value will appreciate over time. Further, crypto tokens have played an enormous role in new methods of capital raising, such as initial coin offerings (ICOs), initial exchange offerings (IEOs), and security token offerings (STOs). Would-be investors purchase a certain number of tokens released by the company raising funds, which come with certain privileges and can later be used or traded on the underlying blockchain infrastructure. ICOs were extremely popular between 2016 and 2018, but the industry has been moving away from these and towards IEOs and STOs due to the additional presence of a third party, which reduces the risk of fraud and the heavy regulation imposed on ICOs (Deng, Huang, and Wu 2018). In the case of IEOs, this third party is the crypto exchange, which works to ensure that the tokens meet requirements. STOs go a step further and ensure that the tokens are backed by actual assets, turning the security tokens into proper securities. These can usually only be purchased by accredited investors and require more stringent regulatory processes, such as KYC and AML verification.

Due to the network effects of fiat currencies and the small or negligible marginal benefits of switching, it appears unlikely that traditional currencies will be replaced by cryptocurrencies anytime soon (Nair and Cachanosky 2017). There has, however, been reasonable success at integrating cryptocurrency payment-processing options into ordinary point-of-sale systems, and payment companies such as Mastercard and Visa have been recently developing crypto debit card solutions, which allow consumers to spend their cryptocurrency more freely. The broader adoption of cryptocurrencies treated as currency is likely to occur most efficiently via such integrations into pre-existing ubiquitous technologies. Regulators around the world have increasingly been calling for tighter restrictions on the use of cryptocurrencies due to many instances of fraud and online crime (Kethineni, Cao, and Dodge 2018) and the perceived threat they pose to anti-money-laundering efforts (Campbell-Verduyn 2018a). For an excellent and in-depth introduction to the terminology and history associated with this topic, see Girasa (2018). Despite the threat of fraud and increasingly onerous regulation, many legitimate businesses will continue to operate using cryptocurrencies, and the financial services industry as a whole will continue to face major disruption from the integration of cryptocurrencies (Avgouleas and Kiayias 2019; Holotiuk, Pisani, and Moormann 2019). For many online merchants and similar businesses, the risk of fraud is simply a cost of doing business which can be quantified and minimized, and the advent of cryptocurrency has merely engendered new developments in their fraud prevention strategies (Stringham and Clark 2018).

References

Alonso, Susal Gongora, Jon Arambarri, Miguel Lopez-Coronado, and Isabel de la Torre Diez. 2019. "Proposing New Blockchain Challenges in EHealth." *Journal of Medical Systems* 43(64): 1–7.

Athey, Susan, and Glenn Ellison. 2014. "Dynamics of Open Source Movements." *Journal of Economics and Management Strategy* 23(2): 294–316.

Avgouleas, Emilios, and Aggelos Kiayias. 2019. "The Promise of Blockchain Technology for Global Securities and Derivatives Markets: The New Financial Ecosystem and the 'Holy Grail' of Systemic Risk Containment." *European Business Organization Law Review* 1–30.

Bauwens, Michel, and Alekos Pantazis. 2018. "The Ecosystem of Commons-Based Peer Production and Its Transformative Dynamics." *Sociological Review* 66(2): 302–319.

Benkler, Yochai, and Helen Nissenbaum. 2006. "Commons-Based Peer Production and Virtue." *Journal of Political Philosophy* 14(4): 394–419.

Bheemaiah, Kariappa. 2017. *The Blockchain Alternative: Rethinking Macroeconomic Policy and Economic Theory.* New York: Apress Media.

Bollier, David. 2015. "The Blockchain: A Promising New Infrastructure for Online Commons." Retrieved February 1, 2019, www.bollier.org/blog/blockchain-promising-new-infrastructure-online-commons.

Boulos, Maged N. Kamel, James T. Wilson, and Kevin A. Clauson. 2018. "Geospatial Blockchain: Promises, Challenges, and Scenarios in Health and Healthcare." *International Journal of Health Geographics* 17(25): 1–10.

Campbell-Verduyn, Malcolm. 2018a. "Bitcoin, Crypto-Coins, and Global Anti-Money Laundering Governance." *Crime, Law and Social Change* 69(2): 283–305.

Campbell-Verduyn, Malcolm, ed. 2018b. *Bitcoin and Beyond: Cryptocurrencies, Blockchains, and Global Governance.* New York: Routledge.

Ciaian, Pavel, Miroslava Rajcaniova, and D'Artis Kancs. 2016. "The Digital Agenda of Virtual Currencies: Can BitCoin Become a Global Currency?" *Information Systems and E-Business Management* 14(4): 883–919.

Coase, Ronald Harry. 1937. "The Nature of the Firm." *Economica* 4(16): 386–405.

Corrales, Marcelo, Mark Fenwick, and Helena Haapio, eds. 2019. *Legal Tech, Smart Contracts and Blockchain.* Singapore: Springer.

Dannen, Chris. 2017. *Introducing Ethereum and Solidity: Foundations of Cryptocurrency and Blockchain Programming for Beginners.* New York: Apress Media.

Deng, Hui, Robin Hui Huang, and Qingran Wu. 2018. "The Regulation of Initial Coin Offerings in China: Problems, Prognoses and Prospects." *European Business Organization Law Review* 19(3): 465–502.

Derks, Jona, Jaap Gordijn, and Arjen Siegmann. 2018. "From Chaining Blocks to Breaking Even: A Study on the Profitability of Bitcoin Mining from 2012 to 2016." *Electronic Markets* 28(3): 321–338.

Dhillon, Vikram, David Metcalf, and Max Hooper. 2017. *Blockchain Enabled Applications.* Orlando, FL: Apress Media.

Dixit, Avinash. 2009. "Governance Institutions and Economic Activity." *American Economic Review* 99(1): 5–24.

De Domenico, Manlio, and Andrea Baronchelli. 2019. "The Fragility of Decentralised Trustless Socio-Technical Systems." *EPJ Data Science* 8(2): 1–6.

Drescher, Daniel. 2017. *Blockchain Basics: A Non-Technical Introduction in 25 Steps.* New York: Apress Media.

Eenmaa-Dimitrieva, Helen, and Maria José Schmidt-Kessen. 2019. "Creating Markets in No-Trust Environments: The Law and Economics of Smart Contracts." *Computer Law & Security Review* 35(1): 69–88.

Feng, Libo, Hui Zhang, Wei-Tek Tsai, and Simeng Sun. 2018. "System Architecture for High-Performance Permissioned Blockchains." *Frontiers of Computer Science* 1–15.

Findlay, Cassie. 2017. "Participatory Cultures, Trust Technologies and Decentralisation: Innovation Opportunities for Recordkeeping." *Archives and Manuscripts* 45(3): 176–190.

Gächter, Simon, Georg von Krogh, and Stefan Haefliger. 2010. "Initiating Private-Collective Innovation: The Fragility of Knowledge Sharing." *Research Policy* 39(7): 893–906.

Gao, Zhimin, Lei Xu, Lin Chen, Xi Zhao, Yang Lu, and Weidong Shi. 2018. "CoC: A Unified Distributed Ledger Based Supply Chain Management System." *Journal of Computer Science and Technology* 33(2): 237–248.

Girasa, Rosario. 2018. *Regulation of Cryptocurrencies and Blockchain Technologies: National and International Perspectives*. Cham, Switzerland: Palgrave Macmillan.

Governatori, Guido, Florian Idelberger, Zoran Milosevic, Regis Riveret, Giovanni Sartor, and Xiwei Xu. 2018. "On Legal Contracts, Imperative and Declarative Smart Contracts, and Blockchain Systems." *Artificial Intelligence and Law* 26(4): 377–409.

Griggs, Kristen N., Olya Ossipova, Christopher P. Kohlios, Alessandro N. Baccarini, Emily A. Howson, and Thaier Hayajneh. 2018. "Healthcare Blockchain System Using Smart Contracts for Secure Automated Remote Patient Monitoring." *Journal of Medical Systems* 42(130): 1–7.

Heiskanen, Aarni. 2017. "The Technology of Trust: How the Internet of Things and Blockchain Could Usher in a New Era of Construction Productivity." *Construction Research and Innovation* 8(2): 66–70.

Herian, Robert. 2018. "Taking Blockchain Seriously." *Law and Critique* 29(2): 163–171.

Hinterstocker, Michael, Florian Haberkorn, Andreas Zeiselmair, and Serafin Von Roon. 2018. "Faster Switching of Energy Suppliers – a Blockchain-Based Approach." *Energy Informatics* 1(Suppl 1)(42): 417–422.

Hofmann, Erik, Urs Magnus Strewe, and Nicola Bosia. 2017. *Supply Chain Finance and Blockchain Technology: The Case of Reverse Securitisation*. Cham, Switzerland: Springer.

Holotiuk, Friedrich, Francesco Pisani, and Jürgen Moormann. 2019. "Radicalness of Blockchain: An Assessment Based on Its Impact on the Payments Industry." *Technology Analysis & Strategic Management* 1–14.

Hsieh, Ying-Ying, Jean-Philippe Vergne, Philip Anderson, Karim Lakhani, and Markus Reitzig. 2018. "Bitcoin and the Rise of Decentralized Autonomous Organizations." *Journal of Organization Design* 7(14): 1–16.

Huh, Jun-Ho, and Kyungryong Seo. 2018. "Blockchain-Based Mobile Fingerprint Verification and Automatic Log-in Platform for Future Computing." *The Journal of Supercomputing* 1–17.

Jamison, Mark A., and Palveshey Tariq. 2018. "Five Things Regulators Should Know about Blockchain (and Three Myths to Forget)." *The Electricity Journal* 31(9): 20–23.

Käll, Jannice. 2018. "Blockchain Control." *Law and Critique* 29(2): 133–140.

Kethineni, Sesha, Ying Cao, and Cassandra Dodge. 2018. "Use of Bitcoin in Darknet Markets: Examining Facilitative Factors on Bitcoin-Related Crimes." *American Journal of Criminal Justice* 43(2): 141–157.

Kim, Hyun-Woo, and Young-Sik Jeong. 2018. "Secure Authentication-Management Human-centric Scheme for Trusting Personal Resource Information on Mobile Cloud Computing with Blockchain." *Human-Centric Computing and Information Sciences* 8(11): 1–13.

Knirsch, Fabian, Andreas Unterweger, and Dominik Engel. 2018. "Privacy-Preserving Blockchain-Based Electric Vehicle Charging with Dynamic Tariff Decisions." *Computer Science – Research and Development* 33(1): 71–79.

Kshetri, Nir. 2017a. "Potential Roles of Blockchain in Fighting Poverty and Reducing Financial Exclusion in the Global South." *Journal of Global Information Technology Management* 20(4): 201–204.

Kshetri, Nir. 2017b. "Will Blockchain Emerge as a Tool to Break the Poverty Chain in the Global South?" *Third World Quarterly* 38(8): 1710–1732.

Lee, Jong-Hyouk. 2017. "BIDaaS: Blockchain Based ID As a Service." *IEEE Access* 6: 2274–2278.

Lerner, Josh, and Jean Tirole. 2002. "Some Simple Economics of Open Source." *The Journal of Industrial Economics* 50(2): 197–234.

Lerner, Josh, and Jean Tirole. 2005. "The Economics of Technology Sharing: Open Source and Beyond." *Journal of Economic Perspectives* 19(2): 99–120.

Liu, Chao, Kok Keong Chai, Xiaoshuai Zhang, and Yue Chen. 2019. "Peer-to-Peer Electricity Trading System : Smart Contracts Based Proof-of- Benefit Consensus Protocol." *Wireless Networks* 1–12.

Lu, Yang. 2018. "Blockchain and the Related Issues: A Review of Current Research Topics." *Journal of Management Analytics* 5(4): 231–255.

Ma, Zhaofeng, Ming Jiang, Hongmin Gao, and Zhen Wang. 2018. "Blockchain for Digital Rights Management." *Future Generation Computer Systems* 89: 746–764.

Mengelkamp, Esther, J. Gärttner, K. Rock, S. Kessler, L. Orsini, and C. Weinhardt. 2018. "Designing Microgrid Energy Markets: A Case Study: The Brooklyn Microgrid." *Applied Energy* 210: 870–880.

Mengelkamp, Esther, Benedikt Notheisen, Carolin Beer, David Dauer, and Christof Weinhardt. 2018. "A Blockchain-Based Smart Grid: Towards Sustainable Local Energy Markets." *Computer Science – Research and Development* 33(1): 207–214.

Milgrom, P. R., and J. Roberts. 1992. *Economics, Organization and Management.* Englewood Cliffs, NJ: Prentice-Hall.

Moyano, Parra, and Omri Ross. 2017. "KYC Optimization Using Distributed Ledger Technology." *Business & Information Systems Engineering* 59(6): 411–423.

Myung, Sein, and Jong-Hyouk Lee. 2018. "Ethereum Smart Contract-Based Automated Power Trading Algorithm in a Microgrid Environment." *The Journal of Supercomputing* 1–11.

Nagasubramanian, Gayathri, Rakesh Kumar Sakthivel, Rizwan Patan, Amir H. Gandomi, Muthuramalingam Sankayya, and Balamurugan Balusamy. 2018. "Securing E-Health Records Using Keyless Signature Infrastructure Blockchain Technology in the Cloud." *Neural Computing and Applications* 1–9.

Nair, Malavika, and Nicolás Cachanosky. 2017. "Bitcoin and Entrepreneurship: Breaking the Network Effect." *The Review of Austrian Economics* 30(3): 263–275.

Nizamuddin, Nishara, Haya Hasan, Khaled Salah, and Razi Iqbal. 2019. "Blockchain-Based Framework for Protecting Author Royalty of Digital Assets." *Arabian Journal for Science and Engineering* 1–18.

O'Dair, Marcus. 2019. *Distributed Creativity: How Blockchain Technology Will Transform the Creative Economy.* Cham, Switzerland: Palgrave Macmillan.

Pathak, Nishith, and Anurag Bhandari. 2018. *IoT, AI, and Blockchain for. NET: Building a next-Generation Application from the Ground Up.* New York: Apress Media.

Radanovic, Igor, and Robert Likic. 2018. "Opportunities for Use of Blockchain Technology in Medicine." *Applied Health Economics and Health Policy* 16(5): 583–590.

Rimba, Paul, An Binh Tran, Ingo Weber, Mark Staples, Alexander Ponomarev, and Xiwei Xu. 2018. "Quantifying the Cost of Distrust: Comparing Blockchain and Cloud Services for Business Process Execution." *Information Systems Frontiers* 1–19.

Risius, Marten, and Kai Spohrer. 2017. "A Blockchain Research Framework." *Business & Information Systems Engineering* 59(6): 385–409.

Roman-Belmonte, Juan M., Hortensia De la Corte-Rodriguez, and E. Carlos Rodriguez-Merchan. 2018. "How Blockchain Technology Can Change Medicine." *Postgraduate Medicine* 130(4): 420–427.

Saberi, Sara, Mahtab Kouhizadeh, Joseph Sarkis, and Lejia Shen. 2018. "Blockchain Technology and Its Relationships to Sustainable Supply Chain Management." *International Journal of Production Research* 1–19.

Savelyev, Alexander. 2017. "Contract Law 2.0: 'Smart' Contracts as the Beginning of the End of Classic Contract Law." *Information & Communications Technology Law* 26(2): 116–134.

Schlund, Jonas. 2018. "Blockchain-Based Orchestration of Distributed Assets in Electrical Power Systems." *Energy Informatics* 1(Suppl 1)(39): 411–416.

Stringham, Edward Peter. 2017. "The Fable of the Leeches, or: The Single Most Unrealistic Positive Assumption of Most Economists." *The Review of Austrian Economics* 30(4): 401–413.

Stringham, Edward Peter, and J. R. Clark. 2018. "The Crucial Role of Financial Intermediaries for Facilitating Trade among Strangers." *The Review of Austrian Economics* 1–13.

Takagi, Soichiro. 2017. "Organizational Impact of Blockchain through Decentralized Autonomous Organizations." *The International Journal of Economic Policy Studies* 12: 22–41.

Trump, Benjamin D., Emily Wells, Joshua Trump, and Igor Linkov. 2018. "Cryptocurrency: Governance for What Was Meant to Be Ungovernable." *Environment Systems and Decisions* 38(3): 426–430.

Unsworth, Rory. 2019. "Smart Contract This! An Assessment of the Contractual Landscape and the Herculean Challenges It Currently Presents for 'Self-Executing' Contracts." Pp. 17–61 in *Legal Tech, Smart Contracts and Blockchain*, edited by M. Corrales, M. Fenwick, and H. Haapio. Singapore: Springer.

Van Der Elst, Christoph, and Anne Lafarre. 2019. "Blockchain and Smart Contracting for the Shareholder Community." *European Business Organization Law Review* 1–27.

Wang, Huaiqing, Kun Chen, and Dongming Xu. 2016. "A Maturity Model for Blockchain Adoption." *Financial Innovation* 2(12): 1–5.

Wang, Yingli, Meita Singgih, Jingyao Wang, and Mihaela Rit. 2019. "Making Sense of Blockchain Technology: How Will It Transform Supply Chains?" *International Journal of Production Economics* 211: 221–236.

Werbach, Kevin. 2018. "Trust, but Verify: Why the Blockchain." *Berkeley Technology Law Journal* 33(2): 487–550.

Williamson, O. E. 1975. *Markets and Hierarchies, Analysis and Antitrust Implications: A Study in the Economics of Internal Organization.* New York: Free Press.

World Bank. 2019. "World Bank ID4D Dataset." https://id4d.worldbank.org/global-dataset.

World Food Programme. 2019. "World Food Programme Building Blocks: Blockchain for Zero Hunger." https://innovation.wfp.org/project/building-blocks.

Yu, Qianchen, Arne Meeuw, and Felix Wortmann. 2018. "Design and Implementation of a Blockchain Multi-Energy System." *Energy Informatics* 1(Suppl 1)(17): 311–318.

Zeilinger, Martin. 2018. "Digital Art as 'Monetised Graphics': Enforcing Intellectual Property on the Blockchain." *Philosophy & Technology* 31(1): 15–41.

Zhang, Aiqing, and Xiaodong Lin. 2018. "Towards Secure and Privacy-Preserving Data Sharing in e-Health Systems via Consortium Blockchain." *Journal of Medical Systems* 42(140): 1–18.

Zheng, Bao-Kun, Lie-Huang Zhu, Meng Shen, Feng Gao, Chuan Zhang, Yan-Dong Li, and Jing Yang. 2018. "Scalable and Privacy-Preserving Data Sharing Based on Blockchain." *Journal of Computer Science and Technology* 33(3): 557–567.

Zhu, Xiaoyang, and Youakim Badr. 2018. "Identity Management Systems for the Internet of Things: A Survey Towards Blockchain Solutions." *Sensors* 18(12): 1–18.

Zhu, Yan, Khaled Riad, Ruiqi Guo, Guohua Gan, and Rongquan Feng. 2018. "New Instant Confirmation Mechanism Based on Interactive Incontestable Signature in Consortium Blockchain." *Frontiers of Computer Science* 1–16.

Zwitter, Andrej, and Mathilde Boisse-Despiaux. 2018. "Blockchain for Humanitarian Action and Development Aid." *Journal of International Humanitarian Action* 3(16): 1–7.

PART V

Discussion and conclusions

Harnessing the Fourth Industrial Revolution in systems building

11

THE NEW ECONOMY

Opportunities, challenges, and what to do about them

In the preceding chapters we have applied the Brisbane Club model of socioeconomic systems as a complex evolving network formed by individuals acting on the basis of their socioeconomic environment and psychology and enabled by the technologies available to them to analyse the mega-technologies of the Fourth Industrial Revolution. This differentiates our analysis from others as it grounds our analysis in psychological, institutional, and evolutionary economics. We applied this model to understand the impacts the internet, artificial intelligence, and blockchain have as the core mega-technologies of the Fourth Industrial Revolution. An analysis of the nature of each technology and its relationship to the psychological process allowed us to understand the behavioural change it might bring about, and we were able to place this at the core of a more macroscopic perspective on how each might bring about disruption and then re-coordination of the socioeconomic system as the Fourth Industrial Revolution progresses.

In this chapter we will combine these analyses of the mega-technologies of the Fourth Industrial Revolution to project a perspective on the likely form and dynamics of the economy it will shape. In doing this we will also draw together our analysis of the various opportunities and challenges presented by the mega-technologies of the Fourth Industrial Revolution to develop a profile of the trends to which individuals and groups will become exposed. We will see that the Fourth Industrial Revolution presents some profound challenges to be sure in terms of the struggle for attention in hyper-competitive global markets, the expanding scope for automation of even the most traditionally secure jobs, and the coordination of responses on the part of individuals and communities to an increasingly chaotic socioeconomic system. But we will also see that the Fourth Industrial Revolution presents profound opportunities for hyper-growth in global markets, for astounding production possibilities to realise these opportunities with a minimum of labour, and for the development of institutional governance solutions to problems facing individuals and their communities by privatised institutional entrepreneurship. We will draw on the behavioural model at the core of the Brisbane Club model in particular, but also its institutional model, to develop recommendations about the strategies which might be formulated by individuals and groups to seize opportunities and mitigate the challenges presented by the Fourth Industrial Revolution. We will see that individuals, groups and communities can take steps to position themselves to seize opportunities presented by the Fourth Industrial Revolution and mitigate challenges by pursuing a generalist education which gives them a moral and practical knowledge which displays what Nassim Nicholas Taleb (2012) calls *antifragility*. We will see that communities can position themselves to seize opportunities presented by the Fourth Industrial Revolution by harnessing institutional technologies to develop institutional governance solutions to the challenges presented to them. We will, in short, chart a map of the likely future, and how individuals, groups, and communities can take action to ensure that that future is closer to a cornucopian utopia than a techno-feudal dystopia.

We will proceed as follows. First, we will draw together our analysis of the various mega-technologies of the Fourth Industrial Revolution in order to project the likely form and dynamics of the economy it will create. We will then draw on this analysis to present a profile of the challenges and opportunities faced by individuals, groups, and communities in the Fourth Industrial Revolution. We will then make use of the Brisbane Club model to derive a view on what individuals and communities can do to prepare themselves to mitigate the challenges posed by the Fourth Industrial Revolution and position themselves to seize the opportunities it presents. We will conclude by considering the "system" of sorts we derive for orienting oneself to the challenges and opportunities we face in the future economy.

1 The new economy: global markets and the struggle for attention, utopia with a hint of plutocracy, and privatised rules

The Fourth Industrial Revolution is characterised by three mega-technologies which drive a host of applications which are transforming economic systems. The socioeconomic system will be transformed by these mega-technologies in ways that we can project by drawing together our analyses of them using the Brisbane Club model of socioeconomic systems as complex evolving networks formed by individuals acting on the basis of their psychology and socioeconomic environment. Drawing these analyses together, we can see that the economy of the Fourth Industrial Revolution is one characterised by global markets subject to hyper-competition and growth as well as an all-important struggle for the attention of prospective buyers, stupendous production possibilities afforded by the in-principle automation of but a select few classes of human labour, and the increasing potential for privatised institutional governance of socioeconomic interaction.

In our first analytical chapter we considered the mega-technology of the internet, which is enabling astounding capabilities in communication, social media, Big

Data, apps, the Internet of Things, augmented reality, and platforms for market interaction. In our second analytical chapter we considered the mega-technology of artificial intelligence endowed with machine learning, which is enabling profound capabilities by allowing the automation of any human labour that can be reduced to an algorithm in the "drone" economy to biomedical science and practice. In our third analytical chapter we considered the mega-technology of blockchain, which is enabling entrepreneurial action in the design and development of privatised, decentralised systems of institutional governance for platforms of monetary and contractual interaction to identity. In each case, the Brisbane Club model allowed us to understand the current effects of these technologies and to project the ongoing effects they are likely to have as the Fourth Industrial Revolution progresses.

The immediate effect of the internet is to allow instant communication at effectively zero marginal cost with anyone, anywhere with an internet connection, which facilitates *search* on a truly global scale. This in turn enables truly global markets to emerge, facilitating value-creating exchange which is increasingly unrestricted by geographical locality. Where existing connective structures in the economy constitute the exchange of goods and services for which substitutes exist in global markets, the effect of the internet is to introduce a degree of hyper-competition, for now connections will only be formed around those individuals and groups which offer the *globally* best price-attribute mix. Where existing structures in the economy constitute the exchange of goods and services for which substitutes do *not* exist, however, the effect of the internet is to enable hyper-growth in newly globalised markets. Both of these dynamics, however, rely on the degree to which opportunities for exchange in global markets will be revealed by internet-enabled search to the attention of buyers. Thus, *attention* becomes the most valuable commodity in the socioeconomic system, so to speak, deciding whether the challenges of hyper-competition or the opportunities for hyper-growth enabled by the internet will be realised. Where attention can be drawn to opportunities in global markets, we will observe disruption of existing structures in the economy as value-creating connections are transferred, and then re-coordination around those individuals and groups who can successfully command attention and/or seize opportunities for hyper-growth by offering world-class or unique niche products and services. Such dynamics are likely to occur on a drastically shorter timescale than we have been accustomed to with such rapid communication, with growth and emergence occurring on timescales of months if not weeks rather than years or decades.

Artificial intelligence is the technology, we could say, that we have made in our own image. It is a technology which mimics not only human action, but human action guided by thought. It offers profound opportunities for expanding production capabilities possible with a minimum of labour input insofar as it offers a substitute for any human labour which can be reduced to an algorithm, and such a substitute as can significantly expand on the production possibilities of such labour. We cannot lightly dismiss the possibility of mass unemployment as artificial intelligence emerges, with value-creating connections between human labour and employers being transferred to the developers of artificial intelligence software and hardware. But there are limits to the substitutability of artificial intelligence for human labour, which means there is a future for certain classes of work, and the effect of artificial intelligence is to *complement* these classes and dramatically expand the range of value-creating connective structures they can form. Artificial intelligence in its current form will *complement*, rather than be substituted for, human labour where production plans require the exercising of *judgment*, deep *creativity* in technology and strategy development, and subtle and sophisticated *tacit knowledge* of the social and physical worlds which are difficult to express. We are likely to observe disruption of existing connective structures in the socioeconomic system as artificial intelligence is substituted for that human labour for which it can substitute, and then re-coordination around those individuals and groups whose capabilities for labour supply lie within the classes which are complemented by artificial intelligence. The production capabilities of such groups of workers enabled by artificial intelligence will be little short of profound and will offer possibilities for forming value-creating exchange connections on a scale hitherto unimaginable.

Blockchain is a somewhat unusual technology insofar as it is an *institutional* technology which facilitates the privatised design and development of decentralised systems of institutional governance. It offers the potential for a new era of community-based solutions to problems which require institutional governance. To implement a substitution between existing platforms subject to institutional governance and new blockchain-based platforms subject to privatised, decentralised institutional governance emergent through entrepreneurial action will require the formation and coordination of expectations concerning the meeting of institutional requirements and offering of complementarities by these platforms. The disruption brought about by this technology will in the first instance be at the level of institutional systems of governance – with the connective structure of the economy not particularly changing so much as the institutional context in which it is formed. But where individuals, groups, and communities can implement substitution of existing institutional systems for bespoke institutional systems emergent from privatised entrepreneurial action, we may see the emergence of a new value-creating structure to address lacunae those groups wish to see addressed facilitated by blockchain-based institutional technology. In a re-coordinated socioeconomic system, we are likely to see a greater variety of bespoke institutional arrangements than we are hitherto accustomed to, including privatised blockchain-based systems designed and developed by individuals, groups, and communities to provide institutional governance for the platforms on which they interact.

Each of these mega-technologies will interact with the others as well to create the new socioeconomic system shaped by the Fourth Industrial Revolution. The internet enables platforms for truly global marketplaces and *agoras* to emerge in which socioeconomic interaction takes place. But it also enables blockchain, which allows for the emergence of systems of institutional governance bespoke to those platforms and the challenges faced by individuals, communities, and groups on them. Blockchain thus interacts with the internet to provide the necessary and sufficient conditions for functioning global platforms for socioeconomic interaction to emerge where there is a current clash of national and sub-national jurisdictions which prevent effective governance solutions from emerging. Likewise, the internet enables artificial intelligences to be distributed over large geographical areas where they may be embedded within an Internet of Things to vastly improve the efficiency of production systems through automation and expanded information processing capabilities. The internet also generates and facilitates the distribution of Big Data, which enables machine learning algorithms and expands the capabilities for artificial intelligence programs to be calibrated, as well as the discovery of new relationships and correlations. Just as it can enable an Internet of Things, which improves the efficiency of production systems, artificial intelligence may be embedded within an Internet of Things within a blockchain-based platform so as to automate interactions within it and implement the system of institutional governance which emerges from its protocols.

So, as the mega-technologies of the internet, artificial intelligence, and blockchain, as well as their many applications, emerge and power the Fourth Industrial Revolution, we will enter an economy which is radically different to that which we are accustomed to, even after some decades of their emergence. We are likely to observe internet-based platforms emerging on a global scale for socioeconomic interaction which are subject to institutional governance designed and developed bespoke by individuals, groups, and communities who interact within them using blockchain technology. We are likely to observe substantial automation of production, exchange, and governance systems within these platforms enabled by artificial intelligence, to the extent that we are likely to see all but a quite restricted class of labour substituted by it. This quite restricted class of labour, that which can provide the necessary exercising of *judgment*, deep *creativity* in technology and strategy development, and subtle and sophisticated *tacit knowledge* of the social and physical worlds will, however, as a result be capable of supporting vast global networks of value-creating exchange. The building of such networks, however, will hinge upon success in the struggle to hold *attention* and success in providing either the globally best mix of prices and attributes in goods and services, or a unique niche product for which no substitutes are available. It will be an economy in constant, rapid flux from hyper-competition and hyper-growth. But it will also be an economy in which individuals, groups, and communities have the communication, production, and institutional technologies which enable them to try to build systems of value-creating exchanges as never before.

Our analysis gives reasons to contradict *both* of the usual perspectives on technological progress on the scale of an industrial revolution. For optimists, our analysis poses a range of challenges that need to be overcome, serious challenges in the form of the significant difficulties which will likely be faced by individuals, groups, and communities living in the Fourth Industrial Revolution. For pessimists, however, our analysis also poses challenges, by suggesting that the possibilities for individuals, groups, and communities living in the Fourth Industrial Revolution to prosper and satisfy material needs with ease are profound. We will now proceed to elaborate on the challenges and opportunities presented by the likely socioeconomic system to emerge from the transformations of the Fourth Industrial Revolution, and then provide some practical analysis using the Brisbane Club model of how the former might be mitigated, and the latter seized.

2 Opportunities and challenges in the new economy

The economy of the Fourth Industrial Revolution is one of global platforms for socioeconomic interaction, enabled by automated and distributed production systems of extraordinary productivity and bespoke systems of institutional governance. It is also one where the ability to build value-creating networks of socioeconomic interaction in this way is contingent on the ability to command scarce attention; discover a talent for value-creation which is globally unique, which requires the exercising of judgment, creativity, or tacit knowledge; and solve coordination problems in the adoption of institutional technologies. It presents both opportunities and challenges which can be approached from the perspective of systems-building.

Creating value in socioeconomic systems, from the perspective of the Brisbane Club model, is properly approached as a process of system-building by the forming of connections (Foster, 2005; Earl and Wakeley, 2010). Organisations become what Foster (2006) calls a "production graph" – a network of interactions which support particular production capabilities – and these are nested within a network of interactions where the outputs of that production system are exchanged with others. The entrepreneur becomes a constructor of connections within the organisation to support its production capabilities, outside of the organisation to support its value-generation in economic systems, and perhaps most importantly within the mind (Earl, 2003). In order to build systems of value-creating connections in socioeconomic systems, it is necessary for the entrepreneur to build *knowledge* of how and why to engage in the formation of those connections within their own mind, within the mind of those with whom they are coordinating in a group or community to support production, and within the mind of those for whom value will be created by their outputs (Markey-Towler, 2018a).

The mega-technologies of the Fourth Industrial Revolution offer profound opportunities for system-building in the socioeconomic systems they will transform. Systems of value-generating exchange may be built within platforms which support truly global markets enabled by the internet as a communications technology. The production of goods and services to be exchanged within those platforms may be supported with next to no labour within organisations enabled by artificial intelligence operating within an Internet of Things with access to Big Data. Those value creating exchanges and production systems may be formed within bespoke institutional systems enabled by blockchains which support their formation rather than constrain them. Not only will the sheer scale of the systems which might be supported significantly increase in the age of internet, artificial intelligence, and blockchain, but so will the efficiency of their function in terms of the allocation of resources and the efficacy of governance aimed at supporting that allocation.

Individuals, groups, and communities have never before been afforded such capabilities for building value-generating systems of exchange as are offered by the mega-technologies of the Fourth Industrial Revolution.

However, the mega-technologies of the Fourth Industrial Revolution also present serious challenges for system-building in the socioeconomic systems they will transform. Systems of value-generating exchange can only be built within global markets supported by internet-enabled platforms if the *attention* of those for whom value might be created can be sufficiently commanded, which takes significant capabilities in terms of resources dedicated to communication. They can also be built if they are substantially inoculated from the effects of hyper-competition within these platforms by consisting of exchanges of goods and services for which available substitutes do not readily exist. Further, these systems do not particularly require labour for their operation given the extent to which the production systems which support them may be automated. Individuals, groups, and communities increasingly will only be able to obtain remunerative work within these production systems if they can provide the necessary exercising of *judgment*, deep *creativity* in technology and strategy development, and subtle and sophisticated *tacit knowledge* of the social and physical worlds which such systems require. Developing institutional governance solutions to the problems that might be thus presented face significant challenges in terms of forming and coordinating expectations about the requirements those systems meet and complementarities they offer. So while opportunities exist for realising value-creating systems on a hitherto unimaginable scale in the Fourth Industrial Revolution, individuals, groups, and communities face significant challenges in developing the characteristics which would allow them to realise these opportunities.

The opportunities we have identified, if seized, will make life in the Fourth Industrial Revolution seductively utopian, so it will be highly desirable for us to discover how they might be seized. The challenges presented, on the other hand, raise the spectre of a techno-feudal dystopia, so it will be even more desirable for us to discover how they might be mitigated. We can now use the Brisbane Club model as a framework for developing practical insight into how strategies might be developed to seize the former and mitigate the latter, and, when applied, facilitate the building of global systems of value-generating networks with astounding scope.

3 Strategies for seizing opportunities and mitigating challenges

Seizing opportunities in the Fourth Industrial Revolution entails the building systems of value-creating exchange enabled by the mega-technologies which drive it, and overcoming the challenges they present even while they enable those opportunities. It entails the harnessing of the global platforms of the internet, the production capabilities of artificial intelligence, and the institutional governance of blockchain to construct networks of value-creating exchange on global scales. It entails the overcoming of challenges presented by the criticality of succeeding in the struggle for attention, the hyper-competition of global markets, the potential for automation of all but a highly restricted class of labour, and the coordination of expectations of institutional governance. It requires the building of networks of value-creating connections within production organisations which can support networks of value-creating exchange in global markets, and that requires the construction of connections within *knowledge* of how and why to form those connections on both sides of the market and within the organisation.

Seizing these opportunities and mitigating these challenges is therefore, as Loasby (2001, 2002) recognised in seminal contributions to the Brisbane Club perspective, a problem largely of developing *knowledge* of how and why to organise socioeconomic interactions to achieve some end. Building systems of value-creating networks within economic systems, Earl (2006) argued in a key contribution, is predicated upon knowledge of how to meet *capability pre-requisites* imposed by non-substitutabilities arising from production technology and consumer lifestyles so that complementarities can be realised which create a valuable good or service. That is to say, production technologies impose certain requirements on production processes such that particular widgets need to be made available to certain elements of the organisation at particular times and in particular conditions before they can produce a good or service which is valuable. When those capability pre-requisites are met, the organisation can function to build complementarities through various parts of the production process to make the good or service more valuable for the customer. The logistical and organisational knowledge of how those capability pre-requisites can be met and organisational functions coordinated so that complementarities can be realised therefore needs to be built and coordinated across the organisation in order for value-creating networks of exchange can be built.

Seizing the opportunities and mitigating the challenges presented by the Fourth Industrial Revolution does not only consist of the building of systems of value-creating exchange within socioeconomic networks, but also *maintaining* those systems. We have seen, in the context of the micro-meso-macro perspective, that economies are constantly subject to disruption as new technologies emerge which are based on mega-technologies such as those of the Fourth Industrial Revolution. Networks of value-creating exchange within economic systems are constantly subject to disruptive pressures, and the organisations within them require what Teece, Pisano and Shuen (1997) famously called "dynamic capabilities," the ability to reorganise to integrate responses to those disruptive pressures. We have seen that such disruption is likely to occur on an ever more regular and rapid basis in global markets enabled by the internet. Economic systems are both dynamically and computationally complex (Rosser and Rosser, 2017; Herrmann-Pillath, 2008), and so the disruption which presents challenges for maintaining the systems of value-creating exchange built within socioeconomic networks is likely to present itself in the form of what Taleb (2007) famously calls "Black Swan" events. Black Swan events emerge from uncertainty about which no expectations are constructed – they are quite unforeseen and unforeseeable. In order to maintain the systems of value-creating exchange built within socioeconomic networks then, those systems must be *at least* robust enough to manage uncertainty and the potential for disruption. But it is better still if those systems display what Taleb (2012) calls *antifragility*. Antifragile systems of value-creating exchange will *grow* in response to uncertainty and Black Swan events.

Action can be taken to overcome the challenges to realising these opportunities for building and maintaining value-creating systems at the level of the individual, at the level of the group, and at the level of the community. At the level of the individual, the problem is a primarily psychological one of developing one's knowledge and cultivating an antifragile personality so that one may occupy a position in a value-creating system of exchange and maintain that system. At the level of the group, the problem is an organisational one of ensuring production systems are organised to secure capability pre-requisites which allow for complementarities to be exploited and ensuring the organisation has an antifragile mindset which allows production systems to be coordinated and maintained. At the level of the community, the problem is an institutional one of harnessing blockchain as an institutional technology to provide governance which enables value-creation and distribution to proceed by forming and coordinating expectations of the solutions it will offer.

3.1 At the level of the individual: seek a "classical" education and cultivate the antifragile personality

The individual faces the most significant challenges to seizing opportunities to build value-creating networks of exchange as the mega-technologies of the Fourth Industrial Revolution continue to emerge. The individual faces challenges to building systems of value-creating connections presented by the necessity of commanding attention in global markets, discovering a unique talent for providing goods and services, and coordinating the formation of networks within organisational systems and the emergence of institutions which solve governance problems. The individual cannot build networks in global markets without the ability to command attention, discover a unique talent for providing goods and services, or coordinate production organisations and the governance to which they are subject – they will simply be lost in the sea of information, overwhelmed by world-class competition, and unable to produce goods or services within a stable governance environment. But perhaps most importantly, the individual faces challenges to building systems of value-creating connections presented by the necessity of being able to exercise *judgment*, display deep *creativity* in technology and strategy development, and apply subtle and sophisticated *tacit knowledge* of the social and physical worlds. Without these abilities, the individual will not be able to supply remunerative labour for long before they are substituted for an artificial intelligence.

What the Brisbane Club suggests (and here again we draw substantially on research published elsewhere by Markey-Towler, 2018b) is that, interestingly, the individual places themselves well to overcome these challenges and seize the opportunities presented by the Fourth Industrial Revolution by seeking to cultivate what used to be called a "classical" education on an ongoing basis. The "classical" education is the education which endows the student with a highly general and expansive knowledge of the physical and social worlds. It includes a scientific and mathematical education, but also an education in history, philosophy, languages, literature, music, art, and physical activity. This, the Brisbane Club model suggests, presents the individual with the knowledge requisite for building systems of value-creating exchange, but it also helps them cultivate an "antifragile personality," which helps them to *maintain* antifragile systems of value-generating exchange.

The classical education has an obvious and straightforward impact on the knowledge of the individual, which allows them to command attention and coordinate production organisations and institutions, but it also makes a somewhat more subtle contribution to the discovery of a unique talent. A classical education by its nature includes an education in rhetoric coupled with artistic design, or in modernity what we would call marketing. It also includes an education in human organisation and institutions by virtue of its inclusion of historical and philosophical study. But further, as Peter Thiel (2014) has argued, the ability to avoid competition by discovering a unique talent for producing goods and services for which no substitutes exist is not a matter of specialisation in a particular niche as we might typically think. This form of uniqueness relies on being the global best. Rather, discovering a unique talent is a matter of discovering a unique *combination* of talents for producing goods and services which emerges from a set of knowledge idiosyncratic to the individual. Amusingly enough, Scott Adams (in his 2013 memoir) argues for the value of this approach to discovering a unique talent with his concept of the "talent stack." The classical education provides the basic general knowledge which, further connected together in a particular idiosyncratic way, can support the development of a unique knowledge set which provides the basis for a unique talent.

The major challenge the individual faces in seizing opportunities to build value-creating systems in the Fourth Industrial Revolution – being able to exercise *judgment*, display deep *creativity*, and apply subtle and sophisticated *tacit knowledge* – is also ameliorated significantly by the general knowledge a classical education brings. In the case of the necessity of being able to apply subtle and sophisticated *tacit knowledge* of the social and physical worlds, the effect is direct – tacit knowledge of the physical world is developed by the physical education a classical education includes, and of the social world by the humanistic education brought by the study of history, literature, art, and philosophy. In the case of the necessity of being able to exercise judgment and display deep creativity in technology and strategy development, the contribution is more subtle.

Arthur Koestler (1964), as we have seen, argued that creativity manifests in the formation of "bisociations" – connections between objects and events in the world which hitherto did not exist. If we understand judgment to be the formation of connections between statements and their "truth values," then we understand such bisociations to also be the manifestation of exercising judgment. Now about the genesis of these connections we can say little. They are by their nature beyond the delimitations of process and procedure. However, about the likelihood of their *incorporation* into the mind and personal knowledge which guides behaviour, we can say more, and it is here that the classical education and the general knowledge it creates contributes to the ability of the individual to exercise judgment and display deep creativity in technology and strategy development. We know from the psychological model at the core of the Brisbane Club perspective that the likelihood that connections which would constitute deep creativity or the exercise of judgment, were they to be incorporated into the mind, will be incorporated into the mind the fewer of them there are, the greater the extent to which they build on existing connections at the periphery of mental networks, and the less they contradict ideas called to mind in any particular environment.

A classical education endows an individual with a general knowledge as a basis for the development of future knowledge. It provides a core set of knowledge so that new knowledge need only build at its periphery, extending general principles into more specialised knowledge. By providing a core set of knowledge, it also allows for fewer connections to be necessary to "complete" any set of knowledge for the purposes of guiding behaviour. But further, with a more general set of knowledge, the likelihood that new connections will contract the ideas that are called to mind in any given environment decreases. Hence by increasing the likelihood that bisociations which would manifest the exercising of judgment and displaying of deep creativity were they to be incorporated into the mind will be incorporated into the mind, seeking a classical education and the general knowledge it contributes to allows the individual to be better able to exercise judgment and display creativity.

The general knowledge an individual obtains by seeking a classical education, we have thus established, positions the individual well to be able to rise to the challenges of seizing the opportunities presented by the Fourth Industrial Revolution for building systems of value-creating connections. It endows them with a knowledge of how to command attention, allows them to better discover a unique talent for providing goods and services, and helps them to coordinate production organisations and the governance to which they are subject. But it also better enables them to be able to exercise judgment, display deep creativity in technology and strategy development, and apply subtle and sophisticated tacit knowledge of the social and physical worlds – and thus supply remunerative labour.

Furthermore, the general knowledge an individual obtains by seeking a classical education also contributes to the development of an "antifragile personality," which helps them to maintain the systems of value-creating connections they build in economic systems by endowing those systems with the characteristic of antifragility. In order for those systems to grow in response to manifestations of radical uncertainty, the knowledge of *how* and *why* they might so grow has to grow in response to manifestations of radical uncertainty. The antifragile personality is that personality which maximises the likelihood that knowledge about and how to respond to Black Swan events – manifestations of radical uncertainty – will be incorporated into the mind when such ideas are presented to the mind by those events (Markey-Towler, forthcoming b).

If we "invert" the analysis the Brisbane Club offers of the likelihood that new ideas will be incorporated into the mind, we can discover what the antifragile personality is. It is one which has an expansive general knowledge which provides a base upon which new ideas can build at the periphery without contradicting them. In this regard a classical education contributes directly to the cultivation of an antifragile personality insofar as it endows the individual with a significant general education upon which more specialised knowledge can develop. But the core mindset of the antifragile personality is also one which does not contain ideas which augur against the incorporation of new knowledge in the belief that this would threaten existing belief systems. On the contrary, the antifragile personality is one which, at its core, consists of what Carol Dweck (2006) famously calls a "growth" mindset rather than a "fixed" mindset – it is a mindset with which the incorporation of new knowledge is consonant rather than dissonant. The antifragile personality, finally, is also one which causes the individual to *seek* manifestations of radical uncertainty and to pay attention to them, increasing the likelihood that they will in fact observe the ideas which would cause their knowledge to grow. The antifragile personality, Markey-Towler (forthcoming b) has argued elsewhere, is isomorphic to the "hero" archetype discussed at length in the works of Joseph Campbell (1949) and Jordan Peterson (1999), or a "scientific" personality characterised by an ethical system which reflects the scientific process.

The challenges presented by the Fourth Industrial Revolution to seizing opportunities to build and maintain value-creating networks of exchange can therefore be addressed substantially, at the level of the individual, by seeking the general knowledge a classical education endows, and cultivating an antifragile personality. This education endows the seeker with a highly general and expansive knowledge of scientific and mathematical matter, but also of history, philosophy, languages, literature, music, art, and physical activity. The knowledge thereby obtained helps the individual to develop knowledge of marketing and organisation required for harnessing internet-enabled platforms and blockchain-enabled institutional systems to build systems of value-creating exchange. But it also helps the individual cultivate their tacit knowledge of the physical and social worlds and their ability to exercise judgment and display creativity such that artificial intelligence is a complement for their labour in such systems rather than a substitute. It also, finally, contributes to the cultivation of an antifragile personality. The antifragile personality, characterised by an expansive general knowledge, a "growth" mindset, and an outgoing curiosity and intense attention to the world, is one which causes knowledge of how and why to maintain systems of value-creating exchange to grow in the presence of Black Swan events. The individual who seeks the general knowledge a classical education endows and cultivates an antifragile personality is better able to overcome challenges to seize the opportunities the mega-technologies of the Fourth Industrial Revolution offer for building systems of value-creating connections of profound scale.

3.2 At the level of the group and organisation: build complementarities and cultivate the antifragile mindset

At the level of the group, seizing the opportunities presented by the mega-technologies of the Fourth Industrial Revolution is a matter of coordinating the actions of individuals in organisations so as to ensure that capability prerequisites are met for providing the complementarities that support the building of value-creating networks of exchange. Maintaining that system in the face of an increasingly chaotic economy is a challenge of cultivating an antifragile mindset across the organisation. Building such networks of value-creating exchange, we have seen, is a challenge of building knowledge within the organisation of how capability prerequisites necessary for providing complementarities can be provided by the interaction of various individuals within it (Loasby 2001, 2002; Earl, 2006). Maintaining them is a challenge of cultivating an antifragile mindset within the organisation so that that knowledge of how to organise interactions to satisfy capability prerequisites and provide complementarities grows in the presence of Black Swan events.

The major challenge identified by the Brisbane Club perspective, particularly by Earl and Wakeley (2010), for organisations when building networks of value-creating exchange in *any* setting is to realise *complementarities* for their customers. The complementarity between various characteristics of the bundle of goods and services offered as the organisation's product make it more preferable than it would be were the product unbundled, and we know (from our considerations of the Brisbane Club model) this can be a deciding factor in behaviour. These complementarities, created by consumer lifestyles (see Earl, 2017), impose the necessity *within* the organisation of meeting the capability prerequisites through individual action to make particular widgets available at particular times and in particular conditions which allow for the production complementarities to be realised which will contribute to their being made available to customers (Earl, 2006). Naturally, even having pursued the generalist knowledge that would allow them as individuals to overcome the challenges presented by the Fourth Industrial Revolution, individuals will have different proclivities and capabilities for satisfying capability prerequisites through their actions. So the challenge for organising individual actions is one of developing knowledge and coordinating it across the organisation of how individual actions can contribute to the meeting of capability prerequisites for achieving production complementarities at various points within the system that is the organisation, and thus providing complementarities for customers which will support the formation of value-creating exchange networks. A good practical way of building this knowledge, and coordinating it across the organisation, is to apply Simon Sinek's (2009) "start with why" management theory. The ultimate complementarities an organisation is oriented towards providing for its customers with its product can provide the anchor point in a process of backward induction which builds knowledge of which capability prerequisites must be met at each point in the organisation in order to build the production complementarities which ultimately support those consumption complementarities.

In the Fourth Industrial Revolution, this organisational knowledge must have particular characteristics which go beyond the usual knowledge required to coordinate an organisation and build value-creating exchange in socioeconomic networks. The production complementarities which are necessary *within* the organisation to realise consumption complementarities require the meeting of new capability prerequisites imposed by the mega-technologies of the Fourth Industrial Revolution. Organisational knowledge has tended in the past to be made up of knowledge of how production techniques can be applied by individuals to transform inputs into outputs to meet capability prerequisites. In the Fourth Industrial Revolution, artificial intelligence can and ought to be substituted for labour in the application of production techniques, expanding production capabilities significantly while saving labour and freeing it up for other roles in the organisation for which artificial intelligence cannot be substituted. Organisational knowledge will comprise more of how artificial intelligence can be complemented by individuals exercising *judgment*, displaying *creativity* in the development of technology and strategy, and applying *tacit knowledge* in physical and social activity so as to meet capability prerequisites for obtaining production and consumption complementarities in hyper-competitive global markets subject to the struggle for attention on a global scale. But in particular, organisational knowledge will need to include knowledge of how individual activity within the group can be coordinated so as for the organisation to command sufficient attention from customers in global internet-enabled markets, and of how individual activity can be coordinated so as for the organisation to offer a unique bundle of attributes with its product which realises unique complementarities for the consumer. If organisational knowledge can include knowledge of how to harness blockchain-based institutional systems to facilitate value-creating exchange by forming and coordinating institutional expectations across the population with whom its networks of exchange will be built, the capabilities of the organisation will be extended further.

Therefore, if organisational knowledge can be developed and coordinated of how to harness the class of labour complemented by artificial intelligence to produce a unique bundle of attributes and complementarities and command sufficient attention to be noticed in global markets, the Brisbane Club model suggests that the group of individuals thus organised in a production system will be able to seize the opportunities presented by the mega-technologies of the Fourth Industrial Revolution. They will be able to overcome the challenges presented by the technologies of the Fourth Industrial Revolution and build value-creating networks of exchange on a scale hitherto unimagined enabled by them. Now in order to *maintain* those networks in an increasingly chaotic socioeconomic system such as will emerge in the Fourth Industrial Revolution, organisational knowledge of how and why to maintain and grow those networks must grow in response to manifestations of radical uncertainty – "Black Swan" events. Organisational knowledge must therefore display *antifragility*.

The antifragility of organisational knowledge is predicated on the antifragility of the institutions which govern interactions within it (Markey-Towler forthcoming b). The institutions which determine appropriate action within the organisation must therefore promote the growth of knowledge within the organisation. Those institutions must, especially when they are internalised to become knowledge structures within the minds of individuals (Markey-Towler, 2018b), promote and encourage the antifragile personality at the level of individuals within the organisation. In order to do so, the institutions which determine appropriate action within the organisation must promote the development of an expansive general knowledge across the organisation, encourage a "growth" rather than "fixed" mindset on the part of individuals within it, and cultivate an outgoing curiosity and intense attention to the world on the part of employees. This is no easy task, as the antifragile personality is, we have seen, a personality which seeks consistently to discover new knowledge and apply it to action. It is a personality which is by its nature highly creative, which goes against the general tendency of organisations to be averse to such displays of creativity Jennifer Mueller (2017) reports in her survey of the literature on organisational attitudes to creativity on the part of individuals within them. Nevertheless, those organisations which develop institutions which cultivate the antifragile mindset within the knowledge of the organisation will, the Brisbane Club model suggests, be able to better maintain and grow the networks of value-creating exchange they build in the context of an increasingly chaotic economy as the Fourth Industrial Revolution progresses.

The opportunities presented by the Fourth Industrial Revolution for building and maintaining value-creating networks of exchange can therefore be seized substantially and challenges thereto overcome, at the level of the group of individuals within organisations, by developing organisational knowledge about how to ensure that capability prerequisites are met for obtaining production and consumption complementarities, and institutions which cultivate the antifragile mindset. Organisations which can develop and coordinate knowledge about how to harness the class of labour complemented by artificial intelligence to produce a unique bundle of attributes and complementarities and command sufficient attention to be noticed in global markets will be able to seize the opportunities presented by the mega-technologies of the Fourth Industrial Revolution to build profound networks of value-creating exchange. Organisations which adopt institutions which cultivate the antifragile mindset of the organisation by promoting the development of an expansive general knowledge across the organisation, encourage a "growth" rather than "fixed" mindset on the part of individuals within it, and cultivate an outgoing curiosity and intense attention to the world on the part of employees will be able, further, to *maintain* those networks. The organisation which develops and coordinates such organisational knowledge, and adopts such institutions, will be better able to overcome challenges to seize the opportunities the mega-technologies of the Fourth Industrial Revolution offer for building systems of value-creating connections of profound scale.

3.3 At the level of the community: harness blockchain for institutional governance by forming and coordinating expectations of governance solutions

At the level of the community, opportunities are presented by the mega-technologies of the Fourth Industrial Revolution particularly in terms of the possibilities for bespoke institutional governance enabled by blockchain to emerge. Institutional systems can be better designed by the communities which will be subject to them and that will promote the formation and maintenance of value-creating networks of exchange. Entrepreneurial action, enabled by blockchain, allows for decentralised institutional governance to emerge as a solution to community-level problems. Blockchain-based systems of institutional governance can be harnessed to promote the formation of value-creating networks of economic exchange by offering organisations a new institutional technology for governance within the organisation. But they can also be harnessed to promote the formation of value-creating networks of economic exchange by offering communities a new institutional technology for governance of solutions to social problems created by the disruptions brought about by the mega-technologies of the Fourth Industrial Revolution. To overcome the challenges posed by the technology to seizing the opportunities it presents requires entrepreneurial action at the community level to form and coordinate expectations of the solutions the institutional system enabled by blockchain will offer.

Blockchain-based systems of institutional governance facilitate the emergence of new systems of value-creating exchange by offering organisations a new institutional technology for governance. In particular, it allows for new forms of supply chains within and outside of organisations, decentralising and dehierarchicalising their form relative to that necessitated by existing command-and-control institutions within firms (Berg, Davidson and Potts, 2018a, 2018b; Allen, Berg and Markey-Towler, 2018). By providing platforms in which smart contracts may be struck and automatically executed by algorithm, it allows for more complex forms of contracting to emerge which account for more states of the world, allowing contracts to be less incomplete, as well as establishing the facts of a contract which lowers the cost of arbitration. It also allows the governance by which arbitration is brought about and contracts are legitimated to be bespoke to the needs of the individuals who will interact within it. Harnessing blockchain-based systems of institutional governance at the community level thus lowers the transactions costs of negotiation between individuals and organisations and thus facilitates the formation of networks of value-creating exchange.

Blockchain-based systems of institutional governance also facilitate the emergence of new systems of value-creating exchange by offering communities a new institutional technology for governance which may provide solutions to social problems caused by the disruption created by the mega-technologies of the Fourth Industrial Revolution. Gans and Leigh (forthcoming) have argued in a different context that much of the disruption created by the mega-technologies of the Fourth Industrial Revolution to existing networks of economic exchange can be substantially addressed by the development of networks of insurance contracts. Security of income, healthcare, and education can be assured by the centralised coercion-based insurance system that is the welfare state, but blockchain offers opportunities for entrepreneurial action in the development of bespoke systems of institutional governance which cause privatised and decentralised insurance systems to emerge.

Blockchain can serve as a smart ledger for smart contracts which record rights, obligations, and empowerments with respect to insurance, which provides for security of income, healthcare, and education as part of a privatised, decentralised welfare system. Potts, Humphreys and Clark (2018) have discussed how blockchain might even enable the development of bespoke, privatised, and decentralised universal basic income schemes through smart contracts embedded within blockchain-based smart ledgers. By harnessing blockchain-based systems of institutional governance at the community level therefore, more bespoke, emergent solutions to providing insurance against the disruption of the mega-technologies of the Fourth Industrial Revolution may be discovered.

To seize these opportunities and harness blockchain as a technology which enables the emergence of institutional governance for solutions to community-level problems and facilitate the formation of systems of value-creating exchange within organisations and community-level insurance schemes requires certain challenges be overcome by entrepreneurial action. These we have identified previously as the challenges in coordinating adoption across the population of individuals who will be subject to the governance of a blockchain-based institutional system. Expectations that the blockchain-based system of institutional governance emergent from entrepreneurial action will facilitate networks of value-creating exchange must be formed and then coordinated across the population who would interact within it. More specifically, expectations that transactions costs will be decreased by the system of institutional governance implemented on a blockchain must be formed and coordinated across the community of organisations and individuals who might interact within it. Similarly, expectations that security of income, healthcare, and education will be sufficiently secured by the system of institutional governance implemented using a blockchain must be formed and coordinated across the community of organisations and individuals who might pool their risk within it. If the entrepreneurial action which develops a blockchain-based institutional system of governance can so form and coordinate expectations at the community level, then blockchain may be harnessed at the community level to pose solutions to problems which require institutional governance, solutions which are bespoke, privatised, and decentralised. The greater the extent to which entrepreneurial action at the community level can form and coordinate such expectations, the greater the extent to which the challenges posed by blockchain can be overcome, and the opportunities its harnessing offers can be seized.

4 Summary: opportunities and challenges in the Fourth Industrial Revolution and what to do about them

In this chapter we combined our analyses of the mega-technologies of the Fourth Industrial Revolution to project a view of the likely economy of the future. We saw that the economy of the future is radically different to that which we are accustomed to even now. We will observe the emergence of internet-based platforms to support socioeconomic interaction on a truly global scale subject to bespoke blockchain-based institutional governance designed and developed by the communities of individuals and organisations who interact within them. We will observe the automation of production, exchange, and governance systems enabled by artificial intelligence on a scale which yields profound possibilities for production by offering substitutes for all but a restricted class of labour which can exercise judgment, display deep creativity in technology and strategy development, and apply subtle and sophisticated tacit knowledge of the social and physical worlds. This will allow for the emergence of networks of value-creating exchange on a scale which is hitherto unheard of with a relatively limited requirement of labour. However, these networks will be contingent upon being able to succeed in the global struggle for attention and provide either globally best mixes of prices and attributes or a unique product within global markets. It will be an increasingly chaotic economy subject to constant flux due to hyper-competition and hyper-growth.

We also drew together our analysis of the various challenges and opportunities presented within this new economy. We saw that the Fourth Industrial Revolution offers some profound opportunities for hyper-growth in global markets enabled by astounding production possibilities and bespoke institutional governance to emerge from private entrepreneurial action. It allows individuals and groups to build networks of value-creating exchange on a scale hitherto unimagined, and communities to develop institutional governance solutions for the various problem facing them. However, we also saw that the Fourth Industrial Revolution presents profound challenges to individuals, groups, and communities as well. The struggle for attention becomes central in hyper-competitive global markets. The expanding scope for automation challenges even the most traditionally secure jobs. The opportunities blockchain offers for institutional governance to emerge presents challenges of forming and coordinating expectations of the solutions offered by that institutional governance across the community that will be subject to it. We then drew on the behavioural and institutional model at the core of the Brisbane Club model to develop recommendations about the strategies which might be adopted by individuals, groups, and communities in order to overcome the challenges posed by the mega-technologies of the Fourth Industrial Revolution and seize the opportunities they present.

At the level of the individual, where the most major challenges will be faced, the profound opportunities for building networks of value-creating exchange can be seized and challenges thereto overcome substantially by seeking the expansive and generalist knowledge brought about by a "classical" education. Such a knowledge set contributes to the ability of the individual to command attention, to develop a unique skill set, but also to exercise judgment, display creativity in the development of technology and strategy, and apply tacit knowledge of the physical and social worlds. This knowledge set allows the individual to substantially overcome the challenges presented by the Fourth Industrial Revolution to seizing opportunities to build networks of value creating exchange. The knowledge endowed by a "classical" education also contributes to the cultivation of an antifragile personality, characterised by an expansive general knowledge, a "growth" mindset, and an outgoing curiosity and intense attention to the world. This facilitates the growth of personal knowledge in response to uncertainty in the world, and allows the individual to *maintain* the systems of value-creating exchange they have built.

At the level of the group, organisations may overcome challenges presented by the Fourth Industrial Revolution to seize the opportunities it presents by developing organisational knowledge about how to ensure that capability prerequisites are met for obtaining production and consumption complementarities, and by cultivating the antifragile mindset. The unique challenges presented by the Fourth Industrial Revolution may be substantially addressed by the development of organisational knowledge which, specifically, includes knowledge about how to harness the class of labour complemented by artificial intelligence to produce a unique bundle of attributes and complementarities and command sufficient attention to be noticed in global markets. Organisations which develop such knowledge and coordinate it will be better able to seize the opportunities presented by the mega-technologies of the Fourth Industrial Revolution to build networks of value-creating exchange on a scale hitherto unimagined. Organisations which cultivate the antifragile mindset by promoting the development of an expansive general knowledge across the organisation, encourage a "growth" rather than "fixed" mindset on the part of individuals within it, and cultivate an outgoing curiosity and intense attention to the world on the part of employees will, further, be able to *maintain* those networks in the face of an increasingly chaotic socioeconomic system.

At the level of the community, the Fourth Industrial Revolution offers new institutional technologies for developing bespoke, decentralised institutional solutions to problems which require governance by privatised entrepreneurial action. Bespoke institutional systems may be developed by entrepreneurial action, which lowers the transactions costs of governance and facilitates the formation of new value-creating networks of exchange for organisations and individuals within a community. But they may also be developed to provide governance which secures income, health, and education for members of a particular community subject to them. Entrepreneurial action which can form and coordinate expectations that this will be the case is more likely to be able to overcome the problems of adoption of such institutional technology and seize the opportunities it presents for developing solutions to community-level problems which require governance.

Our analysis and our recommendations, formulated using the Brisbane Club model as a frame of analysis for the mega-technologies for the Fourth Industrial Revolution, have thus offered us a map, of sorts, of the future economy. But they also offered us a guide as to how to navigate it: how to overcome the challenges and disruptions it presents, and how to seize the profound opportunities it offers. We offered, in a sense, a map of the likely future and a guide as to how individuals, groups, and communities can take action to ensure that the Fourth Industrial Revolution is closer to a cornucopian utopia than techno-feudal dystopia.

References

Allen, Darcy, Berg, Alastair and Markey-Towler, Brendan (2018) "Blockchain and supply chains: V-Form organisations, value redistributions, de-commoditisation and quality proxies", available at SSRN: https://ssrn.com/abstract=3299725

Adams, Scott, (2013) *How to Fail at Almost Everything and Still Win Big*, Portfolio, New York

Berg, Chris, Davidson, Sinclair and Potts, Jason, (2018a) "Capitalism after Satoshi: Blockchains, dehierarchicalisation, innovation policy and the regulatory state", available at SSRN: https://ssrn.com/abstract=3299734

Berg, Chris, Davidson, Sinclair and Potts, Jason, (2018b) "Outsourcing vertical integration: Distributed ledgers and the V-Form organisation", available at SSRN: https://ssrn.com/abstract=3300506

Campbell, Joseph, (1949) *The Hero with a Thousand Faces*, New World Library, Novato

Dweck, Carol, (2006) *Mindset*, Random House, New York

Earl, Peter, (2003) "The entrepreneur as a constructor of connections", in Koppl, Roger, Birner, Jack and Kurrild-Klitgaard (eds.), *Austrian Economics and Entrepreneurial Studies*, Emerald Group, Bingley

Earl, Peter, (2006) "Capability prerequisites and the competitive process", unpublished mimeo, available at URL: https://espace.library.uq.edu.au/view/UQ:8480

Earl, Peter, (2017) "Lifestyle changes and the lifestyle selection process", *Journal of Bioeconomics*, 19(1), pp. 97–114

Earl, Peter and Wakeley, Tim, (2010) "Alternative perspectives on connections in economic systems", *Journal of Evolutionary Economics*, 20(2), pp. 163–183

Foster, John, (2005) "From simplistic to complex systems in economics", *Cambridge Journal of Economics*, 29(6), pp. 873–892

Foster, John, (2006) "Why is economics not a complex systems science", *Journal of Economic Issues*, 40(4), pp. 1069–1091

Gans, Joshua and Leigh, Andrew (forthcoming) *Innovation and Equality*, Oxford University Press, Oxford

Herrmann-Pillath, Carsten, (2008) "Consilience and the naturalistic foundations of evolutionary economics", *Evolutionary and Institutional Economics Review*, 5(1), pp. 129–162

Koestler, Arthur, (1964) *The Act of Creation*, Picador, London

Loasby, Brian, (2001) "Time, knowledge and evolutionary dynamics: Why connections matter", *Journal of Evolutionary Economics*, 11(4), pp. 393–412

Loasby, Brian, (2002) *Knowledge, Institutions and Evolution in Economics*, Routledge, London

Markey-Towler, Brendan (2018a) "A formal psychological theory for evolutionary economics", *Journal of Evolutionary Economics*, 28(4), pp. 691–725

Markey-Towler, Brendan, (2018b) "The economics of artificial intelligence", available at SSRN: https://ssrn.com/abstract=2907974

Markey-Towler, Brendan, (forthcoming a) "Rules, perception and emotion: When do institutions determine behaviour?", *Journal of Institutional Economics*

Markey-Towler, Brendan, (forthcoming b) "Antifragility, the Black Swan and psychology", *Evolutionary and Institutional Economics Review*

Mueller, Jennifer, (2017) *Creative Change*, Houghton Harcourt Mifflin, New York

Peterson, Jordan B., (1999) *Maps of Meaning*, Routledge, London

Potts, Jason, Humphreys, John and Clark, Joseph, (2018) "A blockchain-based universal income", *Medium.com*, available at URL: https://medium.com/@jason.potts/a-blockchain-based-universal-basic-income-2cb7911e2aab (accessed 29/08/2018)

Rosser, Barkley J. and Rosser, Marina V., (2017) "Complexity and institutional evolution", *Evolutionary and Institutional Economics Review*, 14(2), pp. 415–430

Sinek, Simon (2009) *Start With Why*, Portfolio, New York

Taleb, Nassim Nicholas, (2007) *The Black Swan*, Penguin, London

Taleb, Nassim Nicholas, (2012) *Antifragile*, Penguin, London

Teece, David, Pisano, Gary and Shuen, Amy (1997) "Dynamic capabilities and strategic management", *Strategic Management Journal*, 18(7), pp. 509–533

Thiel, Peter, (2014) *Zero to One*, Crown Business, New York

12

EPILOGUE

A call to engage with a brave new world, and to have contingency plans

We began this book with a parallel between Dickens's famous opening of *A Tale of Two Cities* and the modern economy. We live in a world which feels as if it is in the best of times and the worst of times. A world of significant hope, and a world of great fear. We hope that our contribution has offered a unique and valuable perspective on this world – a world in the throes of the Fourth Industrial Revolution.

We have provided an extension of Klaus Schwab's (2016, 2018) work on the Fourth Industrial Revolution and the convergence of technological innovations. Using the General Purpose Technologies framework, we approached the problem of analysing the Fourth Industrial Revolution from an economic perspective by identifying three core mega-technologies, namely the ever-evolving, ubiquitous internet, artificial intelligence, and blockchain, which underlie and enable the various commercial applications which are presently driving the radical, structural transformation of our economic systems.

We then applied the Brisbane Club model of socioeconomic systems as complex, evolving networks, formed by individuals acting on the basis of their psychology and socioeconomic environment, enabled by technology. Combined with an analysis of the *telos* of industrial revolutions as value-creating phenomena designed to help people achieve their ends, this model allowed us to establish a view of how these three technologies are independently and jointly driving structural dynamics in the broader socioeconomic ecosystem.

In other words, this approach allowed us to reduce an immensely complicated modern phenomenon to its core dynamics using a coherent and unique economic framework which combines psychological, institutional, and evolutionary perspectives. From this emerged a systematic analysis of the Fourth Industrial Revolution grounded in theory, which we believe to be a valuable contribution to a body of literature which tends to be somewhat fragmented as a result of its proclivity toward inductive case studies.

We believe that consultants, managers, executives, policymakers, and the interested general reader alike will find value in the content of this book. The Fourth Industrial Revolution is radically altering the structure and function of our socioeconomic systems, and new opportunities are opening up for the creation of a successful life or business. It offers profound opportunities for harnessing its technologies to extend the range of human capability in building networks of value-creating exchange, but it also presents profound challenges for individuals, organisations, and communities.

Our work has allowed us to identify these opportunities and challenges, yielding practical strategies by which the former can be seized and against which the latter can be mitigated. We hope that it allows you, reader, to confront this brave new world with a sense of hope and optimism.

Individuals will continue to face the deep challenges of standing out and being heard in the swarm of chatter and the evolving chaos around them. In hyper-competitive global marketplaces, it is easy for the individual to become lost. This problem can be best overcome by seizing the many unprecedented opportunities which present themselves through global networks of value-creating exchanges. Individuals can also pursue generalist knowledge and a "classical" self-education to help orient themselves in the chaos, develop sound judgment, and cultivate the transferable skills which are highly coveted in the emerging workplace. Building an antifragile personality, with a growth mindset and deep curiosity, will help the individual maintain their personal systems of value-creating exchange.

Companies and organisations, as groups of individuals, are best served by developing and curating organisational knowledge and culture which embraces adaptation, automation, and change, but remains rooted it its core values. Economic principles would suggest that good results are often obtained when automation technology is used to augment human labour, not merely supplant it. By coming to a fuller understanding of the seven penultimate ends of human action, and the implicit hierarchy of value, organisations will discover what motivates the people inside and outside their group, including any customers. The organisation which best satisfies people's needs in a commercial sense will be the most successful, will achieve cut-through in the hyper-competitive global marketplace, and will withstand the Fourth Industrial Revolution to be around for a long time to come.

Entire communities can judiciously utilise new institutional technologies to explore the adoption of bespoke, decentralised solutions to problems which require governance by privatised entrepreneurial action. By lowering the transaction costs of governance, entirely new opportunities may open up for the creation of community networks which create value for the participants. Strong communities are essential for society to withstand all the disruptive forces which the Fourth Industrial Revolution has brought thus far and is still to bring.

As a final note, it is worth bearing in mind that the complex economic systems enabled by the technologies of the Fourth Industrial Revolution are still themselves prone to failure, either by human or natural action. Each of the technologies of the Fourth Industrial Revolution ultimately relies on physical infrastructure, and the compromise of this infrastructure's integrity poses significant risks given how much of modern society and commerce is predicated upon it. Individuals, organisations, and communities must not get so caught up in the promise of new technology that they forget the risks involved with their failure. It is prudent to ensure that adequate redundancies are established within low-tech critical systems so that the catastrophic social and economic consequences of an unforeseen infrastructure failure are minimised.

For example, large solar flares occur semi-regularly, which have the potential to disrupt electricity grids and unprotected electronic devices for extended periods of time. A notable example occurred in March 1989, when a geomagnetic storm shut down the Quebec power grid in Canada. Were a similar or worse event to occur today, the economic damage and disruption to essential services would be potentially catastrophic. Many of the most significant catastrophic events have not yet been seen simply because the world has only become reliant on digital infrastructure in the last thirty years. In January 2019, an undersea cable was damaged which provided internet access to the island nation of Tonga, effectively taking the island off the grid and causing massive disruptions to businesses and the community (Brodkin 2019). Many people had not prepared alternative methods of communication, serving as a stark reminder of the importance of how exposed the modern technologies we rely on actually are in the rough world we live in. Some countries, such as Russia, have reportedly even gone so far as to conduct tests to see if their economy and society could withstand a state of virtual autarky, being cut off from the non-Russian internet (Matsakis 2019).

These threats are not exclusively of natural origin but can also emerge from malicious human action. Some global computer systems are potentially compromised by sophisticated malware, such as Stuxnet, which have the capability to wreak havoc (Anderson 2012). The relative accessibility of important databases and computer networks via the internet has also opened up new opportunities for cyberwarfare, state interference in elections, and grand theft. The ability of individuals, groups, and communities to withstand an extreme event such as a coordinated cyber-attack is crucial for protecting the advances that will be made from the Fourth Industrial Revolution for years to come. It is our hope that many new problems will be solved in coming years and decades, and that in finding ways to deploy new technology, people will consider not just what is most efficient, but most effective and especially the most ethical.

References

Anderson, Nate. 2012. "Confirmed: US and Israel Created Stuxnet, Lost Control of It." *Ars Technica*. Retrieved February 28, 2019, https://arstechnica.com/tech-policy/2012/06/confirmed-us-israel-created-stuxnet-lost-control-of-it/.

Brodkin, Jon. 2019. "Undersea Cable Damage Wipes out Most Internet Access in Tonga Islands." *Ars Technica*. Retrieved February 28, 2019, https://arstechnica.com/information-technology/2019/01/undersea-cable-damage-wipes-out-most-internet-access-in-tonga-islands/.

Matsakis, Louise. 2019. "What Happens If Russia Cuts Itself off from the Internet?" *Wired*. Retrieved February 28, 2019, www.wired.com/story/russia-internet-disconnect-what-happens/.

Schwab, Klaus. 2016. *The Fourth Industrial Revolution*. Geneva: World Economic Forum.

Schwab, Klaus. 2018. *Shaping the Future of the Fourth Industrial Revolution*. Geneva: World Economic Forum.

INDEX

Note: Page numbers in *italic* indicate a figure on the corresponding page.

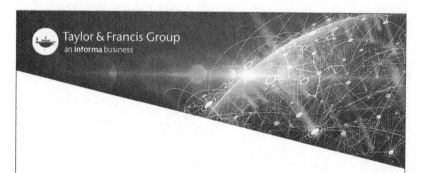